Challenging Religious Studies

Challenging Religious Studies

The Wealth, Wellbeing and Inequalities of Nations

John Atherton

scm press

© John Atherton 2014

Published in 2014 by SCM Press
Editorial office
3rd Floor
Invicta House
108–114 Golden Lane,
London EC1Y 0TG

SCM Press is an imprint of Hymns Ancient & Modern Ltd
(a registered charity)
13A Hellesdon Park Road
Norwich NR6 5DR, UK

www.scmpress.co.uk

All rights reserved. No part of this publication may be reproduced, stored in a retrieval system, or transmitted, in any form or by any means, electronic, mechanical, photocopying or otherwise, without the prior permission of the publisher, SCM Press.

The Author has asserted his right under the Copyright, Designs and Patents Act, 1988, to be identified as the Author of this Work

British Library Cataloguing in Publication data
A catalogue record for this book is available
from the British Library

978 0 334 04649 3

Typeset by Regent Typesetting
Printed and bound by
Lightning Source UK

To Princeton, Uppsala and Chester

Contents

Acknowledgements   ix

1 'That They Might Have Life, And Have It More Abundantly': The Argument Emerges   1

Part 1 Getting Better-ish   25

2 Great Escapes and Divergences   27
3 'I Came That They Might Have Life': Christianity and Wellbeing   62

Part 2 Getting Better-ish in Historical Contexts. Putting Christianity to Work on Progressive Change   103

4 A Nation Under God: The American Case Study   130
5 An Ecclesiastical History of the English Peoples' Journey to Greater Wellbeing: The British Case Study   159

Afterword: On Living in More Than One Place at Once   193
Bibliography   198
Acknowledgements of Sources   207
Index   209

Acknowledgements

Producing this book has been a gradual process of development going back nearly ten years. A grant from two Research Councils, Arts and Humanities, and Economic and Social, enabled us to build a network of scholars to explore, from 2007 to 2009, the relationship between wellbeing studies and religion, producing the volume *The Practices of Happiness: Political Economy, Religion and Wellbeing* (2011). Interestingly, this was published by Routledge in its 'Frontiers of Political Economy' series, reflecting my lifelong interest in religion and economics. The material in this book goes way beyond that research and became focused on the subject of the Wealth and Wellbeing of Nations, the title of a splendid seminar run by that most creative Center of Theological Inquiry at Princeton. Much of this book therefore owes a great deal to its director, Professor Will Storrar, who invited me to pursue my research there as the William Scheide Fellow in Theology in April 2013. This visit widened out, as they invariably and creatively do, and was deeply enriched by a conversation with Angus Deaton, the Dwight D. Eisenhower Professor of Economics and International Affairs in the Woodrow Wilson School of Public and International Affairs and the Economics Department at Princeton University. As a result much of the shape of and research behind Chapter 2 of this book owes a great deal to his seminal *The Great Escape: Health, Wealth and the Origins of Inequality* (2013), the text of which he kindly shared with me before publication. But the feast at Princeton became even more bountiful, through research conversations with Ellen Charry, the Margaret W. Harmon Professor of Historical and Systematic Theology at Princeton Theological Seminary. Her guidance on further reading in biblical studies and systematic theology, particularly in relation to the psychological dimensions of wellbeing, was of great importance for my work.

The core of this book is in Part 1 with its model for connecting Christianity with the economics and psychology of wellbeing. This was developed through a paper 'The Wealth and Wellbeing of Nations: Lutheran–Anglican contributions to future directions for Christianity and political economy' given at the conference 'Remembering the Past – Living the Future. Lutheran Traditions in Transition' at the University of Uppsala in October 2013 and at a research seminar at the Department of Theology at the University through the kind invitation of my friends and colleagues Professors Grenholm and Namli and then at Stockholm Cathedral through the courtesy of the Dean. The core of Part 2 was published in the *International Journal of Public Theology* on 'Public Mission for Changing Times: Models for Progressive Change from American and British Experience'. I have significantly developed this material in this book, including using a relevant section from my *Public Theology for Changing Times* (2000). In terms of commissioning and seeing the book through the press, I am very grateful to Dr Natalie Watson of SCM Press. This is the second book she has sorted out for me!

I need to add to these debts of gratitude some more personal ones. To my colleagues at the William Temple Foundation, and particularly Chris Baker and John Reader, because after 40 years I continue to find it a creative and stimulating home, as I do the Department of Theology and Religious Studies, at the University of Chester. The latter honoured me with a Visiting Professorship in Religion, Ethics and Economics. My first public lecture 'All Shall Be Well. Religion and Progressive Change' in 2010 provided the stimulus and some of the framework of this book. But these acknowledgements get rightly and increasingly into my personal life, for example to my old school friend Eunice Barber, for her assistance with solving various genealogical puzzles and to my dear and glorious parish church of St Katharine's Blackrod with all its friendships and support. They play a significant part in this book, as they have in my life, and not least through my growing

ACKNOWLEDGEMENTS

friendship with its senior churchwarden Margaret Ryding and their and her support for this next (and probably last!) stage of my life.

John Atherton

25 May 2014
Feast of the Venerable Bede

1

'That They Might Have Life, And Have It More Abundantly' (John 10.10) The Argument Emerges

This book is about what matters most to most people most of the time, whether as individuals, families, communities or societies. It is therefore deliberately and primarily about what the American sociologist Robert Bellah has called 'the world of (the) daily life' of people which they face with 'a practical or pragmatic interest'. It is about bringing about 'a projected state of affairs by bodily movements' which Schutz calls 'working'. So it is a world governed by 'the means/ends schema', a world of 'striving' (Bellah 2011, 2). That is how it is so often for most people, and it always has been since the dawn of the human about 200,000 years ago. For other commentators like the archaeologist and historian Morris, surveying human life from 15,000 years ago, it is about society's 'abilities to get things done in the world' (Morris 2013, 5) including in terms of the adequate provision of the basics for human life on earth, as food, clothing and shelter, and increasingly, too, in later periods, in terms of life expectancy, health and education. You can't have a good life if you die before the age of five, and now we don't. In other words, this story is simply about the 'world of daily life', but it is also significantly about, for the economist Angus Deaton, 'how people have managed to make their lives better', so often in terms of 'what makes life worth living' (2013, ix, xiv). And, at the heart of these changes in human development lie the Industrial and then Mortality Revolutions from the eighteenth century, transforming human life in ways never achieved and never really dreamt of in the previous 200,000 years of human history. And all this so often allows and enables that concern to be developed into the pursuit of a good life, a life that turns out well, the basis of a flourishing life and community. It is, as John's Gospel reminds us, the importance of not just having a life, but having it more abundantly. It is very difficult to have the second without the first, as liberation theologians have rightly reminded us.

But this story is also about how these amazing developments in human living have been intimately accompanied by what historians and economists call 'the paradox of development' or the often negative and destructive or damaging consequences of social change (Morris 2011, 28). For example, the astonishing improvements in economic growth, so important for nurturing, sustaining and progressing human wellbeing, have also been accompanied by breath-taking increases in inequalities, particularly between nations, but also within them. The latter is especially the case in the USA and UK and other developed economies, with most people suffering at best a plateauing of incomes and with the super-rich, the top 1 per cent – or even more so, the top 0.1 per cent – taking an increasingly disproportionate share of national income and wealth. And the damage to the economic, political and social life of such nations is beginning to become more evident. For recent generations, parents have fought successfully and hoped realistically (for the first time in human history such progressive change has become achievable) that their children would make a better life for themselves than their parents. That has certainly been the case in my own family, classic English working class (my father was a plumber) and putting their hopes on their one child, born at the end of the Great Depression in 1939, and his ability to escape from their relative poverty into modest prosperity, higher education and more robust health. I was that only precious (to them!) child, on which their hopes for a better life were placed. I am not as confident as they were that my children and grandchildren will realistically have these same opportunities for achieving a much better life. Such inequalities are symptomatic of that paradox of development, but clearly, as the story will recount, they stretch more widely to include, for example, increasingly destructive environmental damage, but also the historic other four horsemen of the apocalypse namely hunger, epidemics, migrations and state failures (Morris 2011, 28–9).

Of course, what matters to people, communities and nations cannot be adequately summarized by their improving wealth and wellbeing, because the world of daily life, however central and essential for human survival and betterment, has always been, at least for 100,000 years, also accompanied by the field of religion, so often of such importance for sustaining and enriching human life. Sociologists talk therefore of humans inhabiting 'multiple realities', which inevitably and invariably constitute 'overlapping realities' (Bellah 2011, 8). So there is now, and always has been deep into human evolution, an acceptance that there is more to human living than the daily struggle for human existence in terms of achieving the necessary basics for human living, of food, clothing and shelter, and now of income, health and education. Without these, you don't survive substantively or gracefully. You either die or suffer so deeply and pervasively from the sheer unremitting struggle to survive. That is still the fate of a billion people today, as it was for most people until two centuries ago. And changing that for the better, as an essential prerequisite for human betterment, is significantly about economics and biodemography. It is not principally about religion. Yet humans, as I have noted, have always recognized that the other dimensions or fields of life – for example, the religious – have contributed so significantly to human struggles to make sense of life by locating it in greater contexts and purposes and acknowledging the necessity and feasibility of translating these meanings into ways of living, including those informed by values or morals.

So this story is about at least both, about the economics and biodemography of life and about the religious dimensions of life and how they have, and need to, come together in ways that recognize and engage constructively the most profound changes the human has ever experienced in such material dimensions of life as income, health and subjective wellbeing.

Of course, this is another way of saying that religions in general, and, in my case, Christianity in particular, have at best persistently refused to take these matters and these changes seriously. They have rarely prioritized them, as the world of daily life does and has to, and they have rather and regularly focused on the negative consequences of the paradox of development and almost never on the processes of social development that contribute to the furtherance of human wellbeing. They have pursued the soft option of prophecy for the hard struggle for construction and reconstruction. They have regularly given the appearance that their priorities (for example, in the current experience and history of my own church, the Church of England) are quite different, instead so often appearing to focus disproportionately (certainly in terms of what the public thinks is important) on issues of human sexuality, or women bishops. But that has so often been the case in these last two centuries of great economic change. In the early twentieth century, after generations of desperate struggle for daily life in the Durham coalfield, the Reverend Alexander Begg from Usworth Parish, concerned over the domination of church life by liturgical reform, noted in his visitation return that 'questions of P[rayer] B[ook] revision fall in importance before [the] social & industrial iniquity [of unemployment]' (Lee 2007, 177). For a Labour MP, in the same period, 'the working man is not interested in the Prayer Book, but in the rent book' (274). So for the historian, Lee, there remained 'a deficit in understanding' from 1860 until 1930 between the 'Church and coalfield community' (276), which I regard as systematic of the Church's failure to engage the world of daily life of the people of Britain. That is the gulf that this story seeks to address.

Finding titles: Describing the argument as the world of daily life

Sexy titles are always appealing to so much of contemporary public life, whether TV programmes, university courses or books. I am just not very good at them. More importantly, I am often left with the feeling that they rarely tell things as they really are. *Challenging Religious Studies: The Wealth, Wellbeing and Inequalities of Nations* communicates, I believe, so much of what this book is about. This is because the world of daily life has, does and will continue to focus significantly on the material or income wellbeing of people, their communities and societies. Income is about far more than money, important as that is in its own right for our wellbeing; its significance also belongs to what it purchases in terms of not simply the traditional bedrocks of social living, – food, clothing and housing – but also education, health care, social security, and governance. So the use of wealth in the subtitle of this book refers to material wellbeing, but also embraces wider human needs, including life expectancy and health. Central as are these perspectives on and for human wellbeing, the concept of wellbeing also involves how people themselves judge their own complex wellbeing. It is no longer sufficient to estimate individual and society wellbeing. It is now also essential to include the views of men and women in such estimations. And central to all these concerns to understand these developments in human wellbeing is that they are equally complemented, at each point of these estimations, by profound inequalities.

But why the wealth, wellbeing and inequalities of nations? Nation states continue to be of central importance to the emergence of our contemporary world, profoundly part, for example, of the stories of the liberation of societies from imperial controls. Yet equally they lie at the heart of devastating conflicts, including in the twentieth century. They are part of the paradox of development. So despite the emerging significance of globalization processes – and the need for international institutions and processes in such fields integral to human wellbeing and development as security, migrations, climate change, disease control, finance and economic life – nations continue to play a central part in the promotion of human wellbeing. Such an agenda of developing wellbeing is both acknowledgement of recent achievements in the last two centuries and their probable likely continuation. It is not a statement that such progress is inevitably going to continue. That would be to contradict the lessons of history, including the paradox of development. Nor is it a judgement that we are morally superior to previous generations. It is to avoid giving such confusing and inaccurate impressions that I have rightly abandoned the early provisional working title I adopted of 'Religion and Progressive Change'.

There are also other reasons why I have developed the concept of the wealth, wellbeing and inequalities of nations. Clearly, the more frequently used concept of countries would have been quite adequate. Yet both nations and countries are used in the research describing the changes in the income, health and subjective wellbeing of peoples. And nations figure prominently in Christian traditions, and particularly in their sacred literatures, the Hebrew and Christian Scriptures, with their over 300 references to nations. But the concept of nation also provides a link between Christian and economic traditions, because Adam Smith's 1776 *Inquiry into the Wealth of Nations* is rightly regarded as the founding text of modern economics. Yet it is its connections to his other projects that add further depth, making his work so relevant to my enquiry. For he himself judged that his earlier 1759 *Theory of Moral Sentiments* was of greater significance, rightly undergirding his *Wealth of Nations*, and therefore economic activities. In his other works, as Nicholas Phillipson's magisterial *Adam Smith: An Enlightened Life* (2011) reminds us, he intentionally linked the two books as integrally related parts of a greater enquiry into the 'Science of Man' (Phillipson 2011, 2), which, unfortunately for us, and particularly for economics, he never completed. That would have made my task in this book somewhat easier, providing a clear bridge between economics and ethics, and so making the project of restoring the historic relationship between economic life and religion, in my case, especially Christianity, more achievable. (Many of these components in this argument were also suggested by the seminar on the Wealth and Wellbeing of Nations, organized by Princeton's Center of Theological Inquiry in 2013, in which Nicholas Phillipson was an important participant.) The title of this book moves rightly and necessarily, therefore, from the wealth, wellbeing and inequalities of nations to their interaction with religious studies, an interaction captured by the concept of 'challenging religious studies' as suggesting and requiring a two-way process of interaction, the one challenging the other, for their mutual benefit, that is, the wealth, wellbeing and inequalities of nations, the stuff of the world of daily life of peoples, communities and societies and its interactive overlapping with the world of religious life.

Weaving themes together: On evolving encounters between Christianity and economics

If economic affairs have deeply informed the world of daily life and its recent dramatic transformations into better ways of living for an increasing proportion of the world's populations, then for a religion like Christianity, that must provide an essential agenda for its constructive engagement with such a world. Any concern for pursuing and promoting abundant life, with its heavy dependence on economic matters, must be increasingly focused on fostering the positive relationship between the two traditions or cultures of religions and economics.

In attempting to suggest how this interdisciplinary engagement needs to proceed if it is to be truly effective in terms of its contribution to developing the wellbeing of all, I have found reflecting on my own personal journey and my publications as almost a bibliographical biography of some use. This is because the stages in it illustrate that relationship's essential features, particularly its strengths and sometimes damaging limitations. This applies to any positive engagement Christianity seeks to develop with economic affairs, but equally, it also illustrates how the agenda for this book evolved, particularly as summarized in the title.

The book's evolution began with the poverty imperative, at the heart of the Christian concern for the vulnerable and marginalized and of modern economics. It is certainly centrally embedded in the works of Adam Smith, its founder, and continuing to be so ever since, for example, in the works of the founder of modern neoclassical economics, Alfred Marshall, and then of recent Nobel economics laureates like Sen and Stiglitz. That concern with poverty and how to address it in both theory and practice powerfully shaped my own life and ministry, initially through the pastoral experience of serving in inner city parishes, in Aberdeen, Glasgow and Manchester, from 1962 until 1974. This was then embedded in research and publications emerging through working with and for the William Temple Foundation, a Christian research and development institute founded in memory of the Archbishop of Canterbury William Temple. His great concern with poverty and welfare was reflected in his lifelong friendship with R. H. Tawney and William Beveridge. In 1903, the latter were instructed by the Master of Balliol College, Oxford, Edward Caird to pursue the great question, why was there so much poverty in the midst of so much wealth, by living and studying in London's East End (Atherton 1979, 30). In my case, living in the midst of such a paradox, and then reflecting on it in a disciplined way, informed my first book, *The Scandal of Poverty: Priorities for the Emerging Church* (1983) and my deep involvement in the founding of Church Action on Poverty, a still important Christian pressure group. Poverty had not been defeated in British society, as many hoped and assumed in the 1960s and early 1970s. It was still, and is still, deeply embedded in a rich Britain. And it therefore remains a scandal for society and therefore a priority for the Church.

This concern in theory and practice provided an essential bridge into the next stage of the journey.

The presence in and threat to the social order, which deeply entrenched poverty represented, led to the formation of a three-year Archbishop's Commission resulting in the report *Faith in the City* (1985), perhaps the most significant action, resourced by impressive interdisciplinary research, which the churches have undertaken in the last 200 years. My involvement in the process of report drafting was as a consultant representing the William Temple Foundation. But what followed was of equal importance. For it became increasingly evident to some that the report did not pursue in any way adequately the question why was there so much poverty in the midst of such wealth. And for my research that therefore meant engaging with economic affairs, with what became, and still is, a lifelong concern with economics. Initially, this took the form of a preliminary study *Faith in the Nation: A Christian Vision for Britain* (1988), leading to a deeper engagement with economic systems, resulting in the publication *Christianity and the Market: Christian Social Thought for Our Times* (1992). The necessity of such a development became increasingly evident to a number of theologians and continues to be so to this day. Yet I began to realize its deep inadequacy in the form of the temptation of the morally obvious and therefore often morally and empirically inadequate. Connecting poverty and economic systems invariably leads church leaders and theologians to condemn the latter on behalf of the former, and therefore to fail both. The fact is, as we will discover in the next chapter, that absolute poverty has been massively reduced for the first time in human history, and that is significantly the achievement of economic activities or systems. For example, in recent years, this reduction in poverty has been the result of changing policies to promote economic growth in China, and then India, and certainly not the result of the work of liberation theologians or bishops.

These concerns therefore drove me to move much wider and deeper than the analysis of economic systems, into the study of economics itself, in terms, for example, of its mainstream discipline of neoclassical economics and into macro and microeconomics (a major academic exponent of the latter, Professor Ian Steedman, has been a close colleague and stringent critic, essential for trying to avoid the routine economic howlers of most theologians and church leaders when pronouncing on economic affairs). The recognition that economics was a changing discipline then led me into its necessary engagement with other related disciplines, particularly psychology, and their combined and robustly creative engagement with wellbeing studies (confusingly and inaccurately collapsed into happiness research), in theory and practice. A research programme involving economists and theologians, and funded by their respective research councils, produced the pioneering publication, *The Practices of Happiness: Political Economy, Religion and Wellbeing* (Atherton, Graham and Steedman 2011).

It was a study leave visit to Princeton in 2013 that provided the creative opportunities to weave all these themes together into a coherent research programme, focused on the wealth, wellbeing and inequalities of nations and its challenge to religious studies. It provoked me to refocus on economics, particularly its central concerns with income, economic growth and inequality. It certainly involved the macroeconomics of economic systems, but equally, the micro issues of economic agents, whether as individuals or households, and economic enterprises. Yet it equally engaged such wider economic concerns as life expectancy and health, and wellbeing studies as subjective wellbeing. Princeton's three institutions – the Center of Theological Inquiry (and its seminar on the Wealth and Wellbeing of Nations), the University (and one of its leading economists, Angus Deaton) and its Theological Seminary (and one of its leading theologians, Ellen Charry) – embedded all these themes in research outputs and opportunities focused around this book's title.

Its first outing was provided by my participation in a Lutheran conference at Uppsala University in Sweden (one of my universities: it awarded me an honorary doctorate in 2004). By concentrating on three classic features of human and national development, income, health and subjective wellbeing, embodied in economic research and practice, including its engagement with such other related disciplines of psychology, sociology, biodemography and economic history, I had begun to develop a model out of religious studies to engage with the third perspective, subjective wellbeing. The Uppsala opportunity drove me, through dissatisfaction leading to critical reflection, to clarify and refine that model and to begin to see the possibility of its transferability to the other two perspectives, income and health, therefore suggesting an ongoing research project and focus. In other words, this research task in religious studies of addressing and contributing to the multidisciplinary agenda of the wealth, wellbeing and inequalities of nations has the major added value of also attempting to bridge the great gulf between Christianity and economics in relation to that greater agenda of clearly mutual concern.

Further thoughts on the emerging agenda's keystone: On Christianity and economics

Of the topics most likely to get people to use the off button, economics and Christianity must be at the top of the list. Christianity's perceived main concerns, for example, sexuality issues, no longer overoccupy the centre of people's lives, if they ever have. And economics is a bit like maths, obscure and daunting. Yet economics lies at the heart of the ongoing journey in human development since 1800, as we will see in some detail in Chapter 2. The impact on ordinary lives of economic change was evidenced by everyone, through, in recent times, the financial near-collapse and the resulting economic recession from 2007–08. And religions, especially Christianity and Islam, are going through major experiences of resurgence. If even the editor of *The Economist*, a journal routinely sceptical of religious issues, can co-author a book, *God is Back: How the Global Rise of Faith is Changing the World* (2009, Micklethwait and Wooldridge), it must be happening on a serious scale. Recent global-reach research (2010, *Pew Forum*) drawing from over 2,500 censuses and surveys, recorded 80 per cent of the world's peoples identifying with a religious group, including 32 per cent Christian, 23 per cent Muslim, and 15 per cent Hindu (Graham 2013, 4–5). This chapter (and this book) has therefore rightly focused both on economics and on Christianity (and other religions, as we will soon see), but particularly on the relationships between them. It is that connection, some of its history and some of its constituent parts, which needs a little further explanation at this point of the emerging argument.

Christianity's relationships to economic life (and economics) moved from a position of assumed and attempted dominance in the Middle Ages to a relationship of its gradual marginalization from economics in the seventeenth and eighteenth centuries as the early stages of industrialization and urbanization emerged. Despite an important attempt to engage early modern economics theologically, through such Christian political economists as Malthus, Whately, Copleston and Sumner, theirs was a brief and in the end unsuccessful attempt to reconcile the two traditions. Whately particularly understood the importance of the task in a letter explaining why he accepted nomination for the Drummond chair of political economy: 'Religious truth ... appears to me to be intimately connected, at this time especially with political economy. For it seems to be that before long, political economists, of some sort or other, must govern the world ... Now anti Christians are striving very hard to have this science to themselves, and to interweave it with their own notions' (Waterman 1991, 206). (Whately is the great-great-grandfather of Kevin Whately, of British TV fame, playing in the detective series *Morse* and then *Lewis*.) And of course, it was the latter fear which came to pass, in terms of not simply the estrangement between the two traditions but how that was accompanied by developments perceived as hostile to Christianity. The great gulf between the two traditions certainly continued to deepen, clearly noted by Keynes from the 1860s: 'The critical moment at which Christian dogma fell away from the serious philosophical [including economics] world in England' (Waterman 2004, 6). And the situation did not change, though maybe modest signs of the reconciliation of the two traditions are beginning to appear in the early twenty-first century. These possibly hopeful signs complement similar, and I believe related, trajectories in this historic and contemporary relationship between economics and ethics. (Ethics is both integrally part of Christianity and also of intrinsic value and significance. The connections between the two are therefore both of historic and logical significance.) For Adam Smith, founder of the modern discipline of economics, the two were intimately related, two key sides of the same coin in his proposed construction of a 'Science of Man', including the *Theory of Moral Sentiments* (written as professor of moral philosophy at Glasgow University in 1759) and *The Wealth of Nations* (1776). My main criticism of Smith is that he failed to link the two explicitly in his introduction to *The Wealth of Nations*, because ever since, scholars and practitioners have either argued over the importance of that relationship (for the Germans, the das Adam Smith problem) or ignored it to all our costs. And that is what happened. As with Christianity, ethics too was gradually removed from the essential core of economics, particularly with the development of economics into its latest neoclassical stage. By the later twentieth century, the gap between the two, as with Christianity, gave almost the appearance of being unbridgeable. So for Chicago school's Nobel economics prize winner Milton Friedman, 'Positive economics is independent of every value proposition or of every ethical position. Its utility is not to describe "what ought to be the case" but "what is the case" ... In short, positive economics is, or can be, an "objective science" in precisely the same sense as any of the physical sciences' (Friedman 1953, 7). It is that unequivocal proclamatory assertion which has been challenged as an inadequate representation of the plural nature of the tradition of economics, for example, by the work of another and more recent Nobel economic laureate, Amartya Sen. He has written persuasively of the two traditions of economics, the engineering or positive (what Friedman focuses on) but also the ethical or normative tradition (Sen 1988). It is the interaction of these two traditions which inevitably and necessarily deeply informs so many aspects of and issues in economic life, and therefore in economics itself, as we will see (Atherton 2010). So the detailed aspects of human development addressed in the next chapter on wealth and wellbeing are both central to the discipline of engineering economics (and other related disciplines) and ethical economics. As another Nobel economics laureate, Fogel, rightly observed 'Many issues that seem purely technical are actually complex amalgams of technical and ethical judgements' (Fogel 2000, 138). It is that inevitable and necessary 'amalgam' of economics and ethics which, I will argue, also can and should involve religions, and particularly in terms of their shared concern for the development of greater wellbeing for all. So the key table in Chapter 3 illustrating the relationship between Christianity and economics (and other disciplines) is titled 'Mapping Christianity's practices, ethics and beliefs from secular and religious sources of wellbeing in the twenty-first century' (pp. 66–67). These shared narratives of the relationships between economics, ethics and Christianity are therefore integral to the arguments, histories and evidences of this story.

Other particular features of this relationship between Christianity and economics also warrant a little further exploration.

The focus on 'the world of daily life' as the world that most people inhabit most of the time, does not, and never has in human history, precluded people inhabiting other worlds, other fields, including the religious, scientific and economic, and they all frequently and inevitably overlap (Bellah 2011, 8). And such different culture systems, like Christianity and economics, often work in different ways towards different ends, even though they also overlap. So it is always important to recognize the clear distinctions between them, where they do and don't overlap, and to acknowledge that all such culture systems develop similarly (whatever their exponents claim otherwise) and all impact on the world of daily life, and vice versa.

In recognizing the significance of such fields of reality in general, and of the religious field in particular, it is important to acknowledge that this argument will focus on Christian traditions because it is the one I inhabit and therefore am most familiar with, but also because Christianity remains the biggest world religion (size is important, as we will later see with China's contribution to global poverty reduction!). It is important, too, to recognize the uniqueness of each religion, and therefore of all religions, even though they are often historically related to each other, and share important features. This will become particularly evident later in this chapter, in Chapter 3, and in the introduction to Part 2, where the world's major religions play an important part in the argument along with the growing significance of spiritualities, both religious and secular. In other words, in this argument, Christianity is both exemplar of and entry point into a plurality of religions and spiritualities.

In developing that relationship between Christianity, religions and economics, the contemporary resurgence of religions globally has ensured the growing importance of religions in the public place where economics is located, including for Christianity, in the form of the emergence of public theology. In other words, theology 'may be "personal"' (Tracy 1981, 6), but it is never simply private, and it contributes, and is accountable, to at least Tracy's three public realms of academy, Church and society. Interestingly, the great public theologian, Max Stackhouse, whom I was privileged to meet in Princeton, has added economy as a fourth public realm, in recognition of its centrality in all public life (Stackhouse 2007, 110). Public theologians, as one could usefully call them now, have attempted, certainly from the 1970s, to engage this public of economics with varying degrees of adequacy and probably with little if any effect on economics. The emerging corpus of such works is growing, including from Munby, Preston, Sedgwick, Brown and Poole in Britain, Wogaman, Meeks, Stackhouse, Long and Tanner in the USA, Grenholm in Sweden, and Goudzwaard and van den Hoogen in The Netherlands (see bibliography).

Importantly, the engagement of Christianity with economics necessarily involves other related disciplines, particularly when addressing wellbeing studies. For example, the collaboration between psychology and economics in terms of, for instance, the economic behaviour of economic agents, whether individuals, households or nations, is gradually influencing and changing mainstream economics. Through the work of another Princeton scholar and Nobel economics laureate, the psychologist Daniel Kahneman, but then spilling out into the work of such positive psychologists as Diener, Seligman and Haidt, this major discipline robustly interacts with economics, thereby making an important contribution to the Christian–economics engagement. This initially focuses on subjective wellbeing, as we will see in Chapter 3. The construction of the table illustrating the resonances over wellbeing between these disciplines is also extended to involve sociology's work on religion and wellbeing. When engaging income and health – the other constituent parts of wellbeing in Chapters 2 and 3 – the involved disciplines extend much wider to embrace economic history and biodemography.

Running through this presentation of the economics of wellbeing and its engagement with Christianity also involves the acknowledgement of the intrinsic importance of evidence-based research, clearly fully implanted in economics and other social sciences, but, in my argument, also beginning to become an integral part of the development of a religious studies which is therefore able to make a more effective contribution to such interdisciplinary studies. It is that evidence-based research – *Kaozheng*, in eighteenth-century Chinese history (Morris 2011, 473), paralleling in some ways, though not sufficient to underwrite an industrial revolution, the model of Western Europe's scientific revolution – which is now beginning to penetrate and resource a more adequate religious studies, as developed in this argument.

Finally, although this thesis focuses on the actual and potential contribution of Christianity (and other religions and none) to human wellbeing, it clearly cannot and must not pursue that important purpose at the expense of not acknowledging the contribution of Christianity and other religions to human ill-being. The deeply negative consequences of human social development are, of course, an integral part of this formal argument, embodied, for example, in the inequalities of nations as one of the great paradoxes of social development. This will spill out into the problem of ceilings for and to human development, reinforced by the always devastating consequences of famines, epidemics, migrations, environmental damage and state failures – graphically portrayed in the Bible by the classic four horsemen of the Book of Revelation, symbolically and tellingly the last book of the Christian Scriptures. In all these deeply destructive aspects of social development, religions have played their damaging part and continue to do so. Reflecting on this perspective on the history of Christianity, Grace Jantzen, in her study of Julian of Norwich noted how she always concluded that 'all shall be well', yet equally recognized, 'it doesn't look well at all to me' as well she might, given the Black Death of 1348, the Peasants Revolt of 1381, the bad harvests and starvation resulting from climate change and the Great Schism in the Church with, at one point, three contending popes. Jantzen therefore rightly concluded that 'we cannot ignore the history of the collusion of Christendom with virtually every human evil of the Western world' (2011, 182, 132, xiv). Three hundred years later, the great philosopher and theologian Pascal, writing in the period of the devastating Thirty Years War of Religion in the seventeenth century, when over 2 million people died and Central Europe's population dropped by one third, commented that 'Men never do evil so completely and cheerfully as when they do it from religious conviction' (2003, 265). And then in our own twenty-first century, Christopher Hitchens would write after 9/11 that 'religion poisons everything' (2007, 15–36). We can't examine religions' contributions to wellbeing in isolation from their negative contributions to life.

Some tools for religious studies' engagement with such an agenda

In engaging the wealth, wellbeing and inequalities of nations, the issue of *how* best to do this as religious studies becomes an integral part of the process of developing such an agenda. Yet, as the title suggests, this challenging of religious studies becomes an inevitable and necessary two-way process. So the first two tools reflect the contribution of economics, psychology, sociology and economic history to constructing a more adequate religious studies for such an engagement. The final two tools reflect more religious studies' added value to secular tools, particularly out of the Christian tradition.

First, economics particularly develops three tools in its engagement with economic life: modelling, in terms of illuminating the world of daily life by 'stripped down representations of the phenomena out there'; locating economics in life's occurrences and ideas in context, particularly using economic history and its increasing use of economic tools; and finally, the measurement of such realities, particularly using 'a statistical approach' (Dasgupta 2007, 9–12). All three will be deployed in developing religious studies' contribution to our agenda, and particularly in Chapters 3, 4 and 5. One of the most important (for me) results of this research is the development of a Christian model to engage the three perspectives of the wealth, wellbeing and inequalities of nations, which also draws on economic history and statistical resources.

Second, one of the most important and useful developments in contemporary religious studies has been the growing interest in practical theology reflected, for example, in pastoral studies, the sociology of religion, public theology and Christian social ethics. But it is the discipline of psychology that has particularly illuminated this significant contribution to human knowledge, in theory and practice, namely what Seligman calls the necessary and mutually enriching interaction between basic and applied research. He rightly recognizes that '[t]he principle that good science involves the active interplay between application and pure science', even though this principle often sits 'uneasily both with the pure scientists and with the appliers' (2011, 61). And that is equally relevant to the assumed dominance in religious studies of 'pure' (often systematic) theology in relation to the reflections on the practice of Christians and their institutions. Correcting this disastrous imbalance will be at the heart of the arguments of Chapters 3, 4 and 5. But its evidential base is also central to the research behind Chapter 2 and the dominant role played in the Industrial and Mortality Revolutions by a knowledge profoundly reflecting that interaction between Seligman's basic and applied research.

Third, one of the problems facing religious studies' adequate engagement with such an agenda is its profound difficulty in reconciling its historic and necessary engagement with the personal, with each human being, made, in terms of its central beliefs and sacred literatures, in the image and likeness of God and therefore of inestimable value and worth. That is, and always will be, its strength, yet on its own it is also a profound limitation, unless it can also engage with individuals in large groups, in the mass, in, in economics' language, the aggregate, the macro. The great changes in material and health wellbeing in the last 200 years are due principally to large forces or collectivities (certainly consisting of myriads of individual contributions, but their sum total is always much greater than the contribution of individual efforts).

Bellah understandably begins to wrestle with this problem in his *Religion in Human Evolution*, dealing as he is with almost unimaginable long periods of time and the processes of organized organic wholes. So he rightly argues that, 'seeing reality' or 'seeing Being' begins with numbers and calculations which 'enables the mind to "view" the great and small in themselves abstracted from their concrete manifestation' (2011, 578). But I find systematic theologian Charry's tool of monovision drawn from optometry, as most useful. For this indicates how one eye is used for reading, for close-up work, while the other eye is used for distance, long viewing, with the brain bringing them together into a cohesive workable whole. It is the placing of the close at hand, including individual lives, in their larger contexts, which allows us, as Charry rightly notes, to stand back from the particular scene in order to give 'the viewer more freedom and time to discern the best response' (2013b, 2, 5). For this book is primarily and necessarily about seeing and analysing the world of daily life on the large scale, in the aggregate, in the context of the nations of the world. In no way does this neglect the experience of individuals, their particular families and communities. For example, the major trend in growing inequalities within developed economies, like the USA and UK, and the consequent disturbing pressures on individual and family standards of living is a disruptive factor from the 1970s to the present. And that is reflected, as such trends always are, in the lives of ordinary people, for example in the 400 food banks across the UK, with even more in the USA. Perhaps the Christian Scriptures give particular added value to such a tool as monovision when it talks of 'the knowledge of the glory of God in the face of Christ' (2 Cor. 4.6). This insight gave such rich meaning to my research in Salford in the 1970s working with the young unemployed, for we uncovered the statistical reality of that unemployment and always saw these facts on the faces of the young unemployed. That's the tool of monovision for developing this agenda.

Fourth, the tool of 'inter-ization' (sorry!), although embedded increasingly, though very insufficiently, in contemporary interdisciplinary studies, as some of my major secular economic sources acknowledge, is given added value when illustrated from the religious studies experience. For the latter, its intrinsic importance also therefore contributes to the wider secular debates on method and process in pursuing greater wellbeing. Christian experience therefore suggests a threefold, three-dimensional 'inter-ization' paradigm for promoting greater wellbeing (Atherton, Baker and Reader 2011, 108f.).

The first dimension is intrafaith, or collaboration within religions, including between Christian denominations, for example the Porvoo Agreement between the British Anglican churches and the Nordic and Baltic Lutheran churches. This then widens out into ecumenical agreements, for example, leading to the historic formation of the British Council of Churches in 1942 at the height of World War Two, and which William Temple rightly and historically referred to in his enthronement sermon as 'the great new fact of our era' (Iremonger 1948, 387). The even more significant founding of the World Council of Churches followed the War in 1948. Given the appalling histories of interdenominational conflict, such emerging collaborations provided a significant positive model for the necessary addressing of often profound differences of opinion and experience.

In the second dimension, this cooperation spills out to embrace interfaith relations between religions, initially, in the later twentieth century, the traditional Western focus on the Abrahamic religions of Judaism, Christianity and Islam, but now rightly and necessarily extending to embrace the great religions of the East – Hinduism, Buddhism and Confucianism – including significantly as recognition of the current rebalancing of the global economy now embracing India and China. These religions and developments will be strongly represented in Chapter 3 and the introduction to Part 2. Yet it is also becoming evident, from empirical research, that interfaith needs to include (it may be a separate category or dimension) interspirituality, as the collaboration between established religious and growing secular spiritualities. This will again feature in Chapter 3.

The third dimension is the emergence of collaboration as the interdisciplinary, as the cooperation between secular and religious disciplines, traditions and experiences. This delivers more adequate theory (through participation in the basic–applied research interaction) and practice (as partnerships between secular and religious bodies and developed particularly in the UK in Chapter 5). The hesitantly possible emerging of a renewed relationship between Christianity and economics clearly also demonstrates such interdisciplinarity. My conclusive view clearly regards this third type of collaboration as now the most important for developing greater wellbeing, with the first two types now feeding into it, though retaining their particular identities.

How the argument evolves: An emerging thesis on Christianity, economics and wellbeing

In many ways this is an exploratory essay rather than a scholarly monograph. Its modest length illustrates this more experimental character. Its arguments are stated in only two parts.

The first part explores the growing and telling evidence for the wealth, wellbeing and inequalities of nations through the three perspectives of income, health and subjective wellbeing in Chapter 2. Chapter 3 then develops a model from the interaction between secular and Christian (and other religions) understandings of the nature and significance of the religious contributions to engage initially the third perspective of subjective wellbeing. This then recognizes the likely feasibility of the model's transferability and adaptability to engaging the second (health) and then the first (income) perspectives. Together, they could constitute a model for Christian engagements with economics (and other disciplines concerned, say, with wellbeing studies, for example psychology). This represents the cumulative result of much research in various fields of religious studies. And it constitutes an ongoing field of activity, not least in terms of further testing and elaboration of the proposed model. It represents, probably, the heart of this thesis.

Yet the second part of the argument's importance lies in the significance of locating this work in a historical context stretching back to the end of the last Ice Age, say around 13,000 BCE, and forward to 2000 CE. This illustrates how social development has gradually increased over that long period, in both the West and East, but how, highlighted by that context of continuing and evolving change, the developments in the last 200 years, from about 1800 CE, represent the most remarkable changes in the whole of human history. This therefore illustrates and confirms the importance of the choice of the two following representative case studies engaging that decisive period from 1700 CE to 2000 CE, and drawn from the USA and UK, two nations at the forefront of such dramatic change. They illustrate what, how, and why Christianity has contributed to increasing human wellbeing.

The argument, initially in the first part, is robustly purposeful yet significantly exploratory, therefore indicating this is an argument in midstream process of development, to be tested further, hopefully, in terms of the wider task of relating Christianity to economics, by a growing number of disciplines. The argument also flows backwards and forwards, across the different chapters, from the economics of wellbeing and then Christianity's contribution to it, but then into how that actually emerged in modern regional histories. Religious studies interacts with and therefore challenges such an agenda and context, and thus it is intentionally developed as an integral part of the emerging thesis. It is not left to the end, as so often is the case, but is woven into and through the secular material. So Chapter 3, Christianity's contribution to wellbeing, is essentially and profoundly complementary to Chapter 2 on the wealth, wellbeing and inequalities of nations. If I had the skill and time, the two chapters could be redrafted (now that I have worked out a model for engaging economics) as one large cohesive structure. As it is, they are robustly two sides of the same coin, the pursuit of human wellbeing.

Finally, at certain points of the evolving arguments, important contributions to the reformulation of religious studies are developed. These include reflections in Chapter 3 on the measurement of religion's contribution to wellbeing; a table incorporating (from both secular and Christian traditions) Christianity's correlative relationship with secular understandings of wellbeing; reflections on the required reformulations of both systematic theology and its location in wider and more important understandings of Christian traditions; and the nature and significance of the transmission processes through which Christianity positively influences the development of human wellbeing.

As an illustration of monovision's focus on the particular, on the short vision of focusing on the individualities of transforming change, I will continue to deploy stories from my own history, essentially as exemplifying the wider facts of the aggregate wider changes of the long-term sighting of monovision but embodied in a very personal face, mine. And from that history, my father was fond of reciting the monologues of the Lancashire comedian Stanley Holloway, and particularly from his version of the Battle of Waterloo, based on 'Sam, pick up thy musket'. It ends with Wellington declaring 'Righto lads, let battle commence'. And so it will in the following argument.

Part 1

Getting Better-ish

> In Christ we are offered the possibility of partaking in the reality of God and in the reality of the world, but not in one without the other. The reality of God discloses itself only by setting me entirely in the reality of the world ... (Bonhoeffer 1995, 193)

From the eighteenth century, two Revolutions – the Industrial and Mortality (Easterlin 2004, 19) – transformed the world and human wellbeing. That process still continues, accelerating and extending its influence for good or bad. Talk of postmodernism was, as most post-isms are, a flash in the pan. These processes are not. They are here to stay. Both revolutions centred particularly on economics and knowledge. Yet from the eighteenth century, relations between Christianity and economics began to deteriorate, a process accelerating into the present. Bonhoeffer's critically clear observation that God's reality discloses itself by setting me entirely in the reality of the world is just not true for most theologians, who have not understood this great gulf with any seriousness. Yet Christianity's and other religions' commitment to pursuing abundant life as central to God's purposes could and should be expected to engage constructively such change.

This first part of the book explores these transformations in national wellbeing and Christianity's contribution to them. First, Chapter 2 illustrates in some detail and through important analyses, the astonishing improvements in the three perspectives of the income, health and subjective wellbeing of nations focusing on economics' contribution to them, but also engaging a variety of related disciplines, including psychology. This is an important reminder that 'human wellbeing has many different aspects, often related but not the same' (Deaton 2013, 55) from health to education, from income to participation in governance. Yet alongside these 'great escapes' from hunger and premature death are the 'great divergences' (Pomeranz 2000), in this case, as illustrated by the breath-taking increases in inequalities in income, health and subjective wellbeing, particularly between, but also within, nations. It is the recognition of the paradoxical nature of social development, in this case in the form and substance of these grave inequalities, which profoundly qualifies the achievements of the Industrial and Mortality Revolutions, and accounts for the addition of '*ish*' to 'better' in the title of this Part 1. 'Ish' is a Lancashire dialect usage, signifying reservations, questioning. It was one of my contributions to many Princeton conversations!

Using Bonhoeffer's words at the beginning of this section, how does the reality of God disclose itself in relation to such pioneering research into the wellbeing of nations? This next task, elaborated in Chapter 3, identifies and elaborates Christianity's (and other religions' and secular spirituality's) contributions initially to the third perspective on the wealth and wellbeing of nations, namely their subjective wellbeing, using, importantly, secular sources interacting with Christian traditions. These outline Christianity's practices, ethics and beliefs, their correlative but also causal relationships to wellbeing, and how such contributions occur and can be measured. Such developments also represent theological understandings corresponding with knowledge developments from the Industrial and Mortality Revolutions. These discoveries generate a tested model which can then begin to engage the remaining two perspectives on the wealth and wellbeing of nations, namely income and health.

2

Great Escapes and Divergences

The greatest escapes in all human history have been from hunger and premature death. And they have occurred in our *recent* history. For, from about the late eighteenth century, there were inaugurated astonishing increases in income and related dramatic reductions in poverty for more and more people. This was accompanied with equally dramatic increases in life expectancy. These processes have continued ever since, and that continuity is again unparalleled in human history. So even since the early 1960s, when I began work as a young clergyman in Aberdeen, 'nearly all countries have become richer and their residents longer lived'. Things have, and are, getting better, for 'both the health and income parts of wellbeing have improved over time' (Deaton 2013, 37). The third perspective on wellbeing, how we feel about such positive change, which will also be examined in this chapter, has also witnessed great change, moving from a concern with 'How can I be saved?' to 'How can I be happy?' (Deaton 2013, 84), how can I seek personal fulfilment, how can we find better ways of improving our lives? And to do that has meant improving the material conditions of daily life and improving our health. Both these achievements feed into how we judge our lives to be doing and how we feel about our daily experiences. And such subjective wellbeing, in turn, influences our material and health conditions.

Lying behind these amazing and historic changes particularly in income and health, are the Industrial and then Mortality Revolutions, revolutions we continue, and will continue for the foreseeable future, to be in the midst of. The first, the Industrial Revolution, beginning in Britain in the late eighteenth century, represented for the American economist Easterlin, the onset of self-sustaining modern economic growth, raising material living standards tenfold among the leaders of the process (Easterlin 2004, 19). The Mortality Revolution began in the later nineteenth century and was driven by public health processes, discoveries of germ theories and then cures for infections. The result has already been a doubling of life expectancy, calculated from birth, in many parts of the world. The combined results of these two ongoing revolutions delivered humanity a freedom 'from hunger and starvation, and from the enormously high rates of infant and child mortality that have plagued humankind throughout history' (Easterlin 2004, 19).

Although both revolutions were deeply informed by economic processes, it was knowledge that played the greater part (Easterlin 2004, 17), particularly in terms of 'improvements in scientific and medical knowledge, or at least' ... (in) 'the greater practical implementation of existing scientific and medical knowledge' (Deaton 2013, 41). And intimately and increasingly part of all these processes was the role of measuring mechanisms. As Deaton rightly observes, '[p]rogress cannot be coherently discussed without definitions and supportive evidence' (Deaton 2013, 15), and enlightened government (and I will add religions in the next chapter!) is impossible without the effective and efficient collection and analysis of reliable data. The arguments running through this chapter are particularly dependent on such measurements.

Yet accompanying these great escapes, and inextricably bound together, are the great divergences, particularly expressed in this argument as the alarming growing inequalities between but also within nations. These are especially reflected in the huge disparities between the incomes of nations, but also in their health, including as life expectancies, what we have already referred to as the profound paradoxes of development. And these disparities are likely to be linked to the processes of industrialization, as Deaton has rightly observed, that '[t]oday's global inequality was, to a large extent, created by the success of modern economic growth' (2013, 4). For the latter can be achieved by some at the expense of others; witness the deployment of empire building to the benefit of mother countries and to the cost of the invaded, or the current exploiting of gross inequalities in say the USA and UK by the top income and wealth holders. As Stiglitz, another Nobel economic laureate, has observed, inequalities are an inevitable and indeed necessary part of any efficient and effective economy, not least because '[s]ome individuals will work harder and longer than others, and any well-functioning economic system has to reward them for these efforts' (2012, 7). Yet when these inequalities become so extensive and concentrated, they increasingly damage growth and impair efficiency to the great detriment, therefore, of the common good of all.

The effects of this great divergence are so great as to challenge both economics and Christianity. For economists, their deployment of what is called the Pareto principle, that if a few get rich and no one gets hurt, then we're all better off, can be, for Deaton (and Sen) 'routinely and incorrectly' applied to income, 'ignoring other aspects of wellbeing' (Deaton 2013, 8; Sen 1988, 31–2). For wellbeing, as we will see in the third section of this chapter, involves far more than material living standards, central as these are; so if the rich undermine the public provision of education, health and governance, that damages the wellbeing of all. This, of course, then leads into affirming what Chapter 1 concluded, that ethics runs through so many of these economic concerns, whether income or health. For economists like Sen, Stiglitz and Deaton, that ethical dimension in economic affairs *also* then extends into a formal recognition of what Deaton calls a 'moral obligation' for those in rich economies to help those in the poor ones – to help reduce poverty and ill-health (2013, 15). And these debates then lead naturally, and, I believe, logically, into Christianity's involvement in addressing inequalities and poverty. Traditionally, it has focused unduly on the poor and the marginalized, on, essentially, the great divergences. Yet the accompanying great escapes from hunger and premature death have been humanity's greatest achievement, even though these have also contributed to growing inequalities. To address the latter without therefore addressing their inextricable relationship to the former – the great achievement in reducing poverty – is both ill-advised and, in the end, not productive of wellbeing, and indeed, may be counter-productive. When Christ lived and ministered in first-century Palestine, the vast majority were poor and often ill-treated by the very small minority of the rich. And, he was lucky to live as long as he did, despite the horrible death he experienced. Now all that has changed and is changing mostly for the better. That requires theologians and church leaders to begin to understand these dramatic and historic changes.

The material assembled for this chapter has been accumulated for at least a decade, but Angus Deaton's *The Great Escape: Health, Wealth and the Origins of Inequality* has provided me with a robust and comprehensive framework for strategically deploying these wider, earlier sources. Indeed, it can also be seen as a useful entry point into them, not least because they often confirm his concept of 'escaping' from pre-1800 history. So I first came across particularly the material on hunger and nutrition and their connection to life expectancy and height (a key indicator of nutritional resources) in Fogel's little classic, *The Escape from Hunger and Premature Death* (2004). The economic historian Clark's *A Farewell to Alms* (2007) continued these themes, as did Easterlin's *The Reluctant Economist: Perspectives on Economics, Economic History and Demography* (2004), and particularly his powerfully researched engagement with the Industrial and Mortality Revolutions and his pioneering work, as the first economist to do so, on subjective wellbeing. The latter takes us into the third perspective, where I early encountered the work of the British economist Richard Layard and his *Happiness: Lessons from a New Science* (2005), but then I moved into the closely related field of psychology, and particularly the works of Kahneman, Diener, Seligman and Haidt. So when I use Deaton as a most useful and viable framework, part of its value is that it confirms so much of this other research. But it does more. It introduces us to new research, some of it challenging the results of these earlier pioneers. But that is as it should be in such rapidly evolving fields of enquiry.

I want to end this introduction with a splendid picture. It's from the ancient parish church of St Mary Magdalene in

GREAT ESCAPES AND DIVERGENCES

Picture 1. *Picturing Death and Riches in England in 1505: panels on the Markham chantry chapel in St Mary Magdalene church, Newark-on-Trent, Nottinghamshire.*

Newark-on-Trent, Nottinghamshire, England. It is taken from the outside panels of the Markham chantry chapel and dates from the very early sixteenth century. It's a remarkable survival given the targeted destruction of such chapels commemorating the dead particularly by Edward VI. It depicts a dancing skeleton flourishing a carnation and pointing to the grave, and on the right, a well-dressed young man with his hand on his purse! The pictures convey the warning that death awaits even the most well-to-do and wealth cannot buy him off! Both death and wealth were as much part of the late Middle Ages in Europe and much of the Middle East, as they are now. But with the most profound of differences, which these two figures of death and prosperity signify. Now death comes to most in old age, not as little children, and prosperity is no longer the prerogative of the elite few, but is increasingly the privileged possession of most people on earth. That's called a better world of daily life for most people on earth. And that's a first, maybe the greatest first, in human history. And you can see why it is from that chantry chapel 500 years ago.

The first perspective on wellbeing: Increasing 'the £ in your pocket': improving material wellbeing, yet what of income inequalities?

> Behold, I make a covenant. Before all your people I will do marvels, such as have not been wrought in all the earth or in any nation. (Exod. 34.10 KJV).

And that's precisely what has happened in God's world in the last two centuries, in terms of astonishing increasing standards of living, reducing poverty, and the positive consequences of both for health and subjective wellbeing. Yet these advances were also accompanied by increasing inequalities which were also of deep divine concern.

Although this survey examines three perspectives on wellbeing, there are others of real importance for wellbeing, including education, participation, families, values and philosophies of life. However, material wellbeing as income is not just central to wellbeing but often essential resource for the effective enabling of these other features. We know, for example, that higher incomes lead generally to higher levels of health and subjective wellbeing. It essentially and profoundly undergirds the world of daily life.

What is material wellbeing regarded as income? Income is important for wellbeing in itself, but also as a key component say of housing, clothing, and food, and as a facilitator of other aspects of wellbeing, including health care, education, governance and security, welfare provision and culture. So material wellbeing is 'typically measured by income' in terms of the amount spent and saved by individuals, households and nations. It therefore represents 'people's ability to buy the things on which material wellbeing depends' (Deaton 2013, 16). The consumer as individual, household and society therefore plays an essential role in the emergence of the Industrial Revolution, together improving the standards of living and quality of life of an increasing number of the world's population. For example, in developed economies like the USA, people spend a third of their money on durable and non-durable goods (importantly moving from providing and consuming more things, to better things), 13 per cent on food, 18 per cent on services like housing and utilities, and 16 per cent on health care – all 'the stuff of material wellbeing' (Deaton 2013, 172). Theologians and moralists regularly denounce such material wellbeing, particularly as consumption, without, as usual, understanding its wider economic significance.

In order to understand better the nature and extent of these continuing transformations in material wellbeing, it helps to contrast these changes with what went before. In 1798, Parson Malthus (as Marx rather rudely called him) published his seminal *An Essay on the Principle of Population*, arguing that increases in population increasingly outstrip the increases in the food, shelter and clothing required to resource them. The gap could only be closed either by education and morality (to marry later and have fewer children, the positive check), or by starvation, war or disease (reducing the population to balance the resources, the preventative check). In demography and economic history, say for Clark, this became known as the Malthusian Trap, and it operated throughout history, and certainly from 14,000 BCE until about 1800 CE. In other words, until 1800, economic life (and so the world of daily life) was shaped by one factor, that 'in the long run births had to equal deaths' (Clark 2007, 19). So before 1800, rates of technological advance in all economies were so low that incomes couldn't escape the Malthusian equilibrium. The only way to improve living standards effectively was to lower the population level by reducing fertility or increasing mortality. Average living standards (for the vast proportion of the population) meant that most people lived 'a pinched and straightened existence' (Clark 2007, 38), working every hour that God sent them, with a very poor diet so low in calories as to produce short people often unable to work, with poor clothing, and crowded into insanitary housing. That was the world for most before 1800, and it was the Industrial Revolution that broke through this trap, changing 'forever the possibilities for material consumption' with all that brings for human wellbeing (Clark 2007, 2). So income per person began its inexorable rise, delivering increasing numbers out of poverty and premature death, *and* accompanied by astonishingly increasing populations (from 1,000 million in 1820, to 7,000 million today – totally breath-taking *because*, for the first time in history, this population explosion was also accompanied by increasing material wellbeing and increasing life expectancy).

Behind these changes lay, for Easterlin (2004, xiii), the recent history of modern economic growth, described by Kuznet's innovatory research of 1966 as 'a sustained increase in per capita income' (GNP divided by population) accompanied by an increase in population (Fogel 2000, 51) and by sweeping structural changes in the economy (including in the distribution of labour among economic activities, such as agriculture, manufacturing and service occupations). So British per capita income resulting from these processes increased ninefold from 1750 (Fogel 2000, 52).

It would be helpful to clothe these historic radical trends in the greater detail of three aspects integral to the shape and performance of material wellbeing: increasing incomes, decreasing poverty and increasing inequalities – essentially the stories of great escapes and divergences.

Increasing incomes

As a result of the Industrial Revolution's 'long-term and continuing economic growth', from 1820 to 1992 the average income of the world's inhabitants grew between seven and eight times, constituting a 'historically unprecedented increase in living standards' (Deaton 2013, 4–5, 167).

In the USA, per capita income rose from $8,000 in 1929, to $43,238 in 2012, a fivefold increase in only 80 years and the result of an economic growth of 1.9 per cent per annum, quite astonishing to our ancestors, yet not to us (Deaton 2013, 170).

In Britain, the average annual rate of growth of per capita national income increased from 0.2 per cent between 1760 and 1800, to 1.98 per cent between 1830 and 1870. Continuing growth in per capita income resulted in the average Briton in

1960 being nearly six times richer than their grandfathers in 1860 (Ferguson 2011, 199).

Inevitably, we have to ask whether this growth in income is worth having. Well, we have escaped from severe poverty; we are all able to purchase new goods and services enabling us to do previously impossible things; for example, we have better transport, clean water, decent sanitation, electronic communications and hip replacements! Yet inevitably there have been damaging consequences from such processes in terms of lifestyles, psychological depressions (what one psychologist has called 'the Age of Melancholy'), inequalities and environmental crises (Seligman 2006, 63). Yet Deaton's conclusion, in surveying all the evidence, is worth considering by Christians: 'No one denies that economic growth has negative side effects, but on balance it is enormously beneficial!' (2013, 174) And we are happier and don't die in childhood!

Decreasing poverty

One of the great consequences of increasing incomes has been the deep erosion of the numbers living in extreme poverty, a key illustration of the breaking of the Malthusian Trap. So between 1820 and 1992 the fraction of the world's population in extreme poverty dropped from 84 per cent to 24 per cent (Deaton 2013, 167). Even between 1981 and 2008, the numbers of the world's poor fell from 1.5 billion to 805 million, astonishingly despite population increases of 2,000 million, mostly in these poorer economies (Deaton 2013, 249–50). For unlike in the USA and UK, after 1970, growth of average incomes after 1975 in these poorer economies 'did much to reduce extreme poverty in the world'. This dramatic reduction was therefore due principally to China and India's economic growth, containing as they do one-third of the world's population and between them, taking over 1,000 million people out of poverty, and constituting 'the greatest escape of all' (Deaton 2013, 247).

Importantly, although such extreme poverty has virtually disappeared from advanced economies, their rightful and necessary refocusing on relative poverty, in terms of the ability to make ends meet and so to be able to participate effectively in society, has revealed the determined persistence of such marginalization from the mainstreams of society. For example, using the official US poverty line reveals 22 per cent living in poverty in 1959, dropping to 15 per cent in 2010 (in 2011, still representing 46.2 million people!) (Deaton 2013, 180–1). In Britain, the Rowntree Foundation 2013 Report identified 13 million living below the poverty line (Cooper 2014, 12). That constitutes one of the great moral and economic challenges to advanced economies, intimately linked as it is to the following trend.

Increasing inequality

Increasing inequality is the classic indicator of the great divergences, a powerful justification of the description of the dramatic changes since 1800 as the paradox of development. According to Deaton, '[t]his historically unprecedented increase in living standards came with huge increases in income inequality, both between countries and between individuals within countries' (2013, 167–8). It was a dramatic change from inequality being located predominantly within nations before 1800 and between the vast majority of the population and rich landowning elites. From 1800 that character of inequality changed to that of inequalities between nations. Note that the living standards of all the world's peoples are now closer together, not least because of China and India's efforts. This does not apply to *nations*, as we will now see.

According to Deaton, income inequality is by far the greatest between nations. The world's very wealthiest countries are now 256 times richer than the very poorest, truly a Great Divergence (Deaton 2013, 20). For the economist Sachs, in 1820 the biggest gap between the richest in per capita income, represented by the UK, and the poorest, represented by Africa, was 4:1. In 1998, the gap between the richest, the USA, and the poorest, Africa, had risen to 20:1. An important – maybe key – reason for this alarming disparity was that US GNP per capita income grew at an annual rate of 1.7 per cent between 1820 and 1998. In contrast, Africa's grew by an average of 0.7 per cent per annum (Sachs 2005, 28–30). Over 180 years, that apparently modest difference produces quite enormous disparities.

Inequalities within nations, and particularly the richest, like the USA and UK, have returned to a disturbing accelerating process. After 1945, all shared in rising prosperity until the mid 1970s, when growth began to slow and incomes began to pull apart. In the USA, the bottom 20 per cent gained very little at 0.2 per cent per annum over the past 44 years; thus, allowing for inflation, their real incomes were no higher than in the late 1970s. In contrast, the average annual income growth of the top 20 per cent was 1.6 per cent. In other words, for the great majority, 'Each generation is barely holding onto the living standards of its parents' (Deaton 2013, 189, 205). For Stiglitz, the national US income going to the top *0.1 per cent* (16,000 families) rose from just over 1 per cent in 1980 to nearly 5 per cent now – a bigger share than in America's notorious pre-1914 'Gilded Age' or the 'Great Barbecue' (Stiglitz 2012, xi–xii). Analysis suggests a variety of factors underlying this acutely growing disparity of incomes, including demand for skills rising more rapidly than supply; lower wages declining in real terms due to globalization (work transferred to Asia); migration (evidence suggests this is a minor cause); and rising health-care costs borne by employees or citizens and so stifling wage growth.

The consequences of such severe and growing inequalities are increasingly recognized as affecting the economic performance of nations and particularly restraining economic growth. In periods of slowing growth, attention focuses more on the distribution of resources than their production – what is called distributional coalitions or special interest organizations, seeking to redistribute incomes rather than creating them, in ways which therefore reduce efficiency and output (Olson 1982, 67). And that means that the fittest (the top 20 per cent, then top 1 per cent, and now even the top 0.1 per cent) gain most through, for example, lobbying, cartels, subsidies, etc. – what is called rent seeking, that is drawing benefits without costs. And the rest, and particularly the poorest, do worst – 'no society rewards those who are least fit to thrive under its arrangements' (Olson 1982, 72).

Yet the implications of such inequalities inevitably stretch beyond economic life into the political arena. Increasingly powerful economic-based elites seek both to extend their resources and to curtail the public resources on which so many citizens, and particularly the more disadvantaged, depend for so much of their wellbeing, whether education (from schools to universities), health care, welfare support, local government services, cultural and environmental services. Deaton rightly regards such developments, in economic and political affairs, as threatening all citizens' material wellbeing and democracy's integrity, since '[i]f democracy becomes plutocracy, those who are not rich are effectively disenfranchised' (2013, 213). Stiglitz summarizes these developments so accurately and succinctly, in the title of his article for *Vanity Fair*, 'Of the 1 per cent, for the 1 per cent, by the 1 per cent' (2012, xxxix). Importantly, Piketty's recent major research findings confirm both the extent of contemporary inequalities and their damaging consequences for both economy and democracy. He argues that 'the rate of return on capital significantly' exceeded the economy's growth rates in the nineteenth century and now in the twenty-first century, so consequently 'inherited wealth grows faster than output and income'. It is therefore 'almost inevitable that inherited wealth will dominate wealth amassed from a lifetime's labor by a wide margin, and the concentration of capital will attain extremely high levels – levels potentially incompatible with the meritocratic values and principles of social justice fundamental to modern democratic societies' (2014, 26).

An issue emerging from this research on material or income wellbeing is of particular interest to Christianity, religions and the morally concerned. I could maybe call it the disease of the morally obvious or economically misguided. The economist Easterlin summarizes it as a question: 'Is Economic Growth Creating a New Postmaterialistic Society?' (2004, 32). He asks the question because the astonishing and continuing, indeed accelerating, increase in incomes and all that brings in terms of wellbeing has led some economists, social researchers and commentators to hope for a life transcending material wellbeing by moving into a postmaterial age, focused on self-realization including spirituality. This deeply human urge began in the mid nineteenth century with J. S. Mill, leading exponent of mainstream classical economics, hoping, in his *Principles of Political Economy* (1850), for a new era of human improvement, culture and morality. One of his successors, but a major reformer of neoclassical economics, J. M. Keynes, looked forward, in 1931, to the day when the '[e]conomic problem will take the back seat where it belongs and ... the arena of the heart and mind will be occupied ... by our real problems – the problems of life and human relations, of creation and behaviour and religion' (1932, vii).

The astonishing increases in material wellbeing, in education, health care and life expectancy since 1945 began to give real hope to such prophecy (as foreseeing the future), so Nobel economic laureate Fogel, in 1997, could write '[I]n the future luxury will be defined increasingly in terms of spiritual rather than material resources. The touchstone of well-being in the future for both young and old will be measured increasingly in terms of the quality of health and the opportunity for self-realization' (1997, 1905). But it was the American political scientist Inglehart who argued that empirical evidence clearly demonstrated the emergence of an increasingly postmaterialist society in the USA and Europe, that postmaterialist values have, in his words 'tended to neutralize the emphasis on economic accumulation' (1988, 1203). This is enough to strongly reinforce all the hopes of the religious and moral idealists, and their deep ill-ease with material wellbeing. But Easterlin has examined surveys between 1975 and 1994, and these reveal a quite different story: that 'the percentage of people naming the materialist response as part of the good life exceeded that of people giving the non-materialist response. But even more important, if we look at the trend in responses reflecting materialist concerns relative to those reflecting social concerns, the excess of those with materialist concerns *rose* between 1975 and 1994 from 7 to 21 per cent points. This suggests a shift toward materialist values, not away from them' (2004, 51, my emphasis). And it is here that Easterlin and Deaton agree, in spite of their conflict over the place of increasing incomes in increasing wellbeing. For in this argument on the postmaterial both agree that the material is still of decisive importance. In other words, material wellbeing is here to stay, but it has always been central to the world of daily life. Christianity, other religions and the morally–spiritually minded do need to come to terms with that. And they are not very good at it at all.

The second perspective on wellbeing: Escaping from premature death

In the mid 1970s, David Landes, doyen of economic historians at Harvard, in lecturing to over 1,000 students in economics, said: 'Look to the left of you and to the right of you. If it were not for the Industrial Revolution, two out of three of you would not be alive' (Fogel 2000, 44). That's how to wake students up, and it's how to get us all to realize the benefits of the last century. We're not dead. So this section examines research evidence and analysis relating to the dramatic and continuing changes in life expectancy and health, and the reasons for them. Much of the material used deploys some of Deaton's findings but with substantial additions from the earlier work of Easterlin and Fogel.

The major astonishing change in the last over 100 years is that we no longer die as children but as old people. And that means a health policy transition from addressing the infectious diseases of infants to engaging the chronic illnesses of the elderly, some of which, at 75, I have! Now the key way of measuring these changes is through examining life expectancy figures. These measure how long a baby born today can expect to live. Provided life is worth living, presumably more years to live is good for our wellbeing. Of course, some criticize this focus on life expectancy as though that is not really what wellbeing is about (it's often the same people who criticize material wellbeing in the same way). Yet, as Deaton reminds us, 'You need a life to have a *good* life' (2013, 24). So this material begins with life expectancy figures, but then moves into other related indices of health improvements, for example, people's height, indicating the profound importance of adequate nutrition for human wellbeing (this therefore links to the first perspective on wellbeing, as the escape from hunger). And running through all these positive changes in wellbeing, as with income, are accompanying inequalities.

In terms of life expectancy, in the USA this increased from 47.3 years in 1900 (20 per cent dying before the age of one), to 77.9 years in 2006, with a white middle class woman born today having a one in two chance of reaching 100 (Deaton 2013, 60, 25). In India, life expectancy is now 64, and in China it is 73, 'surely one of the most dramatic, rapid, and favorable changes in human history' (2013, 26, 89). In rich nations, life expectancy in the last 100 years has therefore increased by 30 years, with now two to three years added in every ten (2013, 6). Yet the Great Divergence also exists in this sector, with poorer nations' health statistics today worse than the USA's in 1910.

What lies behind these changes is the dramatic reductions in infant (dying before one) and child mortality (dying before five). For all history, a significant and tragic proportion of children died early, certainly 20 per cent of children. For example, in Sweden in 1751, one third died before their fifth birthday: it's now three in 1000. In Britain, 20 per cent died before their first birthday in the eighteenth and nineteenth centuries (Deaton 2013, 68–70). Two stories illustrate this tragedy of history. In the parish of Chopwell in the diocese of Durham, between 1900 and 1904, 'some 75 per cent of all burials were of infants less than one year old. The graveyard had been open for two years before its first adult internment, and that of a man aged only 29' (Lee 2007, 250). But then there's my family. My grandmother (on my father's side) gave birth in 1900 to a son, John Robert Atherton, who died well before the age of one. There's every chance I was named after him. In 1910, in the USA, a similar percentage died before the age of five. And the inequalities in life expectancy follow on from this, because in Sierra Leone today, 25 per cent of children born don't reach five years old (Deaton 2013, 25). And although life expectancy is improving, 2 million children still die each year in the world because they were born in the wrong place. That's a human and moral scandal. For each time a child dies, a mother and father will have suffered greatly, as I'm sure my grandparents did at the early sudden death of the infant John Robert.

Yet, since 1945, life expectancy has begun to improve in poorer nations too. In 1950 over 100 nations lost more than 20 per cent of children before the age of one; by 1960, 41 nations lost over 20 per cent by the age of five (Deaton 2013, 102). The story of extending life expectancy across the world is therefore a continuing account of gradual progress.

These developments then shift the focus of health attention from treating the infectious diseases of childhood to the chronic illnesses of the elderly, and particularly cardiovascular diseases, cancers and dementia. Significant progress has been made here since the later twentieth century, but much of this engagement continues to be at an earlier stage of development, particularly in the latter two illnesses. Yet so much has been done to improve the quality of life of older people as well, from hip replacements to cataract operations. As Deaton concludes, '[b]etter health makes life better in and of itself, and it allows us to do more with our lives, to work more effectively, to earn more, to spend more time learning, to enjoy more and better times with our families and friends'. For, '[o]f all the things that make life worth living, extra years of life are surely among the most precious' (2013, 59, 7).

These historic changes are reflected in the fact that we are still alive, but also in our very height. Now height, unlike income and health, is clearly in itself not a measure of wellbeing. To be taller is not necessarily to be happier! Yet when a population is short (not an individual – this is about macro aggregates, not specific persons) that indicates widespread calorific or nutritional deficiencies, particularly in childhood. So variations in populations' heights are an effective indication of degrees of deprivation. Improving nutrition therefore benefits wellbeing as illustrated by height, but it takes generations to impact that height.

In Europe, the average height for adult males in the mid nineteenth century was 166.7cm (5 foot 5.5 inches). By 1980 it had reached 178.6cm (5 foot 10.5 inches). In India the average is still 151cm, shorter than the British average in the eighteenth century (life expectancy in India was only 27 in 1931). At the current rate of increase, it would take 200 years for Indian men to grow as tall as English men now and 500 years for women (Deaton 2013, 158, 160, 127). So once again, increases in wellbeing and inequalities exhibit a 'strong correlation around the world between getting richer and getting taller' (Deaton 2013, 164). It's not the facts on people's faces, as much as the facts in our bodies: 'Global improvements in health and income, as well as global inequalities, can be seen in people's bodies' (Deaton 2013, 26).

To add further value to these analyses, Fogel's work on the 'dimensions of misery' is of some importance (2004, 8). Before the later nineteenth century low levels of calorific intake (food) meant meagre food resulting in a meagre amount of energy available for work and lower stature and morbidity. The bottom 20 per cent of the British population lacked even the energy for sustained work, enough calorific intake to keep body and soul together, but not to move much! In other words, these figures 'show how persistent misery was down almost to the end of the nineteenth century' (Fogel 2004, 18). When the nutritional intake improved, it therefore affected for the better, people's wellbeing, as indicated through increasing heights and their ability to contribute and be rewarded economically. This thermodynamic factor accounts, for Fogel, for 30 per cent of British growth since 1790 (2004, 33). It also, interestingly, resulted in major egalitarian gains to the working class's wellbeing in the next few generations, in terms not just of relative income and life expectancy, but also height. In 1815, 'a typical British male worker at maturity was about five inches shorter than a mature male of upper-class birth'. The gap is now only one inch (Fogel 2004, 143–4).

In examining these statistics of basic wellbeing improvements, important arguments emerged regarding the explanations of such change. For Easterlin (corresponding much with Fogel and Deaton's research) what lay behind these dramatic changes in health was not so much the Industrial Revolution but what he usefully describes as the Mortality Revolution, a quite different revolution focused on increasing life expectancy, particularly from the later nineteenth century, and gradually extending across the world. The result was an astonishing increase in life expectancy from 40 to 70 years or more, with associated improvements in health through the great reduction in contagious diseases (Fogel 2004, 84). In other words, the Mortality Revolution = increasing life expectancy + the associated reduction in morbidity (disease, illness). And this, he argues, did as much for wellbeing improvement as the increase in living standards through the Industrial Revolution. Yet it's the latter we so often focus on, to the neglect or indeed exclusion of the former. They are two distinct but essentially complementary transformations in human wellbeing and should be seen as 'the result of technological breakthroughs in their respective areas' (Fogel 2004, 85–6). They spring, essentially, from a common source, 'the emergence and growing dominance of a scientific approach to the quest for human knowledge' (Fogel 2004, 86). Knowledge, rather than economics alone, drove the two revolutions. Yet they were distinct, including in timing, so knowledge only really began to impact health in the mid–late nineteenth century, at least a century later than the Industrial Revolution. It was driven particularly by the improved sanitation public health movement from about 1850, followed by the discoveries of the germ theory of diseases, reinforcing the public health movement, and finally in the twentieth century, with cures of infections, including through penicillin.

It is interesting, and of some importance, that these economists ascribe the causes of the Mortality Revolution more to knowledge than economics. Yet this apportioning of cause goes further, arguing that major developments in life expectancy and health often owe more to public bodies than to market mechanisms. For example, although Deaton is clear that the evidence indicates that proportionate increases in income are associated with increases in life expectancy, that higher incomes come with more life years (thus contradicting Wilkinson's argument that there is no relation between income and life expectancy in better off economies), he also recognizes that some poorer economies do much better than their income would suggest, for example Nepal, Bangladesh and Vietnam, and some do worse than their high income would suggest, namely the USA (2013, 33, 36). But it's Easterlin who takes this understanding further by arguing that so often public bodies rather than the market have played the greater role in delivering such improved life expectancy and health. For him, '[h]ad it been left to private markets during the last few decades, it is inconceivable that today some 80 per cent of the world's children would be immunized against the six major vaccine-preventable childhood diseases' (2004, 123). In other words, as Nobel economic laureate Arrow concluded, '[W]hen the market fails to achieve an optimal state, society will, to some extent at least, recognize the gap, and nonmarket social institutions will arise attempting to bridge it' (1963, 947).

But there's a further conclusion by the other economist, Fogel, in terms of confirming the extra-market and more knowledge-based contributions to improving health and life expectancy. He develops from his research the concept of technophysio evolution, the 'complex interaction between advances in the technology of production and improvements in human physiology', a synergistic relationship delivering breakthroughs in human life expectancy and health (2004, xv). It represents the evolutionary complement to genetic evolution, which has generated human and animal evolution over the last 7,000 generations of human life on earth. Technophysio evolution is a form of evolution unique to humankind, emerging in the last ten generations (since 1800) and is still continuing apace. It's this, in combination with other forces, which has driven the historic transformations in life expectancy and health. And, for Fogel, these improvements in human thermodynamic efficiency – food, energy intakes – have increased work output by about 50 per cent since 1790 (2000, 79).

The third perspective, subjective wellbeing: Are we happier?

It's never enough to be told how happy you are by experts! It's your happiness and so you are in a unique and indispensable place to contribute to building up our knowledge of happiness. And subjective wellbeing recognizes this by using survey-based self-reporting techniques. Like the previous perspectives on income and health, subjective wellbeing therefore has a particular contribution to make to our understanding of national wellbeing. Income and life expectancy are indispensable resources for wellbeing. Without them, life would really not be worth living. Yet having *worth* is also a profoundly intimate part of wellbeing, belonging equally to how individuals feel about their lives, how they estimate the value of their lives, including recognizing that feelings and valuings are also profoundly interrelated. Subjective wellbeing is about all this, and about how we can incorporate it into the kind of research findings behind income and health, including its measurement. And the task is to do this without eroding unduly its distinctive more personal and relational character (though you can't get more personal than being alive and its dependence on income and life expectancy). The links between the three perspectives are developed even further by the psychologist Seligman, when he argues that a third revolution accompanied the Industrial and Mortality Revolutions, a revolution resourcing a society 'that grants to its individual members powers they have never had before, a society that takes individual's pleasures and pains very seriously, that exalts the self and deems personal fulfilment a legitimate goal, an almost sacred rite' (Seligman 2006, 10).

In introducing and developing this material, the argument begins by examining the research findings of such economists as Easterlin, Graham and Layard, using Deaton's more critical framework. Because of the growing collaboration between economics and psychology, this then requires us to explore both the overlaps themselves and the major contribution made particularly by psychologists to wellbeing studies, and especially in the area of subjective wellbeing. We return finally to that overlap in the form of their agreed recognition of wellbeing's dependence on supportive institutions. And the overlaps between these agendas and findings and those of Christianity will regularly become both implicit and explicit. This will therefore lead naturally and logically into the following chapter on Christianity and wellbeing.

The economics of subjective wellbeing

Economics began to engage with subjective wellbeing in the early 1970s, particularly through the work of the American economist Easterlin and his pioneering 1974 article 'Does Economic Growth Improve the Human Lot?', focusing a continuing interest in the central relationship between income and subjective wellbeing. This research caused major problems for economists because of the required use of self-reporting surveys, deployed from other disciplines in the social sciences. They then adopted the two perspectives seen as constituting subjective wellbeing: life evaluation (how satisfied are you with your life?) and emotional wellbeing (how do you feel about life today?). It was through their work on these perspectives that economists went on to make major contributions to wellbeing studies, particularly in terms of what is now the highly contested question of how, why and to what extent income levels influence wellbeing states. The work of economists on the related contribution to wellbeing of the key realms or domains of life, like marriage, work and health, overlaps with the work of psychologists, as it does on the need to incorporate all such findings into new measurement systems of national wellbeing.

There is a 'long and respected' history in the social sciences of deploying survey research eliciting subjective testimonies (self-reporting) on feelings, beliefs, behaviours, etc. Yet the large amount of knowledge built up through such research was, for Easterlin 'unfortunately largely excluded from economic analysis', which is confusing since economics focuses on the economic behaviour of agents! But it is the form that behaviour is seen as taking that is significant. For 'Economists believe that what people *do* is more relevant than what they say' (Easterlin 2004, 21). For the American economist Carol Graham, economics therefore relies on studying '*revealed* preferences' as the chosen measure of welfare, and not on 'the *expressed preferences*' delivered by studying surveys of self-reporting (Graham 2011, 7–8 – my emphases). This traditional preference of mainstream neoclassical economists, particularly in welfare economics, has ensured that 'it is commonly assumed that higher real income increases wellbeing; that is, with more goods at their disposal, people will feel better off' (Easterlin 2004, 22). It has also, for Graham, meant the continuing and unfortunate reliance on an understanding of 'hyper-rational, calculating "homo economicus"' (2011, 8). There will be the same resistance in religious studies to using self-reporting surveys of ordinary churchgoers as a main basis of the 'consensus fidelium', the consensus of the faithful, rather than the statements of church leaders and theologians (Astley and Francis 2013, 47–8, 70–1).

There are two distinct perspectives on subjective wellbeing which economists also use. The first, life-satisfaction or life-evaluation surveys, are based on individual responses to the question how satisfied are you with your life in general, rating it on a ladder of life with 11 steps, from better to worst (zero). These Gallup surveys conducted in 140 nations allow a nation's life evaluation to be related to GDP per capita, so identifying the connection between subjective wellbeing and income. The second perspective, on emotional wellbeing, reveals 'an emotion, a mood, or a feeling, which is part of experiencing life' (Deaton 2013, 17). This material is elicited by asking individuals how, and to what extent, they felt these emotions the day before the survey (emotions or feelings such as stress, sadness, anger, happiness). These questions deliver very different results from the more important life evaluation or satisfaction questions, as we will see. Yet emotions and feelings are nonetheless of major importance for our wellbeing, despite the general, including religious, wariness of treating them seriously. It is the good life not the happy life which has traditionally been given the greater priority in wellbeing studies – 'Yet feeling happy is better than feeling sad, and stress, worry, and anger reduce wellbeing at the time they are being experienced, even if they sometimes have payoffs in the future' (Deaton 2013, 52). In such a judgement, Deaton is therefore usefully criticizing fellow economist Layard's prioritizing of circumstances only if they promote happiness, and Sen's prioritizing of capabilities rather than what people make of or feel about such circumstances. Deaton, I believe, is more helpful when he recognizes that feelings 'contribute to a good life' and so 'it is important to ask people about them, even if they are not given any special priority in the assessment of wellbeing' (2013, 28–9).

It is in the measuring of subjective wellbeing through its two main perspectives that some economists are now beginning to seriously challenge the traditional findings of Easterlin and Layard, which have been embraced understandably and mistakenly by religious and psychological opinions. They are therefore of some importance for my whole argument, including for the reformulation of religious studies. They also challenge much received economic opinion. There are four dimensions of this highly contested relationship between income and subjective wellbeing. I will give preference to some of the latest research and its criticism of the earlier more established economic opinion of say Layard and Easterlin.

First, within nations, richer people experience greater subjective wellbeing than the poor. This is measured through the life satisfaction self-reporting surveys drawn from 140 nations and asking how one evaluates one's life both over time and in the main realms or domains of life. These surveys indicate relationships between income and life satisfaction as 'remarkably similar', and crucially for the arguments in this field, both at 'high levels of incomes as at low levels' (Sacks, Stevenson and Wolfers 2012, 67). This contradicts earlier economic judgements that the links between income and happiness only really benefit those lower on the income scale and *not* those higher up as well (for some economists therefore, above say $10,000 per capita income, additional income is not associated with extra happiness) (Easterlin 2004, 23–31; Layard 2005, 33; Deaton 2007, 191). These latter interpretations suited far more traditional religious, moral and psychological opinions, which have regularly warned against materialism and have therefore been very wary of material wellbeing. This new conclusion, supportive of the relationship between income and subjective wellbeing at all levels of income, therefore questions both religious and mainstream neoclassical economic assumptions, the latter arguing that the marginal wellbeing impact of 'a dollar of income diminishes as income increases' (Sacks, Stevenson and Wolfers 2012, 61).

Second, across nations, there are now clear, continual and significant relationships between income and subjective wellbeing with *no* evidence of satiation points. This also contradicts existing economic orthodoxy that within nations, the historic GDP per capita rises from 1950 were not accompanied by any increase in subjective wellbeing (Easterlin 2004; Layard 2005).

Third, in time series research (over periods of time), results of surveys now indicate that economic growth translates into greater wellbeing, illustrating a positive relationship between economic growth and rising life evaluation over time (again contradicting the thesis, therefore, that growth in income doesn't make people feel better).

Fourth, emotional or happiness measures of wellbeing are alternatives to life evaluation/satisfaction measures. And particularly interesting and informative, they also *rise* with a nation's average income, yet this general conclusion is much qualified by these surveys of self-reported previous day emotional day experiences like anger and enjoyment, because they also indicate 'a much weaker relationship with national income'. More Pakistanis and Kenyans therefore experience greater such happiness than Italians or Danes (the latter scored much higher than the others on the more significant life evaluation measurements). This 'limited relationship between income and experienced happiness' also holds true for the USA. So beyond say $70,000 a year, 'additional money does nothing to improve happiness, even though those with more money report they have better lives' (expressed as life-evaluation) (Deaton 2013, 52–3). So money matters only up to a point for experiencing happiness, leading to the economist Graham's 'paradox of happy peasants and miserable millionaires' (Graham 2009). These research findings are splendidly summarized and epitomized by the article titled 'High income improves evaluation of life but not emotional wellbeing', co-authored by Princeton economist Angus Deaton and psychologist and Nobel economics laureate Daniel Kahneman (2010).

There is a general recognition that although income plays a central part in all the perspectives of wellbeing, including subjective wellbeing, it is research into the latter by both economists and psychologists which has also robustly widened our understanding of which other influences in different spheres, realms or domains of life have particular importance for our wellbeing. Using economics as an entry point into this material, this will be supplemented from psychological sources. The realms of life especially formative for subjective wellbeing include income, family life or marriage, work or unemployment, health and the ability to participate in governance. They profoundly affect wellbeing for good or ill. For example, marriage is regarded as strongly productive of greater wellbeing, and the divorce or the death of a partner having a contrary effect. They are also, as Graham notes, determinants of wellbeing across nations, but with some local variations. So marriage is an important influence on subjective wellbeing in Latin America, the USA and Europe, but less so in Russia (2009, 53–5).

The easiest way into understanding which realms have most influence on wellbeing is to use the British economist Layard's 'Big Seven' (2005, 62–73). These are based on the US General Social Survey, which enables him to put the first five in order of importance. The greater detail relating to these factors is provided by the World Values Survey, with Helliwell's analysis of the five surveys since 1981 covering 90,000 people in 46 nations. To illustrate how opinions on these seven stretch across the two disciplines of economics and psychology, the psychologist Diener's work will be used to supplement Layard's. The seven are:

1 Income is of central importance to wellbeing, its improvement and its diminishing. Diener, like Deaton in this case, judges that 'the wealth of nations is one of the strongest, if not the strongest, predictors of life satisfaction in societies' (Diener and Biswas-Diener 2008, 94), recognizing that the benefits of money involve not just purchasing power, but issues of resourcing freedom to be and to do, social status, pleasures in life, and the ability to help others. 'Regardless of your actual income, it is your material aspirations that color your mood' (Diener and Biswas-Diener 2008, 111).

2 Family relationships, with the central role and importance of marriage, including compared to other forms of relationships, are also of high importance. Yet this includes recognition of the influence of forms of relationships on the nurturing of children, and their future progress: 'the quality and stability of relationships', in the end, 'matter more than their form' (Layard 2005, 66).

3 Work, as means of acquiring an income, but also as providing 'extra meaning to life' (Layard 2005, 67), is therefore seen as the necessity and ability to contribute to society, and as an important means for sociability. Diener particularly stresses the importance of vocation, with three resulting views of work as its tangible benefits, its career opportunities, and as calling or believing in what you do (Diener and Biswas-Diener 2008, 69, 72).

4 Community and friends, and the relational importance of trust. As Diener notes 'we need others to flourish', for 'other people allow us to love and to be loved' (Diener and Biswas-Diener 2008, 50, 54).

5 Health, including mental health.

6 Personal freedom and peace, the former particularly as the ability to participate in governance, and therefore the connections of greater wellbeing with more democratic forms of government, are also regarded as of high importance.

7 Personal values and philosophy of life, including the relationship to 'disciplining' minds and moods, so 'People find comfort from within' (Layard 2005, 72).

It's these big seven in general which match Diener's important list of essential components for true wealth or wellbeing: life satisfaction and happiness; spirituality and meaning in life; positive attitudes and emotions; loving social relationships; engaging activities and work; values and life goals to achieve them; physical and mental health; and material sufficiency to meet our needs (Diener and Biswas-Diener 2008, 6).

The convergences across so many fields and elements of wellbeing and across so many disciplines and researchers are often quite remarkable, including, as we will see in the following chapter, with Christian practices, ethics and beliefs.

The final contribution of economics to subjective wellbeing regards its robust measurement systems and increasingly, and most importantly, its incorporating such metrics into the accounting systems of nations. This goal is widely shared with the psychologists of wellbeing, like Seligman and Diener, and is reflected in the New Economics Foundation's National Accounts of Wellbeing (New Economics Foundation), which draws particularly from Seligman's wider interpretation of wellbeing. This latter will be noted in the next few paragraphs on the psychology of wellbeing, but particularly in the following chapter. Yet it's the work of economists in this area which is likely to prove of more enduring importance and relevance because their traditional measurements of national wellbeing have dominated the field, even though unduly restricting the metric to measuring the total economic wealth of a nation divided by the population, as GDP per capita. The fact that they are often involved centrally in reshaping by enlarging such systems is therefore of high and telling importance. For example, the Sarkozy Commission's work by leading world economists has produced a new and workable metric of 'economic performance and social progress' (Stiglitz, Sen and Fitoussi 2010) including measuring sustainable environmental development alongside revised understandings of income and the introduction of the measurement of subjective wellbeing. The British government has also encouraged the independent Office of National Statistics to introduce a wellbeing metric in its measurement systems with three dimensions: to monitor life satisfaction, including in its main realms; to use positive and negative emotional wellbeing tests; and finally to measure purpose in life (Graham 2011, 117–18). All these efforts are important not least because they provide tools for promoting policies, practices and institutions to achieve greater wellbeing, human and environmental. As Sarkozy noted in the introduction to his Commission's report, '[t]he kind of civilization we build depends on the way we do our accounts quite simply because it changes the value we put on things' (Stiglitz, Sen and Fitoussi 2010, xiv). For '[i]n an increasingly performance-oriented society, metrics matter. What we measure affects what we do. If we have the wrong metrics, we will strive for the wrong things' (Stiglitz, Sen and Fitoussi 2010, xvii). We have striven for the wrong things, and the pursuit of subjective wellbeing is about changing that for the benefit of us all.

The psychology of subjective wellbeing

The contribution of psychology can be regarded as an important bridge-builder in the argument of Part 1 of this book. It increasingly influences economics, for example, in terms of the emergence of behavioural economics and, as we have seen, in the adoption of self-reporting surveys in, say, wellbeing studies. But it will also play an important part in the next chapter by providing strong linkages between subjective wellbeing and Christianity. We have already noted the significance of the world famous psychologist from Princeton, Daniel Kahneman, in this chapter, with his work with Angus Deaton on the distinctions between life evaluation and emotional wellbeing. But his work, summarized in his *Thinking, Fast and Slow* (2011), when elaborated by the psychologist Haidt, is also of relevance not simply to economics, but also to religious studies, emphasizing, as it does, the greater significance of our intuitive as against our cognitive responses. Haidt's article's title beautifully summarizes this: 'The Emotional Dog and its Rational Tail: A Social Intuitionist Approach to Moral Judgment' (2001). Both Christianity and economics have regularly overemphasized the cognitive to the great neglect of the intuitive. And it's that link to Haidt that also provides a useful way into this brief section. For the most relevant development in contemporary psychology for our agenda has been the emergence of positive psychology since the 1980s, a tradition in which Haidt is involved. Prioritizing, as it does, the focus on health as wholeness over against the usual psychologists' overemphasis on engaging illness, it therefore moves from the negative, pathology view of the psychologist's task to the positive wholeness understanding of health and wellbeing. In this it therefore provides, for a small but growing number of theologians in systematic theology and biblical studies, a bridgehead into an increasingly constructive dialogue between the two disciplines, as we will observe particularly in the next chapter. Their endeavours could be summarized as the promotion of a positive theology, as clear complement to positive psychology (Charry 2013a). They represent an interdisciplinary achievement equivalent to my work with economics and Christianity.

Using material from two of the key exponents of positive psychology, Diener and Seligman, this section will briefly refer to positive psychology's contribution to subjective wellbeing in terms of its emergence as a new science, as new and wider definitions of wellbeing, as work on character and virtues, and finally on the implication of positive psychology for health, including the combating of major illnesses.

The rebalancing of psychology from its increasingly effective focus on treating mental illness, the pathological emphasis, to actively promoting health, the positive wellbeing emphasis, importantly reaffirms the splendid 1946 preamble of the World Health Organization's constitution, that '[h]ealth is a state of complete physical, mental and social well-being and not merely the absence of disease or infirmity' (Seligman 2011, 182). To contribute to that objective, positive psychology has three pillars: the study and promotion of positive emotions, of positive traits as character strengths and virtues, and of positive institutions that support such wellbeing (Seligman 2002, xiii). Importantly, for Seligman, '[t]he skills of becoming happy turn out to be almost entirely different from the skills of not being sad, not being anxious, or not being angry' (2006, iv). And, for positive psychologists, this robust use of evidence and the interaction of basic applied research argue that all this work constitutes, in the economist Layard's words, 'a new science' (Layard 2005). Indeed, for Diener, '[w]e are optimistic that just as science transformed our material world in the twentieth century, it can revolutionize our understanding of happiness in the twenty-first century' (Diener and Biswas-Diener 2008, 246).

Following on from this positive view of health and its emergence as a potential new science, indeed as an elaboration of the latter claim, is the major contribution to broadening, deepening and enriching complex wellbeing constructs through greatly improved definitions, measurements and practices. Seligman's evolving work provides the most useful definition of such wellbeing or flourishing (the latter concept links strongly to Aristotle's *eudaimonia*, and theologians' development of this as a life well lived, a life that turns out well). His latest construct, summarized as the acronym PERMA (Seligman 2011, 16–20), therefore includes:

- *Positive emotions* or the 'pleasant life', particularly engaged through life satisfaction and happiness (emotive wellbeing) measures. These have constituted the basis of subjective wellbeing, especially for economics. Positive psychology has now greatly, and most usefully, extended this definition of wellbeing beyond these original features to also include the following:
- *Engagement* as absorption by a task or interest ('did time stop for you?').
- *Meaning* using character skills and talents to 'belong to and serve something you believe is larger than the self'.
- *Accomplishment* or achievement, tasks often pursued for their own sake.
- *Positive relationships* as, for Peterson, 'Other people'.

The proof of the pudding is in the eating. So in February, 2011, I completed the surveys for each of these five constituent parts of Seligman's flourishing or wellbeing. I decided at first that it wasn't worth doing the initial one, positive emotions, because my wife of nearly 47 years had died suddenly several weeks before. Ours had been a lifelong rich and happy partnership. So I was pretty devastated. I just assumed that any survey beginning with positive emotions was just not worth attempting. I knew what my emotions were, and they were the opposite of positive! Fortunately I read further and realized Seligman himself judged that he was not very good at positive emotions, yet clearly recognized that his life was flourishing. And that was because he scored highly on engagement, meaning, accomplishment and positive relationships. And I did. And that research, confirmed by my completing the personal surveys on the five features of wellbeing, greatly helped me to survive my wife's death gracefully. I might have been down, but I certainly wasn't out. My journey continued based on the other four features, and now the first, positive emotions, is back on stream!

From the late nineteenth to late twentieth centuries, there emerged a strong argument that people are significantly the product of their environments. Rapid industrialization and urbanization created forces which shaped people for good and ill. People became victims of poverty and unemployment rather than creators of their own misfortune. Yet the recognition of the importance of one's character and its ability to make choices affecting one's wellbeing and influence circumstances never disappeared and may be reappearing as a decisive factor interacting with, and not necessarily predominantly shaped by, context. The recent emergence of positive psychology is part of that change, with its commitment to what Seligman calls 'learned' or acquired 'optimism' (2006). Interestingly, this reassertion of character as part of any accurate account of human action (Seligman 2002, 127–31), is confirmed by the reappearance of character as virtue ethics in religious studies. Importantly, too, this material from positive psychology also questions the emphasis in some theology that we are essentially context driven, with no acknowledgement of universals, such as character and virtues, in human behaviour.

Of course, positive psychology, in promoting character and virtues, also recognizes that our actions are significantly genetically and circumstances determined, yet they are equally clear that there are also substantial factors under our voluntary control that we can influence in our own personal development (they represent this set of influences on human behaviour as $H = S + C + V$, with H being our enduring level of happiness, S our set range, C the circumstances of our life, and V factors under our control) (Seligman 2002, 45). It's that opportunity for changing our approach to life that positive psychology focuses on in terms of promoting our health and wellbeing. And it is here that it developed its major research project into classifying and measuring human strengths. Initially they analysed thousands of writings from all the major religions and philosophical traditions, from such secular codes as the samurai, Boy Scouts and Alcoholics Anonymous, across the last 3,000 years of history and across all continents. To their surprise almost every single tradition endorsed six virtues: wisdom and knowledge; courage; love and humanity; justice; temperance; spirituality and transcendence. Taken together, 'they capture the notion of good character' (Seligman 2002, 131–3). Clearly, the details differ in terms, say, of what courage means for a samurai or for Plato. And some virtues are unique to each of these traditions (say, art in Aristotle, and cleanliness for the American Boy Scouts). Yet 'the commonality is real, and to those raised as ethical relativists, pretty remarkable'. To continue to take an unequivocal relative ethical or context determined position is now unsustainable. 'This [therefore] unpacks the meaning of the claim that human beings are moral animals' (Seligman 2002, 133). It is another confirmation and elaboration, running through these first two chapters and reinforced in the next chapter and Part 2, that ethics are an intrinsic and essential part of human wellbeing.

Yet, as Seligman and others recognize, these six virtues are 'unworkably abstract for psychologists who want to build and measure these things' (2002, 133) and so for each virtue, they elaborate different ways to achieve and measure them. So they have usefully and necessarily developed 24 routes, or strengths of character, by which to achieve and measure these virtues, and to build on them in our lives. Thus wisdom's routes include strengths of curiosity, love of learning, judgement, originality, social intelligence and perspective. The task is to help each of us to identify our virtues and which routes are most feasible for us to develop them further in relation to the main realms of our life, from work to family.

Finally, although positive psychology's promotion of subjective wellbeing related to all the main realms or domains of our living, its contributions in the particular field of health are of especial importance and relevance to its place in the three perspectives on national wealth and wellbeing examined in this chapter. For example, its focus on health rather than ill-being does not mean that it ignored the latter, rather, that promoting positive living, of intrinsic value in itself, also thereby contributes to effectively addressing ill-being. Again, the resonances between this section and the following chapter on Christianity and wellbeing, and its proposed work on the second perspective, health, are remarkable.

The task of promoting health, in the WHO's words as 'a state of complete physical, mental and social wellbeing', includes, as we have seen, increasing longevity and decreasing morbidity as a contribution to achieving that greater wholeness. By promoting positive health as not just the absence of mental illness, positive psychology also regards this as the commitment to human flourishing (illustrated in its PERMA acronym). That emphasis, in turn, has very significant measurable results, for example in three spheres of particular contemporary morbidity concern, cardiovascular disease, cancer and infectious illnesses. The former two are of high importance in terms of now addressing the issue of the chronic illnesses of the elderly. First, cardiovascular disease (CVD) is the main killer of the elderly (not cancer, as we are often led to assume by the publicity for it). All the major studies of optimism and CVD 'converge on the conclusion that optimism is strongly related to protection from cardiovascular disease', correcting for all the traditional risk factors. Most importantly, 'the effect is higher with high optimism protecting people compared to the average levels of optimism and pessimism, and pessimism hurting people compared to the average' (Seligman 2011, 190–4). Second, cancer and all-cause mortality. Their survey of cancer literature 'leans quite heavily in the direction of pessimism as a risk factor for developing cancer' with the cancer literature indicating that 'hope, optimism and happiness may well have beneficial effects for cancer patients when the disease is not extremely severe' (Seligman 2011, 203). The latter qualification is of high importance. Third, infectious illnesses. Here the work of Cohen and others in the USA unravels 'the influence of emotion on infectious illness' (Seligman 2011, 195). Again, in facing such illness, including the common cold, the evidence is that 'positive emotion, not negative emotion, is clearly the driving force' in terms of both prevention and cure (Seligman 2011, 199).

Why, in all three illnesses, are optimists less vulnerable to disease (remember, many of us are born pessimists, yet positive psychology has proven ways to correct not to remove that)? Three possibilities emerge, which again link strongly into the following chapter on Christianity and wellbeing: optimists take action and have healthier lifestyles; they have more friends and love in their lives as social support, and biological mechanisms supportive of better health – the least well tested route (Seligman 2011, 205–7). What is particularly impressive in all this material is the growing consensus, in positive psychology and in the much wider fields of research in related disciplines, on the relationship between promoting greater subjective wellbeing and the pursuit of health.

End note: On the common commitment, across the perspectives of income, health and subjective wellbeing, to supportive institutions

It is tempting but ultimately quite unhelpful and inaccurate to assume that wellbeing is primarily about economic growth for better incomes and health and the personal pursuit of virtuous and flourishing lives. It is certainly about all that, but it is even more certainly about far more. As Seligman has reminded us, positive psychology has three pillars: positive emotions, positive traits and 'positive institutions, such as democracy, strong families, free inquiry, that support the virtues, which in turn support the positive emotions' (2002, xiii). Although Diener, in arguing that 'Building a society that maximizes well-being, (and) not just economic growth', might suggest the traditional psychologists' unease with economics, he then continues rightly to state that this wider than economics objective 'should be an aim of the nations of the world' (Diener and Biswas-Diener 2008, 224). So much of the preceding material amplifies that preferred task but in more profound and complex ways than Diener assumes. So economists recognize the centrality of both economics and incomes to wellbeing, but consistently qualify that dominance with other preferred institutions. For example, the Industrial and Mortality Revolutions were clearly integrally part of the momentous post-eighteenth century changes. Although economics played a central part in them, economists have rightly argued that knowledge played a greater part, and particularly in the Mortality Revolution. And knowledge refers not simply to the continuing and accelerating breakthroughs in science and technology, but also to the growing importance of education and its delivery through public bodies and policies (as contributing both to great escapes and great divergences). And this applies to the associated and increasingly important role of improving human capital in economic growth but also to its role in improving life expectancy and combating morbidity. In both, education – particularly of women – plays an important part. When considering the contribution of other institutional realms or domains of life to wellbeing, again, there is strong acknowledgement of the value of participation, of being able to be involved in the various forms of governance, obviously focusing on democracy, but casting its net much wider.

It is helpful to locate these concerns for institutional arrangement which both promote and sustain greater wellbeing in the reflections of two great contemporary economists, both Nobel economic laureates. Thus Sen argues for an 'economic system that is not monolithic' (so involving market capitalism but also public goods like education, health and welfare), which 'draws on a variety of institutions chosen pragmatically, and is based on social values that we can defend ethically' (2009). And it is that additional and integral role of ethical economics in adequate institutional formation which Stiglitz also elaborates in relation to what he calls a 'moral growth': that is one which is 'sustainable', in terms of generating increasing living standards today but also for future generations, that ensures the benefits of growth are shared equitably (so engaging inequalities); and that thereby creates a more tolerant society informed by social justice and solidarity rather than the deep divisions which epitomize so many societies (2005). And it's all that which essentially characterizes what Layard refers to as the common good of all (2005, 95–108).

3

'I Came That They Might Have Life' Christianity and Wellbeing

Although contemporary research on religions' contributions to wellbeing, particularly subjective wellbeing, is of recent origin, 'In survey after survey, actively religious people have reported markedly greater happiness and somewhat smaller life satisfaction than their irreligious counterparts' (Myers 2008, 324). That conclusion is confirmed by economists, for example by Layard's 'one of the most robust findings of happiness research: that people who believe in God are happier' (2005, 72) and by Graham arguing that 'In most countries, respondents that express faith or religious affiliation – as well as those who practice their faith – are, on average, happier than others ... In most of the rest of the world' (2009, 61–2); by psychologists like Seligman: 'survey data consistently show religious people as being somewhat happier and more satisfied with life than nonreligious people' (2002, 59); and finally, by sociologists, for example Putnam: 'As with good neighbourliness, the correlation between religiosity and life satisfaction is powerful and robust ... Other things being equal, the difference in happiness between a nonchurchgoer and a weekly churchgoer is slightly larger than the difference between someone who earns $10,000 a year and his demographic twin who earns $100,000 a year' (Putnam and Campbell 2010, 491).

Why is the relationship between Christianity and subjective wellbeing so positive? Answering that question will occupy the rest of this chapter. But that is not its principal objective. The task is rather to explore the relationship between Christianity and wellbeing, initially and principally through a focus on subjective wellbeing. That entry point will then be extended, at the end of this chapter, to engage health and income, so together embracing the three great perspectives on the wealth and wellbeing of nations that are at the centre of Chapter 2's agenda. The subjective wellbeing perspective has been selected as the main entry point of this research at this stage because achievements in this field, in terms of the contributions of economics, psychology, sociology and religious studies, are most comprehensive, robust and consistent. And it is out of these relationships addressing this shared area of concern – subjective wellbeing – that there emerges a model for Christian engagement with both this perspective, and probably the other two, health and income.

The model can therefore also be deployed to address the relationship between Christianity and economics. As the introductory Chapter 1 noted, one of the tools to be used in exploring this relationship is the deployment of models, reinforced by statistical evidence and located in historical contexts. So the following elaboration of the chosen model will also involve reflection on the nature and role of measurements in religious studies, and Part 2 and Chapters 4 and 5 will explore the historical contexts of such research.

The following material focuses particularly and initially on the task of *mapping* as a way into modelling in some detail those practices, ethics and beliefs of Christianity that resource its robust and positive contributions initially to subjective wellbeing. These are drawn and confirmed from both secular sources and Christian traditions, recognizing their correlative and causal relationships, with their principal features further elaborated with reference to the main Christian denominations, major world faiths and secular spiritualities. This section will conclude with a brief exploration of the model's transmission processes, showing how Christianity influences the development of greater wellbeing in society. The following section will then examine the implications of such a mapping and modelling exercise by developing appropriate measurement tools for religious studies' contribution to human wellbeing and for religious studies itself. The final brief section will then begin to explore the feasibility of deploying the model in relation to health and then income, the other perspectives on the wealth and wellbeing of nations.

Developing the model (1): Mapping and modelling Christianity's contribution to subjective wellbeing

Why do Christians perform better than the non-religious in terms of their subjective wellbeing? Why do secular economists, psychologists and sociologists, given their robust research methods, judge this to be the case?

As with the examination of wellbeing in the previous chapter, it is more strategic and persuasive for wider predominantly secular audiences to therefore begin with the evidence of secular experts as to what and why Christians have better wellbeing, but only if the argument is then developed with reference to what the most interested parties, in this case Christians, judge to be what makes them tick so well. This can then be put alongside an example from secular literatures, in this case psychology interacting with economics, in order to see further the clear resonances between the religious and secular understandings of wellbeing (see Table 1, 'Mapping Christianity's Practices, Ethics and Beliefs ...', pp. 66–67). It is out of these interactions that the content of the model's seven constituent features emerge.

Let's begin by describing these three interacting sources that identify and elaborate what I now describe as Christianity's practices, ethics and beliefs. This will enable us to have an overview of them and the interactive processes generating them, before moving on to develop further their principal features.

First, (and in the first column in Table 1), I have identified the seven features of Christianity's practices, ethics and beliefs regarded as particularly conducive to Christianity's greater wellbeing, from secular sources. The latter include, from psychology, Diener (especially), Myers and Seligman, from economics, Layard, and from sociology, Putnam.

Interestingly, it was from these secular sources, particularly fleshed out by Diener and Biswas-Diener (2008, 117–24), that I first became aware of the actual and potential contributions of religions to human wellbeing as identified in the secular literatures. It was only a decade later, in 2013, that I became aware of both a growing interest in and contribution to wellbeing studies from the Christian tradition, and a recognition of the serious inadequacies, at best, of the dominant and historic Christian understandings of wellbeing in general and happiness in particular.

The seven features of Christianity identified in these secular sources include:

1 Comforting beliefs which generate positive emotions and virtues, including hope and its recognition of an afterlife, compassion, altruism, forgiveness, gratitude, justice and transformation.
2 Connecting to realities greater than the self, as recognition of transcendent realities, including, for Layard, that 'people who believe in God are happier' (2005, 72).
3 Experiences of ritual, including the public and private worship of God, and spiritual exercises such as meditation, including on sacred scriptures.
4 Regulating lifestyle and behaviour, including ethical, through restricting alcohol and drug intakes; acquiring life skills, including participation in society; contributing to society through voluntary and charitable giving; and coping skills for illness, stress and loss and therefore for promoting better health, including mental health.
5 Churchgoing as social support and networking.
6 Nurturing young people in growing up religiously.
7 Generating and sustaining, from these previous six features, personal values and meaningful philosophies of life, including through relationships, extending into a common good.

The cumulative contribution of these seven features constitutes a continuing and evolving Christian tradition, of high importance in resourcing personal and communal wellbeing in past, present and future contexts. Their supportive strength provided by these continuities and embodied in both micro and macro levels cannot be easily overestimated.

Table 1: Mapping Christianity's practices, ethics and beliefs from secular and religious sources of wellbeing in the twenty-first century (Atherton et al. 2011, p. 12)

Supportive Secular Sources of Religion	Christian Tradition (Sweden)	National Accounts of Wellbeing
1. Comforting beliefs (D) – embodied in values generating *positive emotions* (M) including forgiveness, hope, transformation (M), afterlife, compassion, humility, altruism (M,S,P), justice (P).	Hope in context of eternal life; forgiveness through Christ; awareness of sin, humility and responsibility; trust as faith in Christ; love for self, others and God as giving and receiving; justice and peace, especially for the marginalized.	Emotional wellbeing – as *positive* feelings. Satisfying life (*positive* evaluation of life). Feeling optimistic about your *future* (resilience and self-esteem).
2. Connecting to reality greater than self (D) (M): 'people who believe in God are happier' (L, M, S, P).	Engagement with God and the Other.	Meaning.
3. Experiences of ritual as worship (D), including meditation (L, P).	Eucharist, communion, hymns, liturgy.	
4. Regulation of lifestyle and behaviour: as restricting alcohol and drug intake (M); as acquisition of life skills (M), including participation in civic society (L, P); and contributing to society through volunteering and charitable giving (P); coping skills for illness, stress, loss (M) and for better health, especially mental health (S,P).	Lifestyle-choice, courage to be vulnerable, vulnerability-trust, value of love for others.	Resilience and self-esteem (being able to deal with life's difficulties). Competence (feeling accomplishment from what you do, and being able to use your abilities) (as positive functioning).

Supportive Secular Sources of Religion	Christian Tradition (Sweden)	National Accounts of Wellbeing
5. Churchgoing as social support and networking (D,M,S,P).	Church as organization and fellowship; with family relationships, solidary with vulnerable, trust, love-giver and receiver.	Social wellbeing (supportive relationships – families, friends), trust and belonging.
6. Growing up religiously (D,S,P).	The nurturing of children, students, and the study and teaching of ethics.	Seligman addresses this in relation to schools and wellbeing.
7. All sustained by, and in turn generating a philosophy of life, including a common good. (L,M,S,P).	Continuities and meaning, including through Christian tradition, linking involvement with contexts.	Positive functioning – as meaning and purpose – feeling that your own life is valuable, worthwhile and valued by others.
D – Diener; L – Layard; M – Myers, In Eid and Larsen, *The Sources of Subjective Well-Being*, 2008; S – Seligman, *Authentic Happiness*, 2003; P – Putnam, *American Grace*, 2010.	'The Gospel of Today', Strängnäs Diocese, Sweden (2009), with sections on Gospel, Kingdom of God, Conversion, Peace, Freedom, Forgiveness, Atonement, Love, Life, Grace and Mercy, Justification, and Truth.	New Economics Foundation (2009): *Personal Wellbeing*: Emotional wellbeing (positive feelings, absence of negative feelings), Satisfying life, Vitality, Resilience and self-esteem (self-esteem, optimism, resilience), Positive functioning (autonomy, competence, engagement, meaning and purpose) *Social Wellbeing*: Supportive relationships, trust and belonging

Second (and in Table 1's second, middle column), these secularly identified features of Christianity clearly resonate with Christianity's own experiences and understandings. These are illustrated from the Swedish Diocese of Strängnäs's report *The Gospel of Today* (Wikell 2009), compiled by its priests and deacons as part of a conference involving the William Temple Foundation. This was therefore also an example of that intrafaith collaboration, in this case as the Porvoo Agreement between Nordic and Baltic Lutheran churches and the British Anglican churches. Drawn from this published report, these illustrate the seven features from the perspective of the Christian tradition itself:

1 Comforting beliefs embodied in values generating positive emotions including hope in the context of eternal life; forgiveness through Christ; awareness of sin, humility and responsibility; trust as faith in Christ; love for self, others and God as both giving and receiving; justice and peace especially for the marginalized.
2 Engagement with God and the Other.
3 Experience of worship as Eucharist, communion, liturgy, Scriptures and hymn singing.
4 Lifestyle choice; community involvement and service; courage to be vulnerable; vulnerability trust; value of love for others.
5 Church as fellowships and organization; as family relationships; as solidarity with the vulnerable, love-giver and receiver.
6 Nurturing children, students, and the study and teaching of ethics.
7 Continuities and meaning, including through Christian tradition, and linking involvements with contexts.

Third (and as Table 1's third column), it seemed necessary also to illustrate the secular equivalents of the seven features from the source, the British New Economics Foundation's *National Accounts of Wellbeing* (2009). These combine features from positive psychology but also the exercise of economists in developing such measurements of national wellbeing. They draw significantly from Cambridge University's Well-being Institute's

Survey in 2006–07 of 43,000 adults from across 23 European nations, both European Union (EU) and non-EU members. Its criteria for secular wellbeing closely follow Seligman's definition of flourishing as positive emotion, engagement, relationships, meaning and accomplishment (PERMA) (2011, 26–8). They relate to five of the seven features (but not worship, 3, or growing up religiously, 6, although, in other places Seligman develops his positive psychology in relation to education) (2011, 85–8):

1 (Comforting beliefs) as emotional wellbeing, positive feelings; satisfying life (positive evaluation of life); feeling optimistic about one's future (resilience and self-esteem).
2 (Connecting to reality as greater than self) – as the importance of meaning in life.
4 (Regulating lifestyle) – as resilience and self-esteem (being able to deal with life's difficulties); competence (feeling accomplishment from what you do and being able to use your abilities – as positive functioning).
5 (Churchgoing as social support) – as social wellbeing (supportive relationships, families, friends), trust and belonging.
7 (Philosophy of life) – as positive functioning – feeling that your life is valuable, worthwhile and valued by others.

Surveying these seven features of Christianity confirmed across these three different sources (or columns in Table 1), two matters immediately arise: the issues of prioritizing among the seven and the nature of the relationship between the different sources (columns).

To identify seven features resourcing Christianity's contribution to wellbeing does not in itself indicate orders of importance or *prioritizing*. Interestingly, the secular literatures are particularly helpful in this regard. They focus on belief (no. 1) and belonging (no. 5). For Seligman, the emphasis and priority is given to believing, though not before he also comments on the nature of the relationship between religions and wellbeing. So he begins by noting that '[t]he causal relation between religion and healthier, more prosocial living is no mystery. Many religions proscribe drugs, and infidelity while endorsing charity, moderation and hard work'. But '[t]he causal relation of religion to greater happiness ... is not as straightforward'. He then acknowledges that '[i]n the heyday of behaviourism, the emotional benefits of religion were explained (away?) as resulting from more social support'. Yet for him there is now 'a more basic link: religions instil hope for the future and create meaning in life' (2002, 59–60). For him, it is believing that counts most in the end. In contrast, for Putnam, it's belonging that matters by far the most, certainly over believing. He concludes, after much surveying of American religiosity in 2006–07, that 'In short, as with good neighbourliness, the religious edge in life satisfaction has less to do with faith itself than with communities of faith. For happiness as for neighbourliness, praying together seems better than either bowling together or praying alone' (Putnam and Campbell 2010, 491–2). As a classic Anglican, my experience suggests both believing and belonging in equal doses, the one supporting, and being essential for, the robust nature of the other!

In terms of the nature and significance of the *relationship* between Christianity and wellbeing, the model clearly illustrates the correlative connection between Christianity, represented by the Diocese of Strängnäs, and the secular, represented by the National Accounts of Wellbeing, features of wellbeing. Yet this is significantly 'a relationship of meaning' rather than one necessarily implying cause and effect (Astley and Francis 2013, 45). In this sense, Gill rightly cautions with his warning over the 'genetic fallacy', that the evolutionary origins of religion, as say demonstrated by Bellah, cannot be confused with its validity, with the truth of religion's claims (Gill 2012a, 33). The correlative relationship between the Strangnas and the National Accounts of Wellbeing's features of wellbeing do not prove the truth of Christian beliefs, but do indicate their real relevance to greater wellbeing. Yet that relationship is clearly also causal, certainly for Seligman and Putnam. For them, the features of Christianity also explain why it is so effective in promoting greater wellbeing in its members. Again, that does not demonstrate the truth of Christianity, for example, that God exists, but that Christian beliefs do account for greater Christian wellbeing.

This understanding of Christian practices, ethics and beliefs as giving at least critical enriching depths to corresponding secular human understandings also features strongly in Christian social ethics, including in Anglican and Swedish traditions. For example, it is illustrated by Grenholm's partially revelation-based ethics, which 'clarifies and lends depth to the moral insights, which are based upon common human experiences' (1993, 313). This has the additional added value of providing an empirically researched means of religion engaging in the public square as public theology by providing an answer to what Habermas identifies as 'an awareness of what is missing' in secular communicative reason (2010, 15–23; Graham 2013, 46).

Developing such a basic framework for the model provides a working tool, but elaborating its features in greater detail will certainly add value to the exercise. Before that is attempted, the basic framework itself needs to be developed and tested with regard to the basic principle, set out in the introductory chapter, of deploying intra and interfaith dimensions. This exercise, essential as it is, can only be done briefly and selectively, particularly because of my lack of expertise in these other traditions. Yet I hope these rough abstracts demonstrate sufficiently the likely viability of the schema. It's what the archaeologist and historian Morris called 'chainsaw' art, with the only important question for the chainsaw artist being 'whether the tree trunk looks like a bear', or in my case, like the features of a Christianity for greater wellbeing (Morris 2011, 150). I will test this thesis in four stages: within Christianity, within other faiths, then with reference to Küng's global religious ethic and finally with secular spirituality. All are highly relevant and apt, and often quite explicitly so, to wellbeing.

In terms of intrafaith – that is, within the Christian traditions – I have moved beyond the Anglican and Lutheran traditions by selecting two important texts central to and from the Roman Catholic and evangelical traditions, particularly because they represent the biggest Christian denominations in terms of their central position in the global resurgence of Christianity. The first representative text is the Roman Catholic Benedictine, then Abbot of Worth's *Finding Happiness: Monastic Steps for a Fulfilling Life* (Jamison 2008). The second is Rick Warren's *The Purpose Driven Life* (2002). Warren founded and leads the Saddleback evangelical megachurch in California. The book has sold 30 million copies! Remarkably, there are robust resonances between them, but also with the seven features of my model. Although the latter are not in any order of priority, Jamison and Warren clearly begin with belief in and surrender to a transcendent purposeful God, which shapes and resources the whole of your purpose driven life (features 1, 2 and 7) (Warren 2002, 84; Jamison 2008, 31). This is expressed in worship or ritual (3), as constant conversation with God. This also involves the continuous practice of spiritual exercises, particularly using biblical texts for meditation, with the two habits, reading and prayer, being closely linked (Warren 2002, 87; Jamison 2008, 81). Developing such positive habits are central to religious, but also secular, wellbeing. Their religious strength is derived significantly from their location in a wider religious tradition, essentially the cumulative impact of the seven features. In terms of resourcing spiritual exercises, Warren remarkably also deploys such Catholic sources as Brother Lawrence's seventeenth-century *Practising the Presence of God* and the sixteenth century's St John of the Cross's dark night of the soul (Warren 2002, 88, 108). Both are reminders of the centrality, in religious traditions, of the recognition that the journeying to greater wellbeing is always about overcoming obstacles and never ignoring them. Such belief, worship and spiritual exercises powerfully inform and sustain lifestyles, including service in both Church and wider society (feature 4). For Warren, the latter embodies Schweitzer's judgement that '[t]he only happy people are those who have learned to serve' (2002, 276). And all are equally embedded in, and draw great strength from, the commitment to Church as God's instrument on earth (feature 5) (2002, 117–18; Jamison 2008, 98).

The character represented by the seven features is also embedded powerfully in the interfaith dimension. I have selected a presentation to a conference at Chester University in 2011 on 'Spiritual Progression in an Age of Recession' to illustrate a Muslim contribution. Dr Hussain's paper 'Spirituality: A Muslim Perspective' provides strong resonances with Jamison and Warren, focusing again on submission (the meaning of Islam) to God (features 1 and 2) expressed through worship and spiritual exercises (feature 3), emphasizing our inner spiritual being. These are deeply embedded in the Muslim's local and universal community or *ummah* (feature 5) and are also reflected in a powerfully personal and shared communal way of living and commitment to serve the common good through local community and civic involvements (feature 4). The motivating and energizing spiritual force driving such living for others was regarded as being so powerful as to be described as an 'electromotive force', generating one of the largest Muslim charities in Nottingham (Hussain 2011, 3).

The Buddhist contribution, representing the rebalancing of the world economy to fully embrace the East, is provided by the Dalai Lama's *The Art of Happiness: A Handbook for Living* (1998), which remarkably parallels Princeton's Ellen Charry's *God and the Art of Happiness* (2010). Concentrating on the pursuit of inner transformation, particularly through training the mind through the daily practice of spiritual exercises (features 3 and 4) and especially meditation (Dalai Lama and Cutler 1999, 250), the Dalai Lama focuses on compassion and gentleness as counterpoint to the negative emotions of anger and anxiety (1999, 25–6). Note the robust links both to Jamison's emphasis on the Christian virtues counterposed to the seven deadly sins and to Seligman's positive psychology's secular promotion of psychological strengths as against weaknesses. The latter's strong connections to Buddhism were illustrated in a creative public encounter between Diener and the Dalai Lama. That link is reinforced by Buddhism's commitment to health (feature 4) as a 'concrete help in times of trouble' (Dalai Lama and Cutler 1999, 255), with research demonstrating how religion can contribute to happier lives, coping with aging and personal crises, lower rates of alcohol and drug abuse and lower death rates and improved health – all suggesting the benefits for wellbeing derived from beliefs reflected in ways of living (features 1, 2, 4 and 7).

It would not be difficult, indeed it would be profitable, to develop an important dialogue between these findings and Küng's features of a global ethic with its two basic principles of true humanity and the golden rule, both shared by all the main religions of the world, and their informing four ethical directives promoting: life as against murder; truth as against lies; honesty and fair dealings as against theft; and love and respect as against sexual exploitation (2010). This also represents Küng's top-down approach encountering my more bottom-up model.

There are obvious and important resonances between Küng's work and positive psychology's research on the six virtues and 24 character strengths, but also with the Christian, Muslim and Buddhist sources, engaging essentially most of my model's features. Although the focus is initially on ethics informing lifestyles, there is also a strong link to the importance of transcendence, beliefs, belonging and philosophy of life or meaning. It is out of these sets of relationships that we can add the last dimension of interrelationships, namely the increasing importance of secular spirituality, including its interactions with the spirituality so informing the Christian and other faiths' contributions. This section therefore brings into dialogue the Dalai Lama's promotion of what he calls a 'basic spirituality' (following on but distinct from his work on Buddhist spirituality), with Seligman's operating concept of spiritual fitness. The former embraces what it means to be a good human being, 'moral people, without any religion' (Dalai Lama and Cutler 1999, 258–9), and is nurtured by an inner discipline focusing on promoting the positive mental states of compassion, kindness and tolerance, as against the negatives of anger and hatred. There are, once again, remarkable overlaps between this and Seligman's secular spiritual fitness module developed for the US army (Seligman 2011, 149–51). This promotes answerability to a higher moral order (feature 2), the search for truth, self-knowledge and purpose in life (features 4 and 7), again focusing on promoting positive as against negative virtues. To this could be added, for example, the positive psychologist Haidt's research on the emotion of elevation, when we step out of ourselves, whether alone or within a community of like-minded people, whether confronting nature or the arts, and with therefore an additional link to transcendence and ritual (features 2, 3, 4 and 7) (Haidt 2006, 193–200). Maslow's secular study, *Religions, Values and Peak-experiences* (1964) is also a strong embodiment of this dimension.

It's not easy to bring together these very varied selective sources of religious and secular wellbeing, with their profound shared experiences and yet their very distinctive particular identities. But I could use Ellen Charry's concluding judgement, extending her references to Christianity to embrace other faiths and secular spiritualities: 'all their ways of articulating God's purpose for and interaction with creation are entry points into the complexity and subtlety of God's labors for his garden's flourishing' (2010, 277).

The final piece to add to this jigsaw illustrating the model, including by elaborating in increasing detail its main features, draws from the breadth of secular and religious resources used especially in engaging subjective wellbeing. Again, these are both selective and yet representative of main currents of opinion. They therefore hopefully give added value to the model. One source deployed in particular warrants a little further explanation, namely from what is referred to as 'ordinary theology', defined as 'the theological beliefs and processes of believing that find expression in the God-talk of those believers who have received no scholarly theological education' (Astley and Francis 2013, 1). In other words, it examines what the great bulk of church members believe and do, rather than what church leaders and theologians tell them to believe and do. The Church could survive without the latter. It couldn't without the former. So ordinary theology is elaborated using a variety of research tools, including qualitative but in addition the essential quantitative surveys. It's also an equivalent of the use of self-reporting surveys in subjective wellbeing. And because it delivers material on ordinary Christian practices, ethics and beliefs, it provides an invaluable commentary on the model's features as essential complement to the material from academic sources. It's also from reflecting on this material on ordinary theology that I have lately begun to use the concept of 'ordinary church', not the Church which church leaders and theologians think it is, or tell it to be, but the Church as it is, full of ordinary folk doing ordinary things, yet which are also extraordinary, not least because, for example, they produce people who generate higher wellbeing. Another reason why ordinary theology and ordinary church make so much sense is because, for over ten years since I retired, I have sat inconspicuously towards the back of my local church, rarely performing in public office by preaching or celebrating communion, and it's an astonishingly different view of church life, from the roots or bottom up and not from on high. An additional and closely related perspective that confirms and adds to these understandings is provided by Vasquez's development of 'a materialist theory of religion' (2011). This recognizes that 'selves and cultures are material in their own right', as are institutions and environments. So religion is also expressed through 'our own embodiment', seeing reality emerging from our ongoing physical–cultural interactions with the environment (Vasquez 2011, 6). Christianity, like other religions, is therefore primarily about the title of Table 1, about the practice, ethics and beliefs of ordinary embodied individuals and institutions. That's why the model covers seven features, only one concerned with beliefs specifically, and even this is embodied in values and emotions. Four of the rest are even more profoundly practice-based. For Vasquez, the key to religion, and therefore why he develops a 'materialist theory of religion', is not so much beliefs as the actual material practices that constitute the reality of religion in contemporary societies (2011, 8). It's the religious equivalent of my foundational world 'world of daily life'. It is the cumulative results of such researches which begin to form the basis, not simply of my model, but of a reformulated religious studies and experience for the early twenty-first century (I fear so much is still rooted in, at best, the twentieth century). I have selected four out of the seven features of my model for further elaboration.

Comforting beliefs in generating positive emotions

On beliefs in general, and their relationship to attitudes and behaviour, Gill's analysis of 'British Social Attitudes' data and evidence from the 'British Household Panel Survey' suggest that 'churchgoers are indeed distinctive in their attitudes and behaviour'. Although attitudes, say on sexuality, change over time, 'there are broad patterns of Christian beliefs, teleology and altruism which distinguish churchgoers as a whole from non-churchgoers'. These distinctive beliefs are accompanied by 'a strong sense of moral order and concern for other people' – and the latter is reflected in the proven track record of churchgoers to give more, to volunteer more, and to participate in civic affairs more than non-churchgoers (Gill 2012a, 181). Yet the distinctiveness of these beliefs and values is relative not absolute. So 'Many non-churchgoers share their beliefs, values and practices (apart from churchgoing itself), even though these are found more among churchgoers than among non-churchgoers' (Gill 2012a, 217). And that proportionality is also therefore reflected in the fact that non-churchgoers don't not give, volunteer or participate in civic affairs, it's just they do less.

Exploring a little further the nature and influence of beliefs on practice, the research of American theologians Charry and Strawn has produced evidence relating to religious traditions' cumulative power, including its causal connection to wellbeing. They locate such features within biblical and doctrinal narrative frameworks, which, in turn, give them greater cohering and energizing meaning and significance (Strawn 2012). These narratives, for example the Moses story, also generate valuable tools for interdisciplinary engagement, including such emotion-virtues as courage, passion and trust, which inform personal and communal life through processes of moral freighting and the transposition of values into secular life (Roberts 2007). These emotion-virtues linked to the pursuit of justice also play counter-cultural roles, say in struggles against gross inequalities. They therefore allow a robust engagement with debates over the importance for human flourishing of material and subjective wellbeing, health care, education and civic participation.

There is one belief in particular, hope, which attracts special attention. For Seligman, religions produce hope, allowing people to better face the world's trials, and they generate the belief that there is more good to life (and death) than meets the eye (2006, 203). It's the main reason, for him, why religious people have higher wellbeing than others. Interestingly, for Grace Davie, belief in the soul and life after death rises 'markedly in younger rather than older generations' especially in those nations in Europe that have suffered most institutional church decline (2002, 140).

But it's what ordinary Christians might believe about hope relating to life after death that's particularly informative. Here, in terms of research into ordinary congregations, there emerges a deep scepticism over the claims of academics like Tom Wright and church leaders to interpret what the Bible says about life after death definitively (despite the fact that there's a bewildering array of such official views). What emerges is an 'ordinary eschatology', emphasizing the 'nonphysicality of the afterlife'. As the researcher comments, 'potentially damaging disjunctions can appear between ordinary Christians and ecclesial and academic authority' on such central beliefs (Astley and Francis 2013, 103–04). Fortunately, the ordinary Christian keeps going to church, volunteering, giving and serving in civic life. Their actual beliefs must have some real proven value.

Worship

For Diener, the physical trappings of ritual, from beautiful pageantry, music, and buildings to art and festivals, constitute 'experience set apart from everyday life, which translates to feelings of well-being' (Diener and Biswas-Diener 2008, 122). The research projects in *Exploring Ordinary Theology* confirm Diener's observation but are rooted evidentially in the experience of ordinary churchgoers. For such ordinary worship, its 'habitual rhythms and practices' involve 'forms of shared activity' yet which do not 'require a foundation in perfect agreement'. Despite these differences, participation in worship 'offers them a time in which they can recognize themselves yet also encounter something infinitely greater'. Hymns, readings and worship together offer for many 'a new way of seeing the world' (Astley and Francis 2013, 160, 163, 166). The research of David Walker, now Bishop of Manchester, complements this work on regular churchgoing with an analysis of very occasional churchgoers, say at cathedral yearly carol services. His survey on motivations for attending such services (finding meaning, uplifting) also revealed that the more specific the claims made by the Church, the less likely the participants agreed. Their interests reflected more ethical rather than doctrinal concerns. In addition, 48 per cent of those questioned regarded all faiths as leading to God (Astley and Francis 2013, 143) (a finding confirmed by Putnam's survey of even evangelical Christians in the USA, as noted in my Afterword). But it's Gill's research which is of particular interest, especially on the contribution to Christian wellbeing of hymn singing by regular churchgoers. By singing hymns together they 'become carriers of continuity', addressing the unfolding seasons of the Church's year and reflecting on the great Christian doctrines. They thereby link doctrines with lifestyles: 'Make me a channel of your grace'. Summarizing his research, Gill comments 'It may not be too surprising, then, that regular churchgoers who sing hymns together with other worshippers week by week and over many years may assimilate these distinctive features' (2012b, 174, 181).

Churchgoing

For Putnam, regular church attendance, with all the networks this delivers, nourishes and sustains, is the main reason why Christians have greater wellbeing. Diener confirms this judgement from his survey of research, noting the importance of social support, the group mentality of worship and the emphasis on social activities, all as a basis for personal and social outreach. Yet through this contemporary linking to something permanent and important, people are also connected to past and future generations: 'Religious experiences connect people not only to others present, but to the entire group, past and current, and sometimes to all of humanity' (Diener and Biswas-Diener 2008, 121). From the Christian perspective, psychologist Myers confirms this high importance of social support for greater wellbeing, of the value of 'where two or three are gathered together' (2008, 326). Gill, too, writing from the perspective of sociological theology, confirms Putnam's findings that 'religious social networks are a strong more robust predictor' of wellbeing (Gill 2012a, 182). But it's the ecumenical theologian Clements who gets to the heart of what it means to be the ordinary church. Referring to Bonhoeffer's *Life Together*, he notes his judgement on 'community as absolutely of the essence of Christianity', but then elaborates this in terms of churchgoing as involving a 'real community with others in all their awkwardness, bearing and forbearing, giving and forgiving' (2013, 131). And it's that pure unadulterated ordinariness of ordinary churchgoing which sustained me on the sudden death of my wife. For my parish church of St Katharine is full of ordinary folk, doing ordinary things, from coffee mornings, raffles and knitting for premature babies, to singing hymns together and gossiping. And they surrounded me with the normality of ordinary human love and carried me until I could stand alone and begin to sing hymns again. It's that ordinary church which the researchers in ordinary theology have surveyed and generated evidence-based conclusions. And, because it is ordinary and normal, it's quite different from the unnecessary and evidentially inaccurate reified church of some very prominent contemporary theologians (Astley and Francis 2013, 17).

Nurturing children

Growing up religiously, for Diener, encourages a more positive view of the world, one which is more secure and grounded. It generates a stronger sense of community and provides a better moral foundation (Diener and Biswas-Diener 2008, 121). Gill's research, including analysis of church records in York for over 200 years, confirms and elaborates this judgement. Beginning with broad survey work, drawing on the 1991 'British Social Attitudes' data, he notes a 'significant difference of Christian beliefs and values among two groups of adult non-attenders'. Those who had attended church regularly as children score 'significantly' higher (Gill 2012a, 182–3). Moving then to his York church surveys, he concludes that a major factor in the dramatic collapse of church attendances from the nineteenth century, if not earlier, is that 'if a vast majority of children in York today are not being socialized in any of the churches (as appears to be the case) it seems likely that only a very few of them will become churchgoers as adults'. The more recent 'collapse of connection and engagement with children and young people' is clearly linked, from his detailed analysis of York churches, with the major decline of the churches, not least because also '[t]he Christian story is no longer at the heart of the nation' (Gill 2012b, 156, 120, 119). And that's why it's important I take my young grandchildren to church, where we sit together, draw pictures and drink orange juice.

In discussing all this kind of evidence on churchgoing and wellbeing, a very secular major economist observed to me that Christian tradition played a major part in influencing the greater wellbeing of Christians. By that he meant what the seven features of my model summarized about today's Christianity, but that it had also evolved from and been tested by the past. The key here is that of continuity and change, what Brown has referred to as a continually transforming tradition (Astley and Francis 2013, 69). It's what MacCulloch observes in his magisterial *A History of Christianity* from Christianity's earliest origins: that it survived, despite all the odds being against it, because of its 'remarkable capacity to mutate' (2009, 9). It's that continually evolving continuity which lies behind the seven features, and which, for Charry, so often provide 'stable shared environments in which individuals may productively locate themselves' (2013b, 2). Although these combined features of the Christian model are importantly empirically evidenced by economists, psychologists and sociologists, this brief section has also elaborated these features both from that secular perspective but also from within a Christian tradition. And it's the latter which draws much of its value from being precisely from within. In a delightful piece on 'Theology exemplified by music', Gill concludes that '[s]o faith like music may finally require active engagement for a full appreciation' (2012b, 202). But it's the indispensable combination of the two perspectives, secular and religious, which provides both the basis of and justification for the model.

Developing the model (2): Its transmission processes: how Christianity influences wellbeing

Transmission processes are an integral part of this Christian model, particularly in describing and explaining its effectiveness, that is, that the living out of the seven features accounts significantly for the fact that Christians both themselves have high wellbeing *and thereby* influence positively the wellbeing of other people and of society itself. In other words, it's not simply *what* but *how* Christianity contributes to human wellbeing that also reinforces the robust nature of this emerging model for Christian engagement with wellbeing. Transmission processes confirm the importance of the features, which in turn thereby facilitate their transmission. Two ways in which such transmissions of wellbeing occur will be briefly examined: 'transposing' beliefs and values into secular life, using Gill's research; and the 'moral freighting' of beliefs and values into society. This latter begins with Putnam's US research, but significantly elaborates it from the research conducted by Chris Baker, my splendid colleague in the William Temple Foundation. Both transmission models work with very robust, consistent across nations, empirical evidence that the 'religiously observant ... are better neighbours and better citizens than secular [ones] – they are more generous with their time and money, especially in helping the needy ... and they are more active in community life' (Putnam and Campbell 2010, 461).

So drawing from a variety of major secular surveys, Gill concludes that members of British religious groups are more than three times as likely to be involved in voluntary service, and in other caring groups (in parents' associations, political groups, tenant/resident groups and community environmental groups). They are more honest and altruistic than others, and give more to charity, including to overseas aid (Gill 2013, 147, 155). Why is this? It's out of the model's seven features of Christianity's practices, ethics and beliefs, out of what Chris Baker describes as belonging evolving into becoming evolving into participation (Baker 2013). Or, for Gill, it's that 'socially constructed theological ideas, (my beliefs) once generated, may have an influence upon society at large' (2013, 9).

As *why* interacting with *how*, Gill then proceeds to analyse the social significance of theology as 'more typically to be located in theological virtues that have been *transposed* into wider society' (2013, 53). Following in the footsteps of Weber on the Protestant work ethic, he also recognizes that Christian virtues persist in society long after their initial institutional basis has been forgotten. But it's his careful tracking of the current transposing of 'theological virtues' into the contemporary public forum that's most useful. Here, because of his own involvement in such public bodies, he identifies how key religious virtues are gradually being utilized, for example in the 'public discourse about bioethics' and its conscious borrowing from religious traditions because of their adding value to secular discourses – concepts like 'covenant' and 'stewardship' from Judaism, 'solidarity' and 'the common good' from Catholic social teaching and 'mercy' and 'compassion' from Islam. His detailed work in the Nuffield Council of Bioethics allowed him to trace and experience this borrowing 'at first hand' (Gill 2013, 201–06).

Putnam's American research provides the basis of the other transmission process. He clearly demonstrates the robust correlative relationship between religiosity and higher rates of volunteering, giving and civic involvement, but then also demonstrates its development into a causal relationship from his two separate surveys of the same people, in 2006 and then in 2007. It is from this evidence that he concludes 'that religiously based ties are *morally freighted* in a way most secular ties are not'

(Putnam and Campbell 2010, 477, my emphasis). And that's because Christians inhabit a 'density of religious social networks' (such as the number of close friends in your church, participation in small church groups, and the frequency of talking about religion with family and friends) (2010, 470). And it's that correlative and causal relationship between such religious networks and the religious becoming better citizens and neighbours and their proven ability to then inform society for the better that he describes as moral freighting, as the greater capacity of Christians to carry their practices, virtues and beliefs into wider society. And it's that greater capacity of the religious to promote greater wellbeing that lies behind the former British government minister John Denham's recognition in public life, local and national, that 'Faith is a strong and powerful source of honesty, solidarity, generosity, the very values which are essential to politics, to our economy and our society' (quoted in Baker 2013, 343).

The research, using qualitative tools, conducted by Chris Baker has importantly elaborated *how* this moral freighting actually occurs, and has done so most usefully with reference to the contemporary British context. The religious groups he worked with represented major Christian denominations, Muslims, Hindus, Buddhists and members of a secular spirituality group. This has therefore the added value of engaging the interfaith dimension of my multidimensional collaborative model identified in the introductory chapter and in the material elaborating my model earlier in this chapter. Initially, Baker's research distinguished between the religious capital of such religious groups and individuals belonging to them (what they do in the community and wider society – as essentially practical outputs) and their spiritual capital (what motivates them or energizes them including in relation to such practical outputs – this involves the role of sacred buildings, and literatures, public and private worship, social activities and especially Putnam's dense religious networking, etc.) (Baker and Skinner 2006; Baker 2013, 353). His later research then demonstrated *how* such religious and spiritual capital interacted and was then operationalized – *what* were the benefits gained from say church membership and how they were shared or 'freighted' into the wider community. It is this transmission process that he summarizes as the sense of *belonging* to a religious community, which then engenders a sense of *becoming*, in terms of growing in confidence springing from habits, commitments and accountabilities, which can and then do lead to a variety of 'technologies and performances of *participation* in the wider community'(Baker 2013, 355). And it's even happening in China today, witness my conversation in Princeton with a Chinese theologian Zhibin Xie, and his drawing to my attention a number of research reports and articles including empirical studies of Christian family ethics, work ethics and the effects of their moral lives on social and economic public life (Zhibin Xie 2013).

Developing the model (3): Measuring Christianity's contribution to wellbeing

There is, as Gill has rightly acknowledged, a deep unease in theological circles over attempts to quantify religious experiences (2012a, 30). They regard matters of faith to be unquantifiable, not least as the transcendent role of grace in the believer: 'For it is only by God's grace that the church, the visible, concrete product of human actions, institutions and beliefs, is the church' (Astley and Francis 2013, 18). That's alright if you're only talking to yourself, which is what most theologians do, but if you want to engage in conversations with others about what matters so much to men and women, then on their own, such statements are at best useless. But there are other ways of understanding what Christian practices, ethics and beliefs are about, as the rich and robust connection between secular and religious commentators over my model's seven features of Christianity's contribution to wellbeing illustrates. This also includes the emerging research behind the development of ordinary theology with its use of both quantitative and qualitative research tools. Note that both tools are essential, not least to balance religion's propensity to focus unduly on qualitative research, reflecting its overemphasis on the personal and small communities. Engaging the masses, the aggregate, necessarily through quantitative research, is of profound importance in the densely populated urban world of today. And it's also essential in order to engage more effectively with the main social sciences, particularly economics, psychology and sociology. That's why Gill's deployment of both tools is so important and exemplary.

There is a major exception to this measurement reticence, reflecting the often double standards of churches. In their actual practice, churches have increasingly used statistics to measure church performances, whether baptisms, marriages and burials (in the Church of England, from 1541 with the introduction of their parish registers, an astonishingly invaluable source, including for Fogel's work on life expectancy!) or church attendances and finances. As we have also seen from Gill's work – which is very representative of the work in the field, say of the sociology of religion – church-based data is also now powerfully complemented by the use of secular data, including from the World Values Surveys, the UK's BSA, Gallup and the censuses.

In developing measurement systems relating to religious contributions to improving the wealth and wellbeing of nations, for example, as outlined in Chapter 2, I have also begun to explore systems that use complementary secular and religious tools to measure in the broadest terms religions' contribution to wellbeing. Besides their intrinsic value, they also begin to provide an essential additional measurability dimension to my model.

For example, the following three proven secular measurement systems relate to progressive change, using the political scientist Villacort's definition of it as the contributions of institutions, policies and civic agencies and attitudes to enable people to improve their wellbeing (Dasgupta 2007, 159). This is reinforced particularly in terms of the traditions of ethical economics, for example by Stiglitz's (2005) definition of moral growth as: generating increasing living standards today, but also for future generations; ensuring that the benefits of growth are shared equitably and creating more tolerant societies informed by social justice and solidarity.

The three secular tools move from pre-ethical (the first) to the more ethical rest.

1 A social development index, which has been developed by Morris from the historical analysis of statistics and other sources. Its four traits are: energy capture, urban organization, communication and military capacities. Together, these reflect society's abilities to get things done. Although measuring social, and explicitly not moral, development, it generates what the theologian Browning has usefully termed 'pre-moral goods' (2006, 300) by including conditions instrumentally important for achieving progressive change, for example, technophysio evolution's contribution to increasing life expectancy.

2 The Human Development Index (HDI) and the Inequality Adjusted HDI. The former is used by the UN's Human Development Programme to measure a nation's GDP per capita, life expectancy at birth and literacy (Atherton 2003, 162–5). It tests to what extent nations achieve decent standards of living. The theologian Hicks has also developed the HDI to take account of inequalities within nations (2000), which is therefore of particular relevance for my thesis. The aggregate information of the HDI is therefore complemented by distributional information, using the Gini coefficient tool as deployed by economists to measure degrees of inequality.

3 The Index of Sustainable Economic Welfare was developed by the economist Daly and the theologian Cobb (1990) and runs environmental alongside social and economic indicators. The British New Economics Foundation's National Accounts of Wellbeing uses Seligman's PERMA definition of wellbeing in the measurement of human flourishing across European nations, as noted in Chapter 2. Both these systems could now be replaced by the Sarkozy Commission's Measurement of Economic Performance and Social Progress (covering GDP per capita, quality of life or subjective wellbeing, and sustainable development and environment), as noted again in Chapter 2 (Stiglitz, Sen and Fitoussi 2010).

Alongside these secular tools, I have selected three that focus on religious contributions to wellbeing:

1 The Religion and Happiness Index was developed by Leslie Francis, deploying the secular Oxford Happiness Inventory of positive psychology alongside his scale of attitudes to religion (Francis 2011). He uses, for his Christianity surveys, five components: God, Jesus, Bible, Prayer and Church. Valid across age groups, Christian denominations and languages, it has also been tested, appropriately adapted, in Judaism, Islam and Hinduism. It suggests positive associations between attitudes towards religion and happiness, linking therefore particularly to subjective wellbeing.

2 Putnam's Religiosity Index measures American religiosity in terms of frequency of religious attendance, public and private prayer, religion as important in life, its role in identity, and the strength of belief in religion and in God. It applies to Christian traditions, the criteria are all linked, and it also satisfies our intuitive sense of what it means to describe someone as religious. It constitutes a major source of knowledge for exploring the relationship between religion and the development of wellbeing by measuring the extent of religious contributions to volunteering, giving, trust and civic participation, as we have already seen, but also, and this is of particular importance for this book's thesis, by measuring religious commitments to political programmes engaging income inequality and the government's role in poverty alleviation (Putnam and Campbell 2010, 18–23, Appendix 1).

3 Chris Baker's Belonging, Becoming and Participation Index gives greater depth to Putnam's moral freighting transmission process, including by measuring religion's religious and spiritual capital and how they contribute to society's wellbeing. This has been elaborated earlier in this chapter.

These latter three metrics clearly relate significantly to my model, its seven features and transmission processes. They could suggest, for example, incorporation into a single metric or more likely a 'dashboard' (Stiglitz, Sen and Fitoussi 2010, xxiv), the latter representing the need for coordinated multiple metrics which could then also relate to, and draw information from, the three secular tools. What does emerge from this very brief and selective survey of measurement tools, and the work of others in these fields (for example Gill's use of secular surveys already noted), is the possibility and feasibility of developing measurement systems in relation to religion's contribution to improving human wellbeing. 'In an increasingly performance-oriented society, metrics matter. What we measure affects what we do. If we have the wrong metrics we will strive for the wrong things' (Stiglitz, Sen and Fitoussi 2010, xvii). Maybe this introduction to the Sarkozy report by Stiglitz, Sen and Fitoussi has also something to say to a Christianity and religious studies needing to reformulate and reorder themselves for better engagement with and contribution to improving the wellbeing of all, including through the world of daily life.

A matter arising: Maybe some implications for theology and its location in a wider religious studies

Reinhold Niebuhr once remarked that he was a moralist who had strayed into the world of theology. His first great book, *Moral Man and Immoral Society* (1963) (renamed by a student as Immoral Man and More Immoral Society!), was initially treated with scepticism by publishers because it fell between the two stools of theology and politics, and so would be unacceptable to both. That is, of course, one of the most appropriate places for theology to locate itself, within and between disciplines and experiences, within and between the world of daily life and the world of religious practices, ethics and beliefs, the worlds spanned by my seven features of Christianity, what this book is about. And that's a view of religion much wider than theology, than beliefs, because it's also centred on practices and ethics, both of which powerfully pre-date theory, as Bellah's *Religion in Human Evolution* so magisterially demonstrates. That's why I locate theology properly, rightfully and respectfully in the wider field of religious studies.

Since the model I have developed has been modestly and

provisionally tested with regard to subjective wellbeing, the third perspective on the wealth, wellbeing and inequalities of nations (I will shortly consider the feasibility of deploying it for the other two, health and income), this is a useful place to take stock a little. As someone who has worked principally in the field of Christian social ethics (overlapping much with today's public and practical theology), I am very aware that I am not seen to be a professional academic theologian, dominated as that concept has been by systematic theology and biblical studies of various shapes and sizes. So all I can do is to comment on a religious studies traditionally shaped by such theology or theorizing, almost in the spirit of Niebuhr's delightful *Leaves from the Notebook of a Tamed Cynic* (1980) or Easterlin's *Reluctant Economist* (2004).

Drawing on the experience of others much more skilled in systematic theology and biblical studies, all I can do is simply and briefly to sketch some of the implications of this book so far, particularly from Chapters 2 and 3, for religious studies in general, and for theology in particular.

Developments proceeding from the Industrial and Mortality Revolutions were particularly driven by knowledge as scientific discoveries and technological advances. It was their continuing and accelerating interactions which was so mutually productive, as it was between basic and applied research also in the social sciences. The results included the continual generation of a 'set of procedures and attitudes, including the reliance on experimental methods, and an abiding respect for observed facts' (Easterlin 2004, 97). The interactions between such spheres of reality and the world of religious studies should similarly generate an interdependence that drives mutual learning processes. This should result, among other things, in the realignment of the disciplines involved, both within and between them, and particularly if and as they focus on promoting greater human wellbeing. We have already seen the implications of such an agenda on the needed realignment of economics, for example, through the adoption of self-reporting research methods and the implications of the resulting research findings for such basic economic assumptions as the nature of the human as economic agent and on Pareto optimality in welfare economics. Yet the psychologist Kahneman's research, on say identifying the primacy of intuitions over the cognitive function and its implications for risk and decision taking, has profound implications not just for economics (for which he gained the Nobel prize in economics), but also for religious studies. For his findings justify my use, and more importantly, the ordering, of Christianity as practices, ethics and then beliefs or doctrines, and therefore the consequent locating of theology or cognitive religious theorizing, in the much wider framework of religious studies. Recent developments in general theological studies have begun to recognize and reflect this reordering and rebalancing of the relationship between theory and practice (between let us say basic and applied research). The growth of Christian ethics, pastoral theology, practical theology, liberation theology (and its prioritizing of orthopraxis over orthodoxy), sociological theology and public theology, together suggest that this progressive shifting of emphasis is beginning to take strong root in religious studies. This movement is also confirmed by the recognition of the strategic importance of ordinary theology and Vasquez's materialist theory of religion, and the substantial development of more empirical, evidentice-based research. These are some of the main implications of this interactive participation for religious studies through their wider interdisciplinary engagement with wellbeing studies. My model is one of the fruits of all this, and, in turn, therefore becomes a contribution to it.

It is in relation to these findings that I have very recently become aware of certain research developments in systematic theology and in biblical studies relating to wellbeing studies. Although at an early stage of development, some very interesting material is emerging, which begins to add real value to the research findings noted above. I will briefly introduce this material in terms of its implications for methodology and content.

Methodology

The emergence of the scientific revolutions from the seventeenth century and their interaction with technological developments formed the basis of the Industrial and Mortality Revolutions, as we have seen. For systematic theologian Ellen Charry these changes fed into a wider 'epistemological crisis' ... necessarily 'requiring evidence to support truth claims'. It was faced by such historically radical challenges, and particularly for theology's traditional reliance on a correspondence theory of truth and knowledge (that Christian claims were seen as credibly referring to the objects of which they spoke), that systematic theology and dogmatics developed an alternative way of operating, including as 'primarily Protestant enterprises'. Since empirical evidence could no longer support Christian claims, arguing for an alternative truth as the coherence of ideas became the business of the new systematic theology. Its 'rationalist understanding of truth required that conclusions deduced from premises be entailed by the argument being made' (Charry 2012a, 229–30). It generated what became in the later nineteenth and twentieth centuries a modern intellectualist understanding of theology's task. So, for the great German theologian Pannenberg, the project is to establish 'the truth of Christian doctrines' derived from and reinforced by doctrines of God which 'provides the final criterion of truth' and 'that truth itself is systematic, because coherence belongs to the nature of truth' (Pannenberg 1991, 6, 8). So systematic theology's rational claim to be a 'science' comparable to the natural sciences undergirded its claims, with biblical studies, to be the dominant part of any self-respecting Faculty of Theology in and up to the middle few decades of the twentieth century. And that was certainly the case when I arrived in Manchester University's Faculty of Theology in the 1970s. Part of the problem is that such systematic theology thus became increasingly separated from a rapidly changing and developing biblical studies and the latter's increasing reliance on and use of historical and exegetical tools, which were more aligned to the character of the knowledge revolutions. Not surprisingly, therefore, it is in biblical studies that some of the more creative theological contributions to the contemporary study of wellbeing are being located (Strawn 2012). For Charry, such biblical understandings of happiness contrast starkly with her carefully considered judgement on surveying the history of systematic and dogmatic theology, that these biblical concepts of happiness have 'never appeared as a topic, let alone single point of coherence' (2012a, 231). It's that failure which she, with other systematic theologians, are seeking to address, in her terms, as developing a 'positive theology' (2013a). And that's important, because of the historic and contemporary significance of such theology in informing Christian understandings of life. But there are also other signs of positive change in method. For example, the new splendid (female, dear laggardly Church of England) Archbishop of Sweden Antje Jackelén is addressing, also as a systematic theologian, the need to move beyond Newtonian to post-Einsteinian notions of time in terms of how we understand the doctrines of atonement, reconciliation and forgiveness. She has therefore begun to revisit in very creative ways 'common theological understandings of time and eternity' in order to overcome the problems of how we speak about 'the person and work of Jesus Christ in relation to time and eternity' (2013; see also Jackelén 2005). Engaging with foundational dimensions of modern physics and their profound implications for theological understandings, takes us, of course, very much into a relationship with the knowledge-based developments from Newton onwards.

Content

Although I have distinguished this from methodology, it interacts in powerful ways particularly when addressing wellbeing studies. We need to begin by acknowledging that Western theology, from its earlier sources to the present, has been 'skittish about temporal happiness' (Charry 2010, ix) to say the very least! Happiness was rather regarded as a profoundly eschatological matter, so temporary happiness was almost beside the point or, at best, a 'fragile doctrine of terrestrial happiness as relief from fear of eternal punishment through faith in the forgiveness of sin'. Indeed, for Charry, it generated a 'pathology-driven psychology based on God's displeasure with humanity'. Her task, therefore, with other theologians, is to reinforce and elaborate, in conversation particularly with positive psychologists, for example, and with developments in biblical studies, glimpses in the traditions of Christian doctrine, and to develop these into acknowledging and celebrating 'God's full-bodied emotional life' in order to affirm 'God's enjoyment of human flourishing for God's own happiness and to argue that, theologically speaking, happiness is the mutual enjoyment of God and humanity when each fulfils the other' (2012a, 229). The traditional doctrines say of the impassibility of God, as God's supreme sovereignty, as God without emotions, so significant in Christian history, play no part in these contemporary biblical and systematic theologies and their pursuit of happiness. And, of course, that journey into a God of emotions is not new at all. As we commemorate the hundredth anniversary of the start of the great tragedy of the First World War in 1914, I am reminded of the crude but moving poetry of 'Woodbine Willie', Geoffrey Studdert Kennedy. I was introduced to him in the early 1960s (as I was to CND and the Labour Party!) by my old mentor and first boss, Father Strachan in Aberdeen. Living as chaplain with men in the most appalling conditions and suffering in the trenches (he used to give the men Woodbine cigarettes), Woodbine Willie had to re-fashion his very conception of God in Christ:

> And I hate the God of Power in His hellish heavenly throne
> Looking down on rape and murder, hearing little children moan ...
> ... God, the God I have and worship, reigns in sorrow on the Tree,
> Broken, bleeding but unconquered, very God of God to me.
> (Kennedy 1964, 46–7)

It's that God, so full of emotion, which is now being so enlarged to induce, as the biblical material so clearly demonstrates, a God of happiness, of wellbeing, in and through and with all creation human, animate and inanimate.

Great is the Lord, who *delights* in the welfare of his servant.
(Ps. 35.27)
For you shall go out in joy.
And be led back in peace;
the mountains and the hills before you shall burst into song,
and all the trees of the fields shall clap their hands. (Isa. 55.12)
(Strawn 2012, 35, 51)

On beginning to test the model with health and income: From possibility to 'challenging'!

For the model I have developed in relation to subjective wellbeing to be more comprehensibly viable, and particularly for the engagement with economics, it needs to be extended to engage with at least the other two perspectives on the wealth and wellbeing of nations, namely health and income.

There is a clear and robust relationship of compatibility between religion (as Christianity) and health, in terms of their history, traditions and contemporary developments, including in subjective wellbeing studies. These convergences begin to suggest the feasibility and probable viability of extending the model to engage the health perspective. As we will see, for example, the model's focus on Christianity's practice, ethics and theory provides strong bridges with the health field. There has also been interesting use of statistical evidence to support Christianity's contribution to the greater health both of its members (they perform better than the non-religious, as with subjective wellbeing) and of society (through health practices and institutions and through transposing values and beliefs into the medical field). The seven features of Christianity and its transmission processes again play a prominent role in and through such contributions.

But then there's the question of Christianity's engagement with income, surely a central part of its relationship to economics. This is so complex both in terms of the history of that relationship (as income and as economics) and its contemporary manifestations (including as the practices, beliefs and theories of Christianity) that I have neither the time (nor space in this book) nor resources (in terms of those needed to engage this perspective satisfactorily) to go deeper into this first perspective. But it is likely to provide the core of my future research. That's challenging enough, as the title of this final section suggests. But it's even more challenging than that! For Christianity, past and present, has a robust history impregnated with deep suspicion of wealth and money both in themselves and as means of exploiting the vulnerable. One of the most quoted, misquoted and certainly misused relevant biblical exhortations is 'For the love of money is the root of all evils' (1 Tim. 6.10, KJV). With that behind you, who can be against you! So the challenge presented by income is, like that of the so-called 'challenging' parish, pretty hopeless! But the task can and will be done by many others more than me, not least because the material in Chapter 2 demonstrates income's centrality to greater wellbeing. I will now very briefly begin to elaborate the case for the model's efficacy in engaging health, with even less on income.

On health and Christianity: Addressing the second perspective

Health is such a vast and prominent field of human interest, including in religious literatures, that this brief section clearly cannot do any serious kind of justice to it. Yet from my engagement with the wealth and wellbeing of nations and the important role life expectancy and health has played in it, I can at least give hints from this research that could inform the testing and developing of my model in relation to this second perspective.

The place to begin is clearly in the already proven robustly positive relationship between subjective wellbeing and major fields or domains of our lives, including for example, health. This therefore can build on the empirically tested case, as we have seen in the works of Diener and Seligman that better subjective wellbeing leads both to better health and to the more effective challenging of illnesses. And it therefore also builds on the case made in this chapter that there is an effective Christian model for engaging constructively with this material. The material resourcing each of these two cases therefore also provides a clear and tested bridge or route into the development of my model, in this case, now in relationship to health. Thus the material I have already come across provides interesting pointers to the feasibility of making this case for the transferability of the model to health, for example, in terms of measuring Christianity's contribution to health, and then the wider influence of its practices, ethics and beliefs, including through its transmission processes, all constituent parts of my development of the Christian case.

With regard to religion's contribution to health, including its measurement, the Center for Spirituality, Theology and Health at Duke University in the USA reported 'a series of clinical studies which suggest amongst other things: improved rates of recovery for cancer patients who report involvement in faith communities; enhanced longevity (my life expectancy) amongst those who attend synagogues; slower rates of cognitive decline in those experiencing the onset of dementia and [a] marginal impact on aspects of coping strategies in relation to recovery from serious illness for religious people' (Atherton, Graham and Steedman 2011, 13). Likewise, the psychologist Myers (2008) also notes, 'More than a thousand studies have sought to correlate "the faith factor" with health and healing', including the significant [for this book in general, and Chapter 2 in particular] 'religiosity–longevity correlation'. Importantly, he is also *very clear* that 'the religious–health correlation is yet to be fully explained'. Yet Pincus (1997), the deputy medical director of the American Psychiatric Association, also acknowledges that all these findings 'have made clear that anyone involved in providing health care services ... cannot ignore ... the important connections between spirituality, religion and health' (Myers 2008, 335–7).

In terms of religious practice and healing, this has figured prominently throughout history, from at least early hunter-gatherer stages, where, for Bellah, the 'widespread idea and practice of shamanism' accompanied hunter beliefs (2011, 163). In more recent history, these two healing traditions of religion and medicine often converge, for example in Christian history in the establishment, often by monastic orders, of healing institutions like hospices (interestingly, Christianity has also played an important part in their re-establishment as palliative care centres in Britain in the later twentieth century). That tradition has played and is still playing a substantial part in delivering health care, particularly in poorer nations. Linked initially to the astonishing eruption of the missionary movements in the nineteenth century, the institutional health output of Christianity can even now be astonishing, running almost 40 per cent of hospitals and 21 per cent of health centres on the Tanzanian mainland. The Catholic Health Association of India includes 484 large hospitals (Päivänsalo 2013). Catholic institutions even run 10 per cent of hospitals in the USA (*The Economist*, 29 March 2014, 53).

The relationship between spirituality, ethics and health is also significant. As Myers rightly observes, as 'medical science matured', driving the Mortality Revolution, healing and religion often diverged. 'Rather than asking God to spare their children from smallpox, people were able to vaccinate them' (2008, 335). Yet interestingly, as I have noticed in Britain (a departed friend and colleague, Peter Gilbert, was a professor of social work and spirituality), religion and health are converging once again, including in the USA: so of 135 medical schools in the USA, 101 offered spirituality and health courses in 2005, and a survey (1997) found 94 per cent of US health maintenance organization professionals and 99 per cent of family physicians agreeing that 'personal prayer, meditation or other spiritual or religious practices' can enhance medical treatment (Myers 2008, 335). Ethics equally played a prominent role in both medical services and medical technological developments (hospital chaplaincies span and link both spirituality and ethics). Christianity has and does contribute to such ethical formation, including through involvement in national and regional medical ethics committees (Gill 2013, 177), and through the transmission of religious values and virtues into such secular dialogues and practices, as already noted earlier in this chapter.

My seven features of Christianity's contribution to greater wellbeing also play a particularly relevant part in this health perspective model. For example, creative work has been done on the relationship between comforting beliefs and healing. For Charry, beliefs clearly link to emotions, both negative and positive. Her task is to combat the former by developing the latter. So her realizing eschatology 'functions in two directions, suggesting that healing is healing: that is, being healed by Christ strengthens one's ability to heal others ... It is an ever-widening circle. Being healed enables healing, and healing heals' (Charry 2010, 268). A supportive philosophy of life, deeply informed by the other six features, again plays a prominent part in the promotion of wholeness (as it also has in the seventh of Layard's Big Seven contribution to happiness). Both beliefs and philosophies of life again link to the other features, including the social ties of churchgoing, regulatory lifestyles and ritual. Researchers therefore suggest that a set of variables, including a 'stress protection and enhanced well-being associated with a coherent world view, a sense of hope for the long-term future, feelings of ultimate acceptance, and the relaxed meditation of prayer or Sabbath observance', may well be related to mortality reductions, healthier immune functioning and fewer hospital admissions (Myers 2008, 337).

On Christianity, incomes and material wellbeing: Addressing the first perspective

At first sight this is the most difficult task of all. For so much of certainly Christian history, the concept of money dominated understandings of income and material wellbeing. And it has a terrible press, not least through the influence of the Christian Scriptures' pronouncement that the love of money is the root of all evil and Jesus' call to the rich young man to sell all and follow him and his refusal to do so, because he had great wealth. The painting on the Markham chantry chapel from the early 1500s, used hopefully to good effect in Chapter 2, says it all, with the rich young man, with his hand on his purse, warned by Death that even the wealthy cannot buy him off. All these pressures led to the continuing theme regarding money as a god, including by some leading theologians today. This is confusing, unhelpful and inaccurate (I almost said plain stupid!). Historically, money's place in resourcing human life was very limited until at least the eighteenth century. As we have seen, the vast majority of people had very little of it, because they were poor and lived very straitened lives. In such situations money often becomes a symbol of the reality of their marginalization and oppression. When the Industrial Revolution increased and improved the lives of more and more people, income understandably occupied a much bigger part of their lives and the lives of nations. Then it really does become a god for so many theologians and church leaders despite its liberating consequences for the majority poor. What this book tries to do is to correct such general moral confusions, and this is a particular point where that is absolutely essential. Any contemporary consideration of income must recognize its central contribution to contemporary wellbeing both in itself and as key facilitator and contributor to other foundations of wellbeing, from the provision of the basics of housing, food and clothing, to health care, education and governance. And doing that effectively and adequately is what my model has to be able to engage. That is a particularly difficult task because it involves entering the engagement between Christianity and economics (and therefore recognizing and addressing the great gulf between them), and then also developing Christian practices, ethics and beliefs in relation to income and what and how income helps to resource other key foundations of wellbeing, and only then, and from such evidence, can the nature and extent of Christianity's contribution to this first perspective be tested in terms of the viability, or otherwise, of my model.

All I can do now is to give some pointers, out of this research, to highlight the possibilities of this task.

On income itself, particularly as wages, much work has been done from the Middle Ages' understanding of a just wage, to recent and contemporary engagements with a minimum wage, including R. H. Tawney's (1914) work and the promotion of a living wage today. Similar movements occurred in the USA, including the Catholic John Ryan's work for a minimum wage before the Second World War (Frey 2009, 125–9). On income in its various welfare forms (from pensions to social security benefits) again, Christians in the UK were heavily involved, including through the work of William Temple, and similarly in the USA through the social gospel's relationship to the New Deal, both of which are illustrated in Chapters 4 and 5.

In terms of inequalities, again there are strong histories and contemporary Christian involvements, from the development of redistributive welfare mechanisms to volunteering and charitable giving to support the marginalized (witness the contemporary Christian involvement in food banks). Much of the volunteering and charitable giving activities have been measured, for example in North-West England (see the following Afterword), including contributions to overseas aid and to the poorest nations. The condemnation of the exploitation of the poor has been a recurring theme of individual Christians and church bodies.

In terms of the Christian contribution to knowledge, such a key basis of the Industrial and Mortality Revolutions, both Easterlin and Ferguson have particularly highlighted the importance of the contribution of literacy and education, and for Ferguson, the particular role of Protestant Christianity in extending literacy to ordinary people – a key component in the development of human capital – so significant for generating economic growth (Easterlin 2004, 34–79; Ferguson 2011, 77, 125, 263–4). Christianity has also played a significant role, and continues to do so, in the delivery of education at all levels and in rich and poor economies (I'm a visiting professor at a university that emerged from the first Church of England Teacher Training College in the middle of the nineteenth century, interestingly much supported by John Bird Sumner, then Bishop of Chester, but earlier, a leading Christian political economist!).

On the major bases of modern wellbeing for which income is essential, again, there are strong historic and contemporary Christian involvements. For example, in food, housing and clothing, particularly for the poor, then in education and health care: all are informed by Christian beliefs, ethics and practices. It would, almost as an afterthought, be interesting to undertake an equivalent exercise to Chan's 'Biblical Lexicon of Happiness' (in Strawn

2012), but in this case, say on income/money, housing, health and learning, if only to illustrate the wealth of material relating to wellbeing rooted in the Hebrew and Christian Scriptures.

And, finally, on measuring wellbeing, I have already noted the significant material involved in my consideration of Christianity, subjective wellbeing and health. But there are also other sources, including, for example, the theologian Cobb's work with the economist Daly on an Index of Sustainable Economic Welfare, and the theologian Hicks's development of an Inequality Adjusted Human Development Index, to which could be added the work of Sabina Alkire (2005) at Oxford, developing more adequate measurements of poverty (the Alkire Foster Method). Although these are secular tools, they are clearly and demonstrably connected to Christian practices, ethics and beliefs.

In other words, all this very selective and very briefly elaborated material suggests the feasibility of at least taking further forward the testing of my model, or something like it (hopefully better!), in relation to the health and income perspectives, as well as to the more proven subjective wellbeing perspective, on the wealth, wellbeing and inequalities of nations.

Part 2

Getting Better-ish in Historical Contexts
Putting Christianity to Work on Progressive Change

Exploring the great escapes from poverty and premature death and the resulting great inequality divergences is a profoundly modern and contemporary story, as is the development of a Christian engagement with such a grand narrative. Yet it's an account that needs enlarging and enriching but also qualifying and analysing. And that best requires locating it in historical contexts that are both long in extent (and I really mean long, going back to the end of the last Ice Age and before!) and more recent in intensity (since 1750 CE). That will also enable us to see the importance of religious contributions to social development in the more general context, for example through the radical operations of the axial age in the last millennium BCE, but then also in two nations in more recent history since 1700 CE, in the USA and UK.

Such evidence will certainly confirm and elaborate the provisional conclusions emerging from Chapters 2 and 3, that life is getting better for more and more peoples and nations and that Christianity has a robust role to play in that improving of wellbeing. Yet it's equally clearly getting better-ish, with the dramatic damaging increases in inequalities both between and within nations. And it's in that order that hard evidence now locates them, as nations getting better, then that 'better' being qualified. Both these trends, positives and negatives, will also play a prominent part in the long history, with certainly as much emphasis being placed on the negatives through the repeated bumping against robust ceilings of increasing social development, and the regular violent eruptions of my five horsemen of the apocalypse.

There are four brief stages in this introductory argument of locating the themes in historical contexts.

They begin by first using contemporary multidisciplinary surveys of the very gradual progression of social development from the end of the last Ice Age, about 13,000 BCE, until the eighteenth century in modern times. The archaeologist and historian Morris's work, including his deployment of a Social Development Index, is of particular value in tracing and illustrating the improvements in wellbeing over such a long period of time. His use of historical evidence-based narratives also then ensures that the index is tested against the necessary historical detail. This work resonates greatly with the rapidly evolving developments in archaeological science, but also with the contributions of growing developments in evolutionary biology and Bellah's work on religion in human evolution. The latter is also an important source for this section, although, like Morris, I am also very aware of the pioneering contribution of Jared Diamond, a professor of physiology at the University of California's Medical School, but also a major contributor in the fields of ecology and evolutionary biology (1997).

The second section then recognizes that this larger historical context also reinforces the quite astonishing changes in human development since 1750 CE, so influenced by the Industrial and Mortality Revolutions, the basis of Chapters 2 and 3 in this book. The nature and extent of these transformations are illustrated particularly and visually by a series of graphs, drawn from geoscientists, economists, economic historians and psychologists (the latter, Pinker, relates, for example, to a long historical survey of the rise and decline of violence).

Running through these two first sections, and of some importance for this research and the thesis of this book, is the highly relevant critical conversation between two fine historians, Fogel and Elton, the latter representing the more traditional evidence-based narrative approach, and the former the more recent emergence of a more quantitative-based approach to history. This constitutes the third section. Both traditions are clearly essential for a measured and comprehensive engagement with historical contexts, but they have the added value of both confirming the significance of the more narrative approach in religious studies (for example in biblical studies and systematic theology) and also arguing for the now indispensable addition of more quantitative measurement based research.

The fourth and final section then proceeds to introduce two case studies on how, and to what effect, Christianity has contributed to increasing wellbeing in the USA and Britain from 1700 to the present. It's about moving from more general to more specific contexts, from the arguments about and evidence of the growth of wellbeing and Christianity's contribution to it in Chapters 2 and 3, to how Christianity has actually contributed to it through the more detailed historical processes in two nations at the centre of the dramatic changes in wellbeing since the eighteenth century. It's another illustration of the value and relevance of monovision, of bringing together the long and short range perspectives on human life.

Putting the argument in long historical contexts

Although this section will concentrate on the long historical context from the end of the last Ice Age, this, in turn, can be located in an even longer story. To begin at the beginning in terms of our universe's emergence about 13.5 billion years ago, and our development after this, is beyond most people's imagination. Bellah helps greatly by using David Christian's schema by collapsing that history by a factor of one billion, so each billion years is reduced to one year. And the results are intriguing (Bellah 2011, 51). The universe's beginning through the Big Bang 13.5 billion years ago therefore becomes 13.5 years ago; 'the sun and solar system 4.5 years ago; the first living organisms on earth, single-cell organisms between 4 and 3.5 years ago; multicellular organisms, seven months ago; *Homo sapiens*, about 50 minutes ago; agricultural communities, five minutes ago [when our story begins, from the end of the last Ice Age]; and the great explosions of science and technology, in the midst of which we live [and the focus of this book], within the last second'! Most history focuses on the last three minutes. In terms of religion's contribution, the earliest sources of which go back to our pre-human animal existence, most research is involved with the last period, from 14,000 BCE (less than five minutes ago), beginning with tribal religion and its 'production of meaning' (a key concept in contemporary well-being studies), its transition to archaic religion and its focus on gods and kings, as the interaction between meaning and power (beyond which religions, including Christianity, have never moved cleanly) (Bellah 2011, 117–18, 171–2, 210–11). It is in relation to the latter – meaning and power – that the significant axial age initially engages in the first millennium BCE, as Greek philosophy, Judaism, Buddhism and Confucianism, for its great first historian, Jaspers, the time when 'Man, as we know him today, came into being' (Morris 2011, 255).

Morris begins his analysis near the end of the last Ice Age, 14,000 BCE, therefore tracking the movement from hunter-gatherers to the emergence of agriculture and its associated early settlements, initially from 9500 BCE in the 'Hilly Flanks', along the border line of today's Iran, Turkey, Syria, Lebanon, Israel and Jordan (Morris 2011, 93–7). Similar patterns emerged in China, 2,000 years later. Importantly, this larger context powerfully questions the basic underlying conclusions of more traditional historians like Elton. For him, 'Recorded history amounts to no more than about 200 generations. Even if there is a larger purpose in history, it must be said that we cannot really expect so far to be able to extract it from the little bit of history we have' (Morris 2011, 581). Yet for contemporary research, using archaeology, genetics and linguistics, we can now go back 500 generations. Which is where we, like Morris, Diamond and Bellah, can more usefully begin our narrative.

I have found it helpful to begin with a measurement system in order to provide a viable framework which can then be tested in detail by more traditionally researched historical narratives and analyses. Morris's Social Development Index (SDI) is the most useful tool to deploy, not least because it emerges out of a critical engagement with the relevant multidisciplinary literatures and because it is a provisional working tool to be tested and adapted in the light of appropriate evidence. As we have noticed, in the introductory first chapter and its use of concepts like the world of daily life, Morris complements this through his definition of social development as 'basically, a group's ability to master its physical and intellectual environment to get things done', or, more formally and usefully for our arguments in Chapters 2 and 3, 'the bundle of technological, subsistence, organizational, and cultural accomplishments through which people feed, clothe, house, and reproduce themselves, explain the world around them, resolve disputes within their communities, extend their power at the expense of other communities, and defend themselves against others' attempts to extend their power' (Morris 2011, 144).

Morris uses a number of criteria by which his measurement system must be judged, including Einstein's supposed and splendid one that 'in science, things should be made as simple as possible, but no simpler' (2011, 145). Out of such critical analysis he develops a tool using four traits: energy capture, without which we can't survive and reproduce, and on which (and on our ability to find better ways to exploit it) improving our wellbeing depends so much (as set out in Chapter 2); urbanism – as our ability to organize and therefore resource our communities; communications and information processing; and finally, sadly, our capacity to make war. It is, as he acknowledges, a crude yet effective tool, essentially 'chainsaw art' (2011, 643), providing a good enough approximation to social development, evidence informed and within tolerable margins of error. He uses these traits to build up an SDI score for Eastern and Western 'cores', the West's core, for example, moving from the Hilly Flanks where it all began, to the Eastern Mediterranean and then including Italy, and moving north and west into Europe and to North America. The Eastern core moved similarly, from the original Yellow Yangze River zone, expanding, much later than in the West, to include Japan and South East China. What the SDI reveals, moving backwards from today (which has a maximum of 250 for each of the four traits, so making 1,000 in total for the highest achievement in 2000), and then for us forwards from 14,000 BCE, is a very, very gradual growth, with severe ups and downs, never attaining more than 50 combined, and before 1700 CE, reaching an important peak of around 45 points in East and West (the West being the Roman Empire) around 1 CE (see Morris's Figure 1 – p. 114 – on this historical range of SDI). That threshold of 45 points was not broken through until around 1700 CE in either East or West. Note that the West (the Hilly Flanks) began with a 2000-year advantage over the East for most of the period before the common era (an issue of geography, not intelligence), but by the fourth century CE, China overtakes the West until the mid eighteenth century CE. The West's social development was therefore higher than the East's for 92.5 per cent of these 14 millennia. The idea that the only serious increase in social development occurred after 1750 CE is just plain inaccurate. It's the sheer speed, depth and extent of increasing social development *after* 1750 that was breath-taking.

Out of the wealth of fascinating historical detail in Morris, Diamond and Bellah, which fills out and tests with strong historical evidence this broad measurement tool, two matters arise that are of particular relevance to my thesis. The first focuses more on the secular material, the second on the more religious evidence.

Matters arising 1: Elaborating the paradox of development in historical context

This is a necessary reminder that increasing social development is neither even in pace nor inevitable, that progress is not forever and always, and, at the very least, social development is invariably accompanied by damaging consequences, as we have seen in Chapter 2 in terms of the gross inequalities between and within nations. There are two useful illustrations of this paradox of development.

First, even when the SDI had risen to its highest score of only 45 points since 14,000 BCE in first-century Rome, despite having an astounding one million inhabitants, it still had the urbanizing capacity to develop impressive sanitary mechanisms to deliver clean water and remove waste, indeed, vastly superior to Manchester, the great Cottonopolis of the mid nineteenth century CE. Yet regardless of these developments, most people lived lives of grinding poverty and premature death. The Malthusian Trap operated even then, at the height of empire, and until the late eighteenth century CE. And the effects of scarcity, then, as now, were to ensure for the vast majority, stunted lives of daily and relentless stress and anxiety, impairing the acquisition of new skills and technologies, and lowering productivity. For the poor today, as then, living under scarcity so often leads to choices that significantly exacerbate the conditions of scarcity, which the richer rarely encounter.

Second, the survey of long history from 13,000 BCE to 1750 CE regularly reveals rises in social development; yet they always hit ceilings, frequently followed by falls in the SDI. For example, such a ceiling was reached towards the end of the second millennium BCE, when, in 1200 BCE, social development stalled in the West, followed by a Dark Age, itself then stimulus for the axial age, for example in Greece. A similar ceiling was reached, particularly in the West, in the fourteenth century CE, from which the population of Britain did not really recover until the sixteenth century. Complementing, and indeed frequently and robustly interacting with these hard ceilings, were my classic five horsemen of the apocalypse in the form of epidemics, famines, migrations, climate change and state failures. The histories of both Eastern and Western cores regularly witness the most dire effects of such Book of Revelation horsemen. For example, the Old World Exchange route from east to west along the steppes brought trade, art and ideas, but also pathogens and Mongols, and particularly epidemics in the second to fourth century CE. But even this was dominated by the Columbian Exchange from Europe to Central and South America in the sixteenth century CE, bringing with it measles, smallpox, typhoid and meningitis, and destroying three out of four of the indigenous colonized population of 'epidemiological virgins' (Morris 2011, 295).

Matters arising 2: Elaborating the axial age, including religion's role

The world of religion has exercised a powerful, continuing and evolving influence on the world of daily life, for example, as sketched and analysed in some detail by Bellah from its pre-human sources through early human, and then emerging into the axial age in the first millennium before the common era when 'Man, as we know him today, came into being' (2011, 255). Morris is another source, but only covering the story from 14,000 BCE, and again emphasizing a turning point significance of the axial age. Against the background of this long history of religious involvement, the detailed historical narratives with their agreed recognition of religion's contributions to the axial age particularly illustrate its influence on how we understand and locate our lives, including in wider contexts. In addition, this acknowledgement of the axial age has the added value of illustrating the major and continuing contributions to social development of both the Eastern and Western cores through their main philosophies and religions, including Greek philosophy, Judaism, Hinduism, Buddhism, Confucianism and Daoism (all strongly linked to Chapter 3's recognition and deployment of the world's main religions). While I will use two main sources, Morris and Bellah, the latter provides richer and more focused accounts as befits a study of *Religion in Human Evolution*. Both confirm my use and interaction of secular and religious sources.

The axial age was a response to the paradox of development towards the beginning of the first millennium BCE as bigger more complex cores created bigger problems for themselves, not least renewed challenges from their margins. And the axial age leaders often spoke from those margins, from small peripheral states. They were radical thinkers in terms of how they saw the world working, the worlds of both daily and religious life, and their continuing substantial and robust interactions. And in doing so they also 'defined the meaning of life for countless millions ever since'. Their ultimate subject was 'a transcendent realm beyond our own sordid world', a realm ultimately beyond language

(Morris 2011, 255). Yet their skill was to enmesh that view with the world of daily life, thereby generating a radical questioning of the traditional relationships between religion and power, with the resultant radical reordering of how people practised, moralized and believed about life. These different voices from different parts of Eastern and Western cores, from different philosophies and religions, from about 800 to 400 BCE, all asserted, in their different ways that 'we do not need god-like kings to transcend this sullied world. Salvation is within us, not in the hands of corrupt, violent rulers' (Morris 2011, 255). Perhaps the most significant consequence of such perspectives on life, strongly present in Greek philosophy, Judaism, Buddhism and Confucianism, was giving the primacy in life to the ethical, to how to attain such visions of the good life, a flourishing life of capacious wellbeing for all.

Bellah summarizes these transformations as the radical innovatory eruption of thinking about thinking, of a profoundly theoretic culture (from which religious theologies significantly emerge), of the capacity for 'questioning all human activity and [so] conferring upon it a new meaning' (Jasper), as 'reflection for its own sake', as the 'ability to think analytically rather than narratively, to construct theories that can be criticized logically and empirically' (Bellah 2011, 269, 274).

Importantly, too, the axial age's more rational strands encouraged and informed important and often radical developments in law, maths, science, history, logic and rhetoric, all increasing our intellectual mastery of the world (Morris 2011, 263). In effect, these models of realities 'either mystically or prophetically or rationally apprehended, are propounded as a criticism of, and alternative to, the prevailing models' (Bellah 2011, 275). And it was this unity in diversity, this astonishing range of ideas, which contributed to raising social development, reaching its highest point in 1 CE, before the breakthroughs of the late eighteenth century.

A further axial wave in the early to mid first millennium CE confirmed and extended the achievements of the first wave. The emergence of Christianity, of a renewed and reinvigorated Buddhism particularly in China, and then of Islam again represented a revolt against, and challenging of, established traditions, and their consequent reformulation. What was particularly remarkable was their astonishing growth, often testimony to their intrinsic worth and strategic skills, with two of them – Christianity and Islam – also experiencing and achieving major resurgences in today's world. In this second wave, for example, Buddhism in China grew from a few hundred in 65 CE to 30 million by the sixth century (an increase of 2.3 per cent per annum, so doubling every 30 years). Christianity similarly experienced early dramatic growth, from a few hundred followers of Jesus in 32 CE to over 30 million in the fourth century (a growth rate of 3.4 per cent per annum or a doubling every 20 years) (Morris 2011, 323–7). And, as with the first wave, much of the impact of this axial age thinking occurred when states learned to tame it, to make it work for them, whether Greek philosophy, Hinduism, Buddhism, Confucianism, Islam or Christianity. Any disproportionate or exclusive focus on the importance of the prophetic character of axial age thinking divorced from such processes of assimilation and incorporation is both profoundly inaccurate and misleading. It's the paradox of axial age thinking, a subset of the paradox of development, the interacting once again of secular and religious agendas, of the worlds of daily life and the worlds of religion.

The transformative Industrial and Mortality Revolutions seen through the long historical context: After 1750 and all that

Running through this book is the influence on national wellbeing, for good and then for bad, of the dramatic changes inaugurated and continued by the Industrial and Mortality Revolutions. A particularly effective way to grasp the timing, nature, extent and significance of these transformations is visually, using classic well-proven tools from the social sciences. What emerges is a multilayered picture, drawn from key perspectives embedded in the analysis of the wealth, wellbeing and inequalities of nations elaborated in Chapter 2. It therefore moves from a survey measuring social development in the East and West from 14,000 BCE to 2000 CE (Figure 1), to Cook's estimates of per capita energy consumption, again from (for our argument) early agriculturalists to today (Figure 2), and then to Fogel's survey of world population growth and the major events in technology's history again covering the same period (Figure 3). We then move on to Chapter 2's key indices of national wealth, wellbeing and inequalities: to a survey from 1 CE to 2000 CE of world average per capita income (Figure 4), then to a survey of global poverty from the modern ages 1820 to 1992 (Figure 5), then a survey of global inequalities in terms of GDP per capita by region, 1820–1998 (Figure 6), and finally a survey of life expectancy in England, the USA, India and China, 1725–1990 (Figure 7). I have added, as a quite different but very relevant survey for wellbeing of the percentage of deaths in warfare, from 12,000 BCE to the present (Figure 8).

We begin with Morris's survey of social development from 14,000 BCE to 2000 CE (Figure 1). This allows us to link and locate this section with and in the previous one on the long historical context. Using his social development index (measuring, as we have seen in the previous section, energy capture, organizing capacity, communications and information, and military capacity), this 'presents the scores, highlighting the relative rates of growth in the East and West and the importance of the thousands of years of change before 1800 CE' (Morris 2011, 166). Yet it equally and dramatically illustrates the staggering leap in social development since 1800. It also shows the East and West scores, including recognition that the West has not always been higher than the East, particularly from around 300–500 CE until the late 1700s CE. There is no reason to assume the West will continue to be dominant, given the growth of China in particular in the present world.

Cook's survey of daily per capita energy consumption (Figure 2) runs from the proto human period, but for our purposes we should begin with the early agriculturalists around 9000 BCE, so resonating in terms of timing (and much else) with Morris's survey. In 1971, the *Scientific American* asked Earl Cook, a geoscientist, to contribute an article 'The Flow of Energy in an Industrial Society'

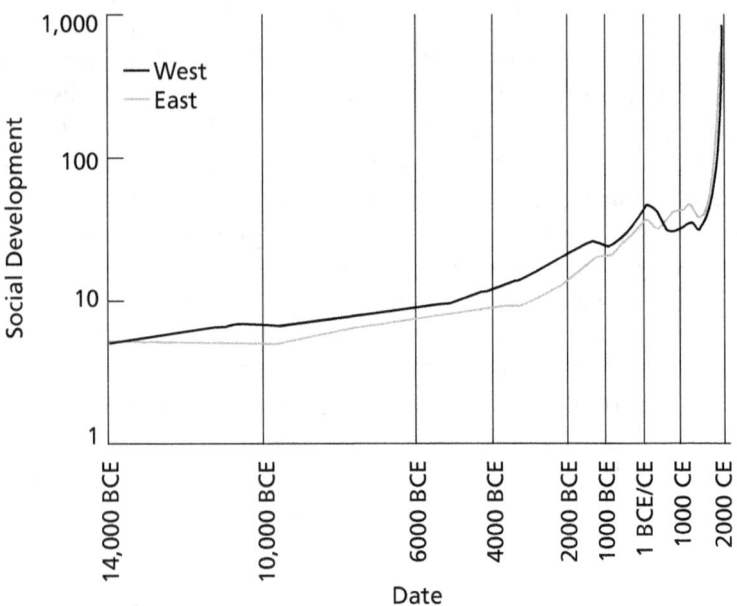

Figure 1: Growing social development in the East and West, 14,000 BCE–2000 CE (Morris 2011, p. 166).

(Morris 2011, 154–7). This contained Figure 2, his estimates, from varied sources, of per person daily energy consumption, including from (in terms of our work) the early agriculturalists (farmers of South-West Asia around 5000 BCE), the advanced agriculturalists (North-West Europe in around 1400 CE), industrial society (Western Europe about 1860) and ending with our own late twentieth-century technological societies. The scores were divided into four categories: food (ours and feed for animals that are eaten); home and commerce; industry and agriculture; and transport. His guesstimates have stood up 'remarkably well to nearly forty years of comparison with the results gathered by historians, anthropologists, archaeologists and economists' (Morris 2011, 155). Note the take-off with industrial society.

The economist Fogel's figure (Figure 3) brings together figures illustrating the growth of world population and major events in the history of technology, two of the major driving forces of the

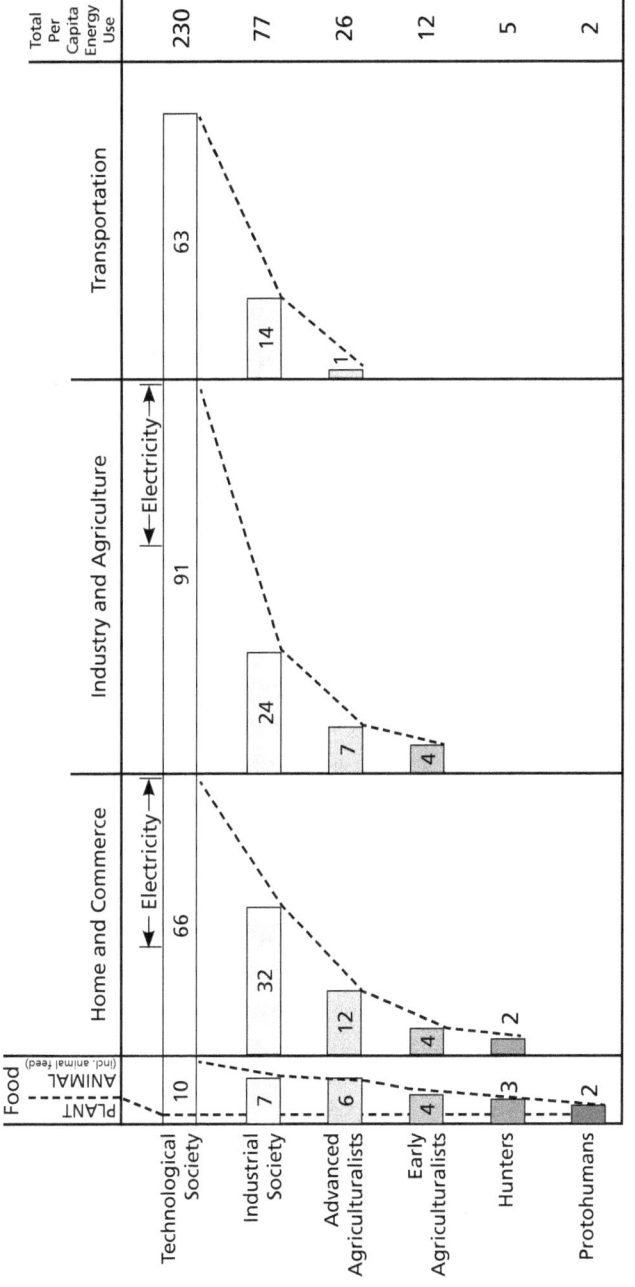

Figure 2: Growing per capita energy consumption (in 1000 kilocalories), from hunter-gatherers to today's technological society (Morris 2011, p. 156).

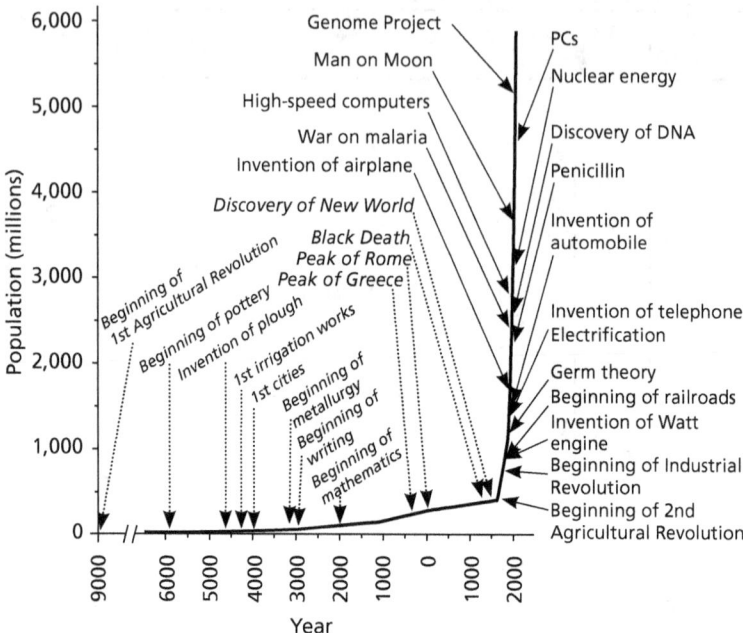

Figure 3: Growing world population and major technological events, 9000 BCE–2000 CE (Fogel 2000).

dramatic accelerating changes from the eighteenth century. Again, he works from 9000 BCE to 2000 CE (Fogel 2000, 75).

With regard to the key three indices in Chapter 2's analysis of income and life expectancy, the economist Sachs's measuring of increases in world average per capita incomes is particularly relevant (Figure 4). Stretching from 1 CE to 2000 and linking to the previous Figure 3's use of population statistics (Sachs 2005, 28), Sachs acknowledges that in the period of modern economic growth both population and per capita incomes 'came unstuck, soaring at rates never before seen or imagined' in world history. So, although global population grew sixfold from 1800 to 2000, global per capita incomes grew even faster, around ninefold between 1820 and 2000 (Sachs 2005, 27–8). For population to grow so much *and yet* to be outpaced so significantly by income resources is the clearest illustration of the breaking of the Mal-

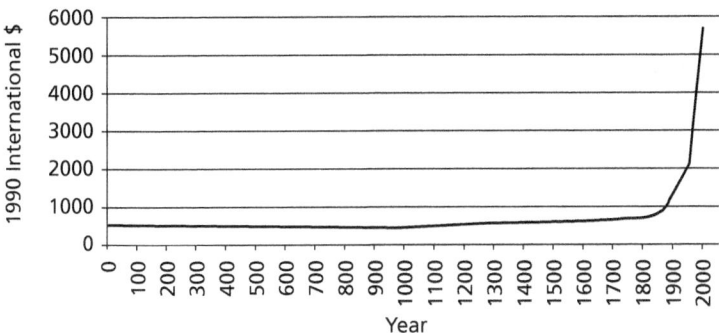

Figure 4: *Growing world per capita income, 1 CE–2000 CE* (Sachs 2005, p. 28).

thusian Trap, which had held the world fast in its grip for all previous history.

Global poverty figures show a decline equivalent to the rise in incomes. In Figure 5, Sachs traces these changes in global poverty from 1820 to 1992 (Sachs 2008, 51). They reveal, as he observes, that 'The world has seen an astounding reduction in extreme poverty since the beginning of the Industrial Revolution'. Before 1800, perhaps about 85 per cent lived in what we count today as extreme poverty; it's now about 15 per cent (Sachs 2008, 50).

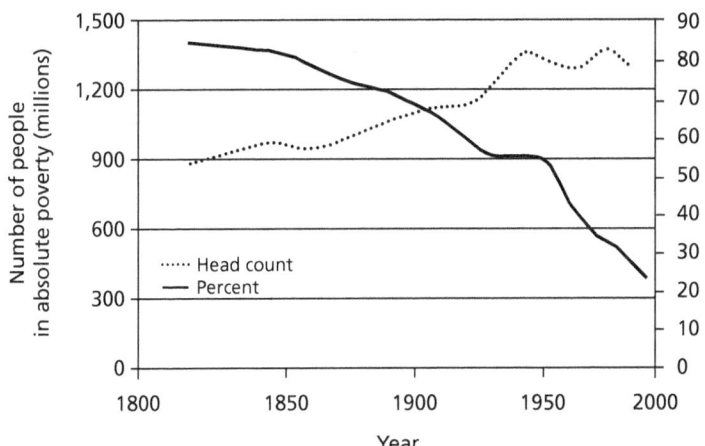

Figure 5: *The great escape from global poverty, 1820–1992* (Sachs 2008, p. 51).

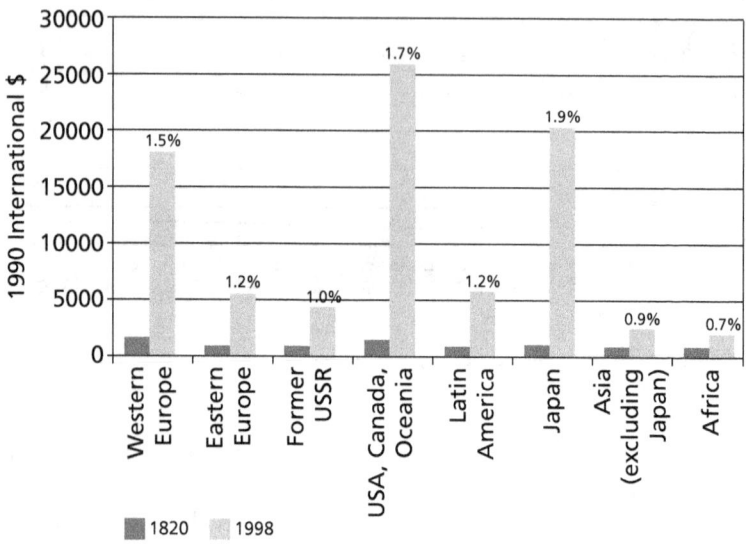

Figure 6: The great divergences in per capita incomes between regions, 1820–1998 (Sachs 2005, p. 21).

The global extent and location of income per capita inequalities is the obverse side to these great improvements in material wellbeing, as we have seen in Chapter 2. They represent, therefore, in Figure 6, the Great Divergence, the paradox of development. Here Sachs charts GDP per capita, by region, between 1820 and 1998 (2008, 29). They reveal that the growing and dramatic gulf between the richest and poorest nations rose from a ratio of 4:1 in per capita incomes in 1820 to a widening gap of 20:1 by 1998. 'Today's vast income inequalities illuminate two centuries of highly uneven patterns of economic growth' (Sachs 2008, 29).

With regard to the life expectancy–health perspective in Chapter 2, the work of the economic historian Ferguson (Figure 7) surveys the life expectancy figures at birth from 1725 to 1990, across four key nations from East and West, namely, India, China, England and the USA (2011, 147). At around 1800, average global life expectancy was only 28.5 years; by 2001 this had more than doubled to 66.6 years. The inequalities between nations are

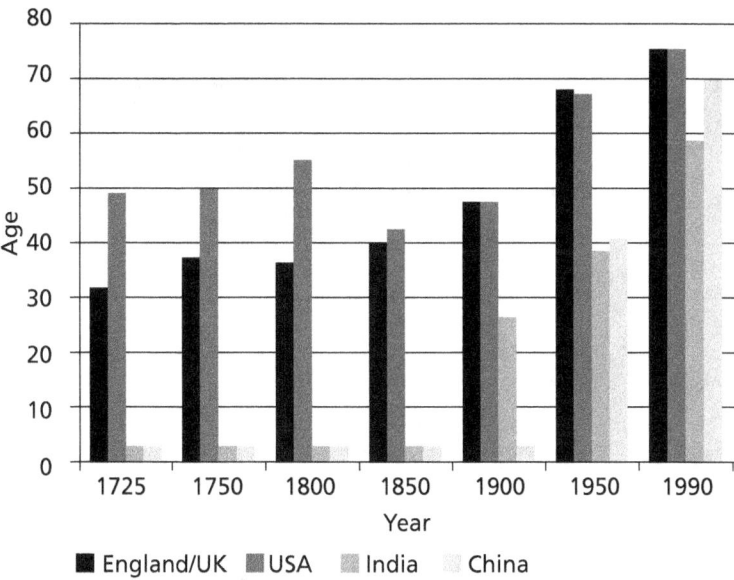

Figure 7: Escaping from premature death: life expectancy at birth in England, the USA, India and China, 1725–1990 (Ferguson 2011, p. 147).

revealed here in terms of timings of this 'health transition', as the beginnings of improved sustained life expectancy. In Western Europe this occurred from the 1770s to the 1890s, in modern Asian nations from the 1890s to the 1950s, and lastly, in Africa from the 1920s to the 1950s (Ferguson 2011, 146–7).

Finally, Figure 8 measures the percentage of deaths caused by 'state' violence or its equivalents (Pinker 2011, 49). I've put it here because it indicates the dramatic decreases in such deaths which contributed to improving social wellbeing in general, and life expectancy and health in particular. The American psychologist Pinker has collected these statistics from non-state peoples using prehistoric and archaeological sites, hunter-gatherers and hunter-horticulturalists; and then from a variety of state societies. They reveal, for example, that the two most violent centuries in European history were the seventeenth-century Wars of Religion and the two World Wars in the twentieth century. Yet the major cleft

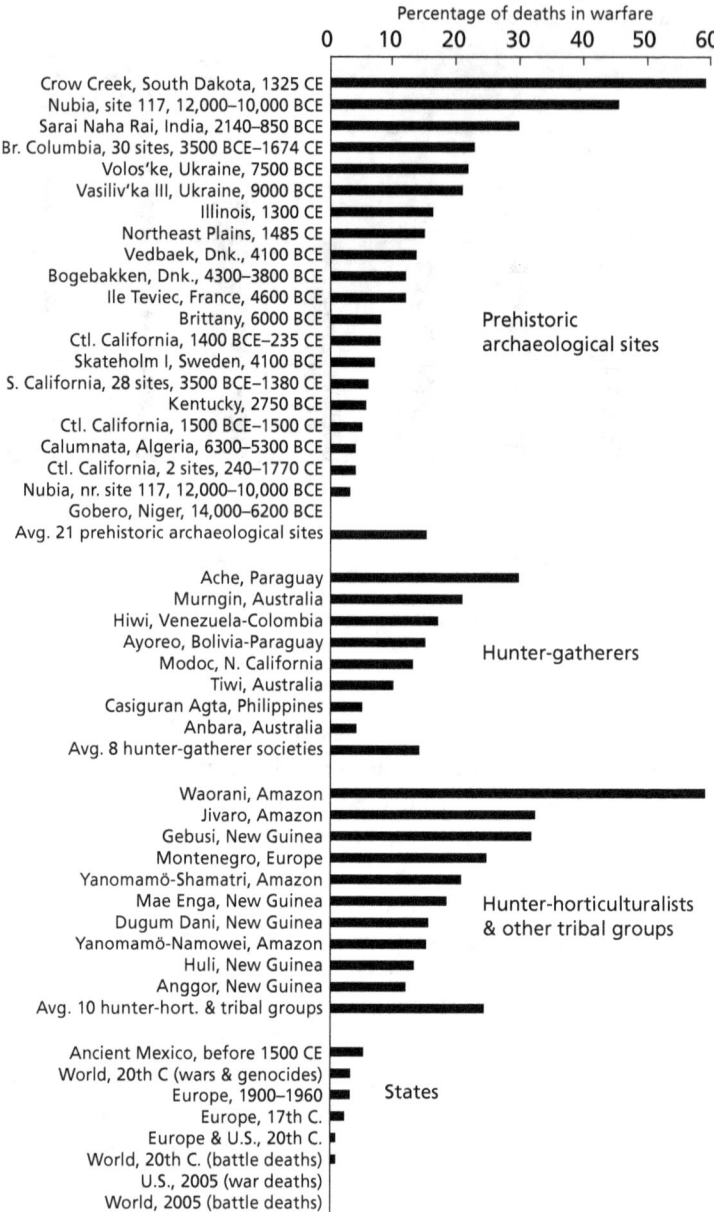

Figure 8: Declining violence: percentage of deaths in warfare, 12,000 BCE–2000 CE (Pinker 2011).

in the graph is not there at all, but is between the 'anarchical bands and tribes' and the governed states at the beginning of our long history survey (Pinker 2011, 48, 51).

To put these eight figures together is to highlight visually the dramatic changes in wellbeing since the eighteenth century, but even more so to powerfully illustrate the facts on the people's faces of the world. All we need to do is to look at the faces, but then do something about the facts, which is what the final two chapters will narrate.

On 'traditional' and 'scientific' histories: The implications of cliometrics for religious studies as religiometrics

Running through this whole argument is the issue of what matters for the wellbeing of nations and how to count it, whether as income, life expectancy or subjective wellbeing. What is not really in doubt is their significance for human flourishing today. And running through these means to and ends of lives that turn out well there are a number of complementarities, the world of general trends and the world of particular people; of income and what it enables us to do and be; of life expectancy and what that allows to happen through greater lifespans; of subjective wellbeing as how we judge our lives are doing over the long term and as how we felt yesterday. It's another way of describing the processes of monovision, enabling us to see the longer view along with the more immediate shorter view, and, more importantly, how the brain then puts them together. That is what this argument has tried to do, to weave these distinctive and different perspectives into one tapestry, to see the facts on people's faces. Yet also running through this argument is what it all means for religions, for Christianity in particular, and for religious studies, and what they can all contribute to promoting greater wellbeing. And, in that process of interaction, the case is also being made that that means changing religious studies in order to change wellbeing for the better. Part of that change, indeed quite central to it, is a religious studies taking to itself these two complementary long- and short-view modes of operating into its practices, ethics and beliefs.

What does this begin to mean for religious studies and how can it be achieved? Since this second part of the argument includes locating all this material in historical contexts, it seemed very appropriate to search historical sources for corresponding struggles with such complementarities. Mutual learning has been a key part of this book, for example with economics learning from psychology and vice versa. By following up references and sources in the histories resourcing this part of the argument, I came across a little book (often the best!), which I believe does this. It's called *Which Road to the Past? Two Views of History* (Fogel and Elton 1983) and is essentially a critical but highly constructive conversation between two great historians, Robert Fogel and Geoffrey Elton, embodying two contrasting but ultimately and necessarily complementary views of history. It becomes of real added value for my thesis because Fogel was awarded the Nobel Prize in economics for his contribution to 'cliometrics' (interacting history, its muse Clio, with advanced statistical analysis, economic theory and modelling). Should there be two views of religious studies, similarly very different, but essentially developing as complementary parts of the same task? I am clear that there must be, but let's briefly learn for our wider project from these two historians, these two views of history, the 'traditional' and the 'scientific'.

Traditional history expounded by one of its masters, Elton (his work being a key source when I studied Tudor history at University College, London and the London School of Economics in the late 1950s), focuses on particular individuals, institutions, movements, occurrences and ideas, relying mostly on literary evidence. For Elton, history is 'ideographic', it particularizes; it is not 'nomothetic', it is not about establishing general laws. For another fine 'traditional' American historian, Schlesinger, and maybe like 'traditional religious studies', 'almost all important questions are important precisely because they are *not* susceptible to quantitative answers' (Fogel and Elton 1983, 20–1). Traditional historians were reluctant, maybe like traditional theologians, to embrace statistical evidence.

The other view of history, the 'scientific' or 'cliometric' view, is expounded by the American economic historian Fogel, whose great classic *Time on the Cross* (1974 co-authored with Engerman) in its second volume became a model for quantitative history through its deployment of economic models and statistical techniques to examine how profitable slavery in America was. This view, therefore, focuses on collections of individuals, categories of institutions, repetitive occurrences, and relies much on quantitative evidence. So Easterlin's understanding of historical experience uses quantitative time series to help define problems and test hypotheses (2004, xvi). A traditional historian might seek to explain why the poet Keats died 'at the time, in the place, and under the particular circumstances that he did'. The 'social-scientific' historian is less interested in these particular circumstances of Keats's death and rather focuses on why death from tuberculosis was so prevalent in the early nineteenth century (Fogel and Elton 1983, 29).

How can we decide whether a historian belongs to one or the other view of history? Six characteristics or sets of questions enable us to locate where a scholar or approach belongs (Fogel and Elton 1983, 42–65):

1 Subject matter: the most fundamental difference between the two histories:

- Traditional history focuses on particular individuals or events.
- Scientific history tends to focus on the collectivities of people and on recurring events.

2 Preferred type of evidence (both traditions use documentary evidence, yet they differ over which evidence-type is preferred):

- Traditional: firmly biased to literary, non-quantitative sources.
- Scientific: leans strongly to quantitative, preferring information on enacted behaviour rather than opinions (the old economics' emphasis on revealed preferences, now

challenged by self-reporting surveys of subjective well-being). Note, as Morris and Cook's work on energy capture measurements reveals, limited information can be sufficient to produce robust estimates. Also, most of the scholars I have encountered in researching this book clearly work with *both* literary and quantitative evidence, although they differ in terms of emphasis.

3 Standards of proof and verification:

- The traditional approach uses a variety of tools, including the model of the legal questioning of witnesses; testing authenticity, reliability, provenance, ordering and interpretations of documents; and reasoning by analogy.
- The scientific or cliometrician's approach: proves/disproves by empirical–scientific models; makes explicit the implicit empirical assumption; and searches for quantitative and qualitative evidence (the former often located in tables rather than footnotes).

4 Role of controversy:

- Traditional history certainly experiences controversy, yet success 'normally turns on how widely and how well a work is perceived' (Fogel and Elton 1983, 54).
- Scientific history demonstrates arguments more prominently often because they perform different roles compared to their use in traditional history. This is also reflected in the protracted process of verification which such studies, for example, on the economics of US slavery, or on the demographic transition in the UK, require. Cliometrics is also 'heavily influenced by the intellectual styles of the physical sciences' (Fogel and Elton 1983, 58), yet it still remains history – essentially, the thesis of this book's argument is for a reformulating of religious studies which robustly includes both traditions. This means incorporating a 'religiometrics' into an interactive relationship with the traditional approach together constituting an evolving religious studies.

5 Attitudes towards collaboration:

- Traditional history values the individual and personal voice, therefore with no robust reliance on collaboration. Their interpreters often therefore differ 'not so much in the statement of facts as in their moral stance' (Fogel and Elton 1983, 61).
- Cliometrics is far more concerned with collaborative research, often technically based, and representing the views of all the concerned spectrums.

6 Connections with the history-reading publics:

- Traditional historians emphasize communication with a wider public, seeking to inform 'a people's conception of its past'.
- Cliometrics 'do not generally address this wider public', relying rather on the views of the narrow groups capable of assessing their 'scientific labors' (Fogel and Elton 1983, 64–5).

Oddly, traditional theologians, in this regard, overlap substantially with the cliometricians in terms of so often talking to themselves. Ordinary theology and church may involve features of both histories in terms of relating to the public. By recognizing the wider religious publics, they link to traditional histories. By subjecting their material to a more cliometristical approach, they link to the scientific histories. This is but to reinforce the conclusion of this conversation between two views of history, that neither mode of itself is in any way adequate to deal with the questions historians (or practitioners of religious studies) need to address. Each has a comparative advantage in certain research domains, and so they necessarily complement each other. So working with aggregates and the model-building out of quantifiable data and analytical reliance on mathematical techniques which generate them has to work with a whole host of contingent factors of particular events, institutions and people. Yet the facts on people's faces, institutions, systems, cultures and religions creatively and substantively recognize both views of history, economics, psychology and religious studies. But that's called mutual learning processes, knowledge transfer, or learning from each other for our and the others' mutual benefit.

Putting Christianity to work in promoting greater wellbeing: Two case studies of America and Britain from 1700 to today

The financial and economic crises of 2007–09 constitute events of continuing global significance and are restatements of the central importance of economic affairs for human wellbeing. The nature and extent of that significance of economic life for our agenda has been reinforced and elaborated particularly in Chapter 2. Christianity shares that concern for human flourishing, as Chapter 3 has illustrated to some effect. Yet the links between the two, between Christianity and economics, was, and still continues to be, negligible (Bateman and Banzhaf 2008).

That disturbing judgement is elaborated by a recent study of Christianity's relationship to culture in the USA. For despite a globally resurgent religion, not simply in the global South, but also in the USA, its impact on culture in the latter is claimed to be negligible despite the obvious and acclaimed (or denigrated) contribution of Christianity to the American culture wars. For Hunter, irrespective of the fact that 88 per cent of people 'adhere to some faith commitments ... our culture – business, culture, law and government, the academic world, popular entertainment – is intensely materialistic and secular' (2010, 19). This judgement on religion's irrelevance to economic and cultural affairs applies equally to Britain despite the Canute-like rearguard actions of some Christians in the courts and press to defend their religious identities.

Attempts to rectify this marginalization from public affairs are importantly becoming recognized tasks within the academy in terms of the growing interest in public theology, but also with regard to renewed concerns to recognize the contributions of faith communities to community and national wellbeing. The task is complemented by an additional focus on developing new (or more historically accurate, revised) forms of mission to contemporary society. Yet rarely do such attempts to reverse religion's irrelevance persuade the secular, and certainly they do not 'change the world', especially the world of family life, in the way Hunter regards as central to Christianity's origins and history. That requires recognition of 'the complexity of the world and Christianity's relationship to it' (Hunter 2010, 29). That's what this argument tries to demonstrate.

Although addressing these problems and questions is occupying the attention of some theologians and missiologists, albeit with little impact, an alternative route of enquiry, as we have seen, is to examine secular interpretations of religious interactions with economic, political and cultural change correlatively corroborated by Christian understandings. Given the importance of economics in shaping modern societies including through economic crises, the perspectives of economists on such change and of Christianity's constructive contribution to it would bring added value to the argument of this book, as we have already noted.

Two examples from American and British contexts provide such evidence for understanding the intricate yet positive connections between secular and religious contributions to developing human wellbeing. Each locates such enquiries in historical contexts beginning with the dramatic changes in human experiences from the eighteenth century and through the nineteenth and twentieth centuries. But, as the introduction to Part 2 has demonstrated, this can and should be also located in a much more extensive longitudinal framework, following, for example, also in the paths of Arrighi and Landes, but also in the case of this argument from the end of the last Ice Age (Arrighi 1994; Landes 1998). This long view reinforces the focus on examining religion's contribution to greater wellbeing from the eighteenth century.

The American example is more empirically based, not least because it deploys some of Fogel's work, who, as we have seen above, is a leading contributor to scientific history or cliometrics. Yet part of this evidence also crosses American and British experiences. Both begin with such secular frameworks, which, because they confirm religion's contribution to wellbeing, allow, enable and justify the elaboration of that case also from a religious perspective. Again, as with the examination of Christianity's contribution to subjective wellbeing, proven initially from secular sources, this demonstrates a working model for developing the case for Christianity's contribution to and involvement in the shared promotion of wellbeing. Of particular importance, therefore, is the dependence of both case studies on these interdisciplinary engagements with human development. Together, they constitute comparable models for interpreting Christianity's role in change processes over this most crucial 300 years in human history.

Both examples also acknowledge the breadth of these shared experiences of Christianity. Hunter's judgement that such interactions between secular and religious values must recognize 'the complexity of the world and Christianity's relationship to it' (Hunter 2010, 29), therefore also needs to acknowledge the complexity of Christianity itself in these processes, involving, as both cases do, a great variety of Christian practices and beliefs. Further, because the models recognize the proactive as well as reactive character of religion in the complexities of change, they can be described as contributions to the development of religious engagements with the public realm. Taken together, Niebuhr's *Christ and Culture* and Hunter's *To Change the World* illustrate this historical and contemporary two-way engagement between Christianity and contemporary societies. They can also be described as public responses to God's call to change the world for the better. In addition, they confirm and elaborate the importance of locating models in historical contexts as well as the measurement of their contributions (Dasgupta 2007).

Although the American model is examined first, there are important connections with the British model. For example, the American makes considerable use of Fogel's work, and particularly his *Fourth Great Awakening and the Future of Egalitarianism*. This also has strong links with the earlier material examined in this book, particularly relating to income and life expectancy, but also to the engagement with inequalities. Fogel's book was published in 2000, when my *Public Theology for Changing Times*, the basis of this British model, was also published. I only became conscious of this date coincidence after later immersion in the American model, leading to major revisions and extensions of the British model in 2011. There are other obvious connections between the details of the two histories, as will soon become evident. For example, there are strong resonances between the American First and Second Great Awakenings and the British Age of Atonement and Voluntarism. Both recognize the more evangelically oriented contributions to resurgent religion and its impact on wellbeing. That reappears in the American Fourth Great Awakening today. There are resonances, too, although more tenuous, between that Fourth Great Awakening and the present British emergence of a Third Age of Partnership and Reconciliation.

Both case studies are stuffed full with particular examples of the practices, ethics and beliefs of Christianity engaging with the three perspectives on the wealth, wellbeing and inequalities of nations. The original British draft and earlier American draft had not set out to illustrate this, so were not done to this effect. Yet clearly they work; they can now be seen clearly, robustly and very tangibly to demonstrate Christianity's contributions to developing human wellbeing. It's an example of economics' law of unintentional consequences! So I came to redraft the following two chapters with the renewed and excited interest of the recognition that although they have intrinsic value they also have the remarkably added value of clearly illustrating the contribution of Christianity to the wellbeing of nations and peoples in this most decisive period in human history.

4

A Nation Under God
The American Case Study

Given the extraordinary growth in the wealth, wellbeing and inequalities of nations since the eighteenth century, a growth involving more and more nations and peoples, an important part of this whole argument needs to move on to examine how particular nations engaged with and in such change, to move from the more general contexts to the more particular. The United States presents a distinctive case to deliver this aim because a framework or model already exists for exploring such change processes. This involves peoples and institutions being awakened to change in response to disruptive transformations in social, economic and political life. These Great Awakenings are particularly relevant to my argument because they include, in a formative role, but always alongside other factors, the contribution of Christianity to the struggle for greater wellbeing.

Although there have been four Great Awakenings (the most recent fourth, running from the late twentieth century to the present, is more contested), the first in the eighteenth century, the second in the nineteenth century and the third spanning the later nineteenth and deep into the twentieth century, it has rightly been argued that modern America (clearly it was populated by *Homo sapiens* over 15,000 years ago) was 'born in an awakening' with the arrival and successful colonization from Europe of the north-eastern periphery in the early seventeenth century. These early settlers were driven by 'conscience and faith as much as by the hope of bettering their condition' (McLoughlin 1978, 24). Myles Standish was one of these early Puritan leaders, sailing on

THE AMERICAN CASE STUDY

the *Mayflower* and becoming a military leader in the Plymouth colony. He was born in Chorley in 1584, my local town, and I drive along the Myles Standish Way whenever I go to shop at the supermarket! But it was John Rolfe, one of the early Virginians, who best summarizes this sense of this religious Puritan calling to and in a New World, as chosen of God for a special mission in it, a world view quite different from, and in conflict with, the established British Anglican order, and which it both rejected and escaped from. For Rolfe, these early settlers in Virginia were 'a peculiar people, marked and chosen by the finger of God, to possess it, for undoubtedly He is with us' (McLoughlin 1978, 36). It was out of this initial awakening, confirmed and elaborated by the others, that there emerged a 'common core of beliefs' giving shape and continuity to American culture: that 'Americans are a chosen people', destined 'to lead the world to the millennium', with their 'democratic–republican institutions', abundant natural resources, and a 'concept of the free and morally responsible individual', all informed by a 'Judaeo-Christian personal and social ethic', and including the belief that the general welfare thrives best by giving 'the greatest possible free play and equal opportunity to each individual to fulfil his or her potential' (McLoughlin 1978, xiv). But, of course, how such contested core beliefs emerged and adapted to great change is then tested on the hard anvil of history. And it's the contribution of this awakening thesis that can be seen to play an important part in that account.

The interaction of the struggles of an emerging nation with the economic, social and political changes associated with the impacts of industrialization and urbanization generated experiences shared across nations, yet transformed by the particular contexts of the American narratives. It was in response to such turbulent change, the paradoxes of development, that the Great Awakenings emerged. It was in these awakenings that religious revivals played a prominent part, leading the reaction to dislocating change that threatened the credibility and relevance of established practices, ethics and beliefs. It was out of these reactions that reforms emerged, contributing to the development of greater wellbeing. Although often religiously inspired, these awakenings and reforms always involved a variety of other contributions. Their combination, secular and religious, informed the resulting changed practices, ethics and beliefs.

Although these combinations of 'Revivals, Awakenings and Reform' form the basis of the historian McLoughlin's thesis, which instituted much of this debate over awakenings, it is the later reformulation of this argument by Fogel that links more clearly to the thesis of this book. For him, the pronounced lag between comprehensive technological–economic transformations and human adjustments to them generated periodic crises which ushered in profound 'reconsiderations of ethical values' and their implications for new agendas of social reform. Great Awakenings constituted that ethical–political–economic response. And they were initially and powerfully informed by 'enthusiastic religion' ('religion characterized by spiritual intensity linked to conversion) which emphasizes individual responsibility' (Fogel 2000, 9, 6). Although the evolving character of the Great Awakenings is the creative development of McLoughlin's thesis, for Fogel, this becomes the interactions between three realms: technophysio evolution (itself the interaction between technological–economic change and physiology), enthusiastic religion and political realignments. The latter occurred when 'a dominant coalition ushers in an extended era of legislative reforms'. For example, the Republican Party's taking control of the federal government after Lincoln's 1860 election led to two generations of Republican-led economic, social and political reform. Similarly, the Democratic coalition of Franklin Roosevelt captured the federal government in 1932, leading to two generations of Democratic-led reform from the New Deal in the 1930s to Johnson's Great Society of the 1960s (Fogel 2000, 8). It was the interactions between these three realms which therefore drove these reforms, resulting in greater wellbeing. Given Fogel's commitment to scientific and traditional history, it's the former which is deployed in building up the technophysio evolution and political realignment cases, with the rigorous methods of traditional history substantiating the religious case.

From these two sources – McLoughlin and Fogel – further useful clarifications emerge.

McLoughlin, using Wallace, describes six stages of the awakenings' revitalization of culture (1978, 12–22). The first represents the initial response to troubling change as a 'period of individual stress' with people losing their bearings and identities; the second stage is a 'period of cultural distortion' when people see that the problems are not personal but result from institutional malfunctions – in churches, schools, society and politics. In response, people return initially to old-time religion and values, called in the literatures 'old light theology' and religion; it also leads to scapegoating. This then widens into searching for new and better ways to live well together in the new circumstances, to find new ways of seeing and engaging the changing 'world of daily life'; the third stage involves building the new world vision, including by modifying Christian practices, ethics and beliefs as the emergence of 'new light' views; the fourth stage sees the new light prophets attract more flexible, often younger people willing to experiment with new lifestyles; in the fifth stage, the new light prophets now win over large groups, not necessarily through conversions, but because people were persuaded that this constituted better ways of seeing and doing things; and finally, in the sixth stage, the prophets continue to win over large groups of undecided people again sufficiently impressed by the doctrines and practices of the new lights. And it's from this 'thesis and antithesis of the revival generation a new synthesis emerges'. Yet, always, 'the old light never quite dies, and the process is never finished' (McLoughlin 1978, 22). That's why the Great Awakenings are a continuing process in American history. And their effects have transformed American life in terms of family patterns and sex roles, and educational, economic and political reform. For McLoughlin, 'It was through following the new guidelines of our revitalization movements that Americans abandoned allegiance to the King, abolished human slavery, regulated business enterprise, empowered labor unions, and is now [in 1978] trying to equalize the rights of women, blacks, Indians, and other minorities' (1978, 22–3).

For Fogel, reflecting on these religious–political cycles in American history, with their related upsurges in religious enthusiasm, they tend to run in about 100-year cycles (for McLoughlin, they are much shorter), each involving three phases, and each about a generation in length. The first phase is the response to turbulent change initially through religious revivals, intensifying religious beliefs and practices and their ushering in a reinvigorated or new ethics and theological principles. In the second stage the new ethics and theologies precipitate powerful political and economic programmes and movements, all conducive to achieving greater wellbeing. The third and final stage ends with the ethics and politics nourished by religious revivals being challenged by new movements, and their associated political coalitions also going into decline. It is here that the end of one awakening overlaps with the emergence of the next (other models working with cycles and their phases or stages, for example Arrighi's, come to similar conclusions on such overlaps).

As can be seen in this chapter, I am very reliant on the work of other scholars, expert in their respective disciplines. As an early proponent of the Great Awakenings and reform thesis, McLoughlin provides a basic operating framework in his *Revivals, Awakenings and Reform* (1978). Yet as part of embedding such material in my argument's wider framework, I also saw the added value of developing McLoughlin's work through two other perspectives central to my main and earlier arguments: namely Fogel's research on economics and economic history, and his use of the methods of scientific history, or cliometrics, and particularly his *The Fourth Great Awakening and the Future of Egalitarianism* (2000); and Putnam's research on American religiosity, in his (with David Campbell) *American Grace. How Religion Divides and Unites Us* (2010). These therefore contribute to developing a more cohesive argument in terms of weaving together very different perspectives and disciplines. Interestingly, my first introduction to this American material was as an important part of a course I taught for 20 years on contemporary Christian social ethics at Manchester University from the mid 1980s. This included examining the contributions of American Christian social ethics from the mid nineteenth century to the present. Looking back on this material, so much resonates with this later research on the Great Awakenings.

THE AMERICAN CASE STUDY

These important, substantial and robust connections between contemporary arguments for the increase of wellbeing and Christianity's contribution to it, and their location in the modern contexts of histories of America and Britain, can be elaborated further in two areas, secular and Christian, which again overlap significantly. Both case studies also confirm and develop some necessary and valuable detail on the connections between the two parts of this book.

In terms of the more secular, both histories illustrate the importance of personal lives and communities for wellbeing, but also the great significance of developing institutions more supportive of greater wellbeing. This regularly involves major reform movements and programmes, from the abolition of slavery in the nineteenth century to the institution of welfare systems to support the elderly and poor in the twentieth century. Again, there is a recognition that a variety of factors constitutes wellbeing, from income, health and subjective wellbeing, to education, family and community life, and greater participation in civic affairs and governance, as reflected in the corresponding agendas for reform of the Great Awakenings.

The more religious connections are both distinctive and also overlap with the secular. For example, the relationship between religious revivals and reform movements illustrates the transmission processes by and through which Christianity both engages with and influences for the better wider society. Religious revivals are both response to disturbing change and agents of further change. Yet such contributions also invariably combine with other contributions. It's their interactive cumulative significance which counts most in the promotion of greater wellbeing in American society. The histories also contribute to rebuilding the relationships between Christianity and economics. This is because the explorations of Great Awakenings generally deploy models, measurement systems and location in historical contexts – the three features of economics identified by Dasgupta in his *Economics: A Very Short Introduction*. But they also reveal strong detailed practical involvements by Christianity, often with others, in reform programmes relating to economic affairs. Sometimes the overlap between general and particular is embodied in important economists, for example the work of Ely and his formative influence in the founding of the American Economic Association in 1885. These connections and interactions constitute, through their combined contributions, the development of greater wellbeing. So Hunter's conclusion from his study of the reciprocal relationships between culture and religion in contemporary American society applies equally to this study of the history of Great Awakenings, that 'when culture and symbolic capital overlap with social and economic capital and, in time, political capital, and these resources are directed towards shared ends, the world, indeed, changes' (2010, 43). And so it did.

The First Great Awakening (1730–1820)

The processes of secularization affected even the writings of history, particularly around the mid twentieth century and in both Britain and America. It's out of these experiences that Martin Marty comments on the public neglect of the importance of the First Great Awakening for American history. In 1976, the bicentennial celebrations of America's Declaration of Independence, polls of historians and news reporters never included that awakening in their top 100 selections of key events in their history. The significance of the religious contribution in modern history was ignored by secular historians, just as the sociopolitical implications of religious revivals were ignored by ecclesiastical historians who focused instead on narrow denominational and theological matters. Both were profoundly inaccurate because evidence continually appears illustrating that this First Great Awakening was 'perhaps the most extensive intercolonial event' reaching into and across most communities in all the states as shared experiences howbeit locally interpreted. Its influence was often 'profoundly unsettling to the established order', out of which emerged new ways of understanding and practising, which certainly reshaped religious life, but, through a variety of transmission processes also then informed the social, economic and political life of the

THE AMERICAN CASE STUDY

nation. By questioning traditional religious authorities, the new light thinking and living easily transferred into the questioning of traditional political authorities, including British rule. Not surprisingly, Miller and Heimert argued that the awakening inaugurated 'a new era, not merely of American Protestantism, but in the evolution of the American mind' (McLoughlin 1978, viii). Through these crises came turning points, conversion experiences across so many areas of the 'world of daily life'.

Like all the awakenings, as with the founding of America itself, this first one began as response, as reaction, to greatly changing contexts which had profoundly dislocating consequences. From the 1690s to the early 1700s, the generally prosperous colonies were also 'far from stable'. The inherent dynamics of growth in rapidly expanding 'frontiers', geographically, economically and socially, inevitably and invariably challenged established ways of doing and thinking in church, civic, economic and social affairs. What emerged was a 'growing incongruence between prescriptive norms and prevailing circumstances' (McLoughlin 1978, 52).

The features of that creative but disruptive transformation included rapid social change which questioned stable community life and patriarchal systems increasingly unsuitable for rapidly expanding populations. The latter influence was confirmed and exacerbated by ever-extending frontiers with dispersed populations full of enterprising individuals necessarily looking after their own interests. These features all fed into a rising bourgeois capitalist system with its commercialism and materialism, and generating the inevitable inequalities between rich and poor. As Bushman observed, by 1730 such '"estrangement" between ordinary people and their leaders in church and state inevitably created unbearable stress' (McLoughlin 1978, 55). It was such pressure points which enlarged into and reinforced an increasingly changing relationship with the mother country, particularly after the latter's 1688 revolutions. And, to cap it all, the Calvinist and Puritan worldview, so formative in both inspiring the colonization and early construction of America, and affecting all areas of life, public as well as private, was challenged by all these changes, but also, additionally and increasingly, by Enlightenment views.

But above all, the routinization of religious life (no longer was conversion required for church membership), translated into authority structures, beliefs and mores, created that increasingly foundational dissonance between such traditional norms of living and these emerging new circumstances. That waning of religious enthusiasm became quite incapable of engaging and resourcing this new world of daily life. What could and did was the 'new surge of religious feeling', the beginnings of the First Great Awakening (Fogel 2000, 19).

It began as a series of private explosions of and in profound emotional conversions from the 1720s and 1730s in very scattered communities across the colonies. These gradually developed a common shape from the late 1730s, though expressed through the particularities of the different denominations in their different geographical areas of influence. For McLoughlin, by the 1760s, these different denominations, leaders and communities were all 'at approximately the same point in the new ideological consensus and were thus ready to move on together into political reformation' (McLoughlin 1978, 60).

In the early stages of this transition the initiatives were particularly taken by itinerant prophets, for example, George Whitefield, a leader of the English Methodists. The moralizing and dry doctrinal sermons of the routinized church life were turned upside down by such preaching 'with an explosive emotional power' (Fogel 2000, 19), appealing directly to each person's heart (this was powerfully a religion of the heart and feeling) to repent of their sins and be saved. It was a preaching characterized by histrionics and charisma, focusing on the emotions, emphasizing personal accountability and responsibility. And, in doing so it both directly challenged the established orderings in church and civic life and engaged far more effectively the new emerging patterns of life. For example, the young Isaac Backus, from the town of Norwich in Connecticut, member of a prosperous farming family, brought up in the security of the routine congregational habits of church and family life, and living a 'careless and secure life' never interrupted by conversion, was suddenly confronted by the invading force of Whitefield's preaching. A little later, when 'mowing in the field alone' on 29 August 1741, 'the justice of God shined so clear before my eyes in condemning such a guilty Rebel that I could say no more – but fell at his feet'. And his life was transformed, for 'now my Burden (that was so dreadful heavey before) was gone: that tormented fear that I had was taken away, and I felt a sweet peace and rejoicing in my soul'. He went on, as so often happened, to himself become an itinerant preacher and then pastor of a Baptist church. And that kind of 'intensely personal relationship of God to the convert' became a common feature across all the awakenings into the present (Mcloughlin 1978, 63–5). In particular, it spread across all the colonies, from the New England, to the Middle and Southern colonies.

The old light ways of doing and thinking were then increasingly challenged by these developments, leading to the construction of new light ways of understanding and practising. Jonathan Edwards, minister and theologian from the Congregational church in Northampton, Massachusetts, led the revival in New England and beyond. He became the principal new light theologian, strong Calvinist, yet then developing a modified Calvinism and understanding of predestination, holding out 'hope that unregenerate sinners might yet be saved through conversion' (Fogel 2000, 20). Linking Locke's epistemology to such a revitalized Calvinist theology, he generated principles of conversion along with a concept of disinterested benevolence in the service of others (remarkably resonating with Adam Smith's *Theory of Moral Sentiments* and its impartial spectator). It was this which therefore, but often inadvertently, also contributed to the awakened Christian involvements in social and civic concerns, in what became movements for progressive reform in this, but particularly in the later awakenings. But all beginning from what Edwards recognized in 1742, that '[o]ur people do not so much need to have their heads stored as to have hearts touched' (McLoughlin 1978, 74). It's a similar, if related, energizing force to that identified by Baker in Chapter 3 above as spiritual capital in the early twenty-first century in religious communities in Britain. And it's that contribution to a revitalizing of lives, communities and cultures, which so influenced families, churches and civic life for the good. As Jonathan Lee then put it in words now so central to this argument for Christianity's contribution to wellbeing today, 'the happy tendency of vital piety to heal the maladies and rectify the disorders of the church of Christ' would expand, under the continuing power of the revival, to a 'blessed tendency of vital piety to *happify* the civil state' (McLoughlin 1978, 80; my emphasis). And that glorious concept of happifying, that pursuit of a wider wellbeing, rippled outwards into contributing to that greater intercontinental unity, to what Wood called the religious contribution to 'the rise of ordinary people into dominance', to arousing and resourcing the spirit of humanitarianism, the notion of equal rights, and the inclinations to and for democracy. The result was a combining of such religious experiences, Deism and Enlightenment views which challenged and overcame the tradition of British ascendency in 1776 (Fogel 2000, 29). For Wood, it was this 'Republican Regeneration' which made explicit, among other things, the 'fundamental link between the First Great Awakening and the Revolution'. For '[t]he traditional covenant [remember Gill's use of covenant in today's bioethic public discourse] theology of Puritanism combined with the political science of the eighteenth century into an imperatively persuasive argument for revolution'. The Revolution was therefore, in so many ways, 'the secular fulfilment of the religious ideas of the First Great Awakening'. For '[i]n liberating *their* country from British tyranny, the colonists were both freeing their consciences from a rebellion against the authority of their fathers and asserting the rising (postmillennial) glory of America' (McLoughlin 1978, 96–7).

The Second Great Awakening: (1800–1920)

The years leading up to and following the successful Revolution reinforced 'the optimistic world view' of Americans, including their belief that they were God's chosen people and that their land was 'the potential scene of the millennium'. They had united the 13 states into a republic with a written federal constitution–covenant. And they developed a form of cultural consensus from

THE AMERICAN CASE STUDY

the First Great Awakening, which was significantly 'theologically' Calvinistic but now modified to emphasize God's willingness 'to save those who truly repented of their sins'. Yet in many ways it began to become evident that this was also a fragile unity not least as its revolutionary zeal began to fade. The Revolution had produced some clarities over the American identity of intercontinental unity even though fused out of the differences especially of fiercely independent states. But what did it really mean 'to be an American' (McLoughlin 1978, 98)? An answer to that question was hammered out on the anvil of the Second Great Awakening, and particularly out of the great tragedy of the American Civil War.

The complex continuing and evolving search for national unity and identity involved engaging a series of profound differences over how to implement such identity, differences that had been provisionally addressed in order to deliver the Constitution. The Jeffersonians supported an English alliance against Napoleon, whereas the Hamiltonians moved for a revolutionary alliance. The Revolution's profound recognition of the common man now addressed the always present power of the elites of the educated, the wealthy and the 'well-born'. This, in turn, was reinforced economically by the Jeffersonian commitment to small farmers and therefore to westward expansion, as against the Hamiltonians' commercial and manufacturing vision for the nation, and therefore to strong relationships with emerging European power in production and global trade (McLoughlin 1978, 98–9). Even more unsettling was the growing conflict between the Calvinist consensus of the First Awakening's new light thinking and a powerful emerging Enlightenment rationalism. The hardening of Jonathan Edwards's teaching by his followers, particularly by Samuel Hopkins, led to a 'discordant, unbelievable formula'. The 'willingness-to-be-damned' for God's glory did not fit at all well with the emerging world of daily life following the successful Revolution and the growing prosperity of an America of self-made people (McLoughlin 1978, 100–1). That increasing gulf generated the crisis, and the Second Great Awakening forefronted the response.

Its first phase from about 1800 to about 1840 was pioneered not so much by the itinerant preachers of the First Awakening as by great organized camp meetings. These delivered similar outcomes of mass conversions, characterized by 'barbarous emotional outbreaks', especially on the frontiers, and initially generating a return to old time, old light religion (McLoughlin 1978, 107). It therefore had strong links with the similar use of camp meetings particularly by the Primitive Methodists in England in the same period. Methodism also played a formative role in this American revival in the form of the Methodist Episcopal Church, organized from 1784. Its evangelical growth was astonishing, surging to 1,250,000 members by 1850 and becoming thereby the largest Protestant denomination in America (Fogel 2000, 92). Its influence, theologically and therefore practically, was to erode the dominance of Calvinism and confirmed its major transformation. The latter's New England theologians therefore developed a modified Calvinism, the New Divinity, which recognized the ability of sinners 'to realize salvation through personal struggle against inner and outer corruption'. This had clear links to Methodism's Arminianism, which, despite its rejection of predestination doctrines, also acknowledged that ability of sinners to 'realize salvation through personal struggle' (Fogel 2000, 92). For the Methodists, it went still further in terms of meaning converted Christians could achieve not just salvation but also the perfection of sanctification. Yet, despite these resonances with Methodism, the New England New Divinity was more sedate, less emotional, certainly stressing conversion but linking it to a 'rationalistic Scottish philosophy' that recognized, so importantly, 'the human capacity to (thus) act virtuously'. This reformed new light Calvinism was therefore to become engaged in fighting inner corruption by engaging in movements for 'moral reform and social benevolence' (Fogel 2000, 93). Taylor and Beecher's leadership in New England of this theological reshaping of tradition as revivalism and perfectionism was confirmed and elaborated in the Midwest states by Finney. The difference was that he repudiated Calvinism for a 'new scientific theory of revivalism', which shaped his mass evangelism adapted from the rural camp meetings but now used strategically in the cities and larger towns. These were the first great organized evangelical campaigns, forerunners of Billy Graham's in post-Second World War America and Britain (McLoughlin 1978, 127). And, again, the effect of Finney's preaching and new light theology was the promotion and development of a salvation through rebirth into unselfishness and altruism – the energizing of Christian involvement in reform. Initially, much of this religious fervour for change was transmitted into the founding and strategic deployment of voluntary societies in the early nineteenth century. These included Bible societies (108 by 1815) in all the states linked also to educational concerns including literacy, so important for the knowledge revolutions, and tract societies producing guides for Christian behaviour (Fogel 2000, 94). Both were connected to the significant growth of the Sunday school movement, important for the nurturing of children in Christian living and values. Many of these initiatives were paralleled by similar developments in Britain through the activities of the Methodists and the Anglicans, including through the work of the evangelical and reforming Clapham Sect. And, so significant for our argument for Christian involvement in furthering wellbeing, the great success of the 'united front' of missionary and educational organizations in 'reviving religious zeal led evangelicals to return to their broader goal of shaping the moral and political character of the American nation' (p. 95). This, importantly, developed into the recognition of the social origins and character of sin, to an understanding of structural sin to complement its personal nature.

This movement, my transmission processes, led from Christian involvement in such benevolent reform into social action and into the great historic campaign to abolish slavery. Out of these interactions, and indeed informing them, profound political realignments also occurred – what Fogel refers to as the political phase of the Second Great Awakening – from 1840 to 1870. The emerging reform agenda was both diverse in the variety of its involvements and in their continuing importance and relevance for the following Third Awakening. It included the search for justice for indigenous Americans, and particularly their protection from white exploitation; campaigns for women's rights and temperance (the two were often closely linked), with the work of the early feminist leader, Elizabeth Cady Stanton, including her seminal *Declaration of Sentiment* (1848) still of significance today; the commitment to extensive and good quality public education, springing largely out of the great Puritan tradition of Bible reading and therefore of the promotion of literacy and out of the Sunday school movement, and these became forerunners of the later evolving commitment to non-sectarian, free, universal and compulsory elementary education; the promotion of progressive urban change accelerated as a key reform priority with the rapid, indeed explosive, growth of cities, and the accompanying and extensive social problems (these included housing, sanitary conditions, poverty and security) and the attempts to address them resulted in the emergence of civic corruption, politically focused, which in turn led to campaigns for clean politics for the common good, including through political parties, campaigns and increasingly interventionist municipal governments. These all gained in reform momentum particularly in the following Third Awakening (Fogel 2000, 95–109).

The final reform, the abolition of slavery, was the most radical, complex and politically informed of this Second Awakening. Campaigns by evangelical reformers meant that American abolitionism began more as a theological than a political movement, as a consequence of the founding belief that 'all men were equal before God', and so combining the religious (personal freedom as essential for heavenly salvation) and the political (the importance of political democracy). It was a religious agenda which also split the churches, particularly dividing North and South, but also within the North, and especially over more radical arguments and tactics. For example, Beecher, a prominent new light leader, even raised money to purchase rifles for the North in the Civil War, obviously known as 'Beecher's Bibles' (Putnam and Campbell 2010, 250). The latter radical pursuit disturbed many in the churches and drove its proponents into the more necessary field of political campaigning, with all its required compromises. The achievements were both profound and lasting, not simply and primarily for human beings, but also because they were enshrined in constitutional reform, along with other objectives and achievements of the wider reform movement. The resulting seven constitutional amendments included 'the Thirteenth (outlawing slavery), the Fourteenth (due process), the Fifteenth (black male suffrage), the Sixteenth (federal income taxes), the Seventeenth (popular election of senators), the Eighteenth (Prohibition), and the Nineteenth (women's suffrage)' (Fogel 2000, 30). Although of such intrinsic importance, these achievements also demonstrated to both church and society that, faced with increasingly complex social challenges, 'legislative' action in democratic societies could become 'an instrument of radical reform' (Fogel 2000, 107). That became particularly significant in the Third and Fourth Awakenings and will continue to be so for the pursuit of agendas addressing the wealth, wellbeing and inequalities of nations. In addition, it was in this Second Awakening that Fogel's thesis of the interactions of technophysio evolution, religious revivals and political realignments became particularly apparent, with the movement in the 1850s, given their anti-slavery commitments, of evangelicals out of the Democratic Party into Lincoln's Republican Party, which then retained political control for two generations. It was the support of the social gospellers and their successors that helped to bring the Democrats back into control in the 1930s to introduce another and equally significant reform programme.

Interestingly, the principal economic theorist of this awakening, the Reverend Francis Wayland, President of Brown University, was also an important figure in the Northern Baptist Church before and in the Civil War (the Southern Baptists rejected this link). His *The Elements of Political Economy* (1837) was a key economics text book before the 1860s (Wayland 1837). Like Adam Smith and Thomas Malthus in Britain, he regarded economics 'as a subfield of moral philosophy', focusing on 'the science of wealth' as discovery of God's laws and confirming the importance of individual liberty and private property, and therefore of 'industry and frugality' (Fogel 2000, 108; Frey 2009, 42–7). Like Malthus, he opposed charity for able-bodied workers, because it led to indolence and dependency. Again, he was similarly critical of labour unions because they challenged competition law. These views therefore resonated with the British Age of Atonement and Voluntarism, and are then challenged by deep changes in economic structures in the later nineteenth century.

The Third Great Awakening (1870–1970)

Beecher was not simply a new light leader of progressive reform in the Second Awakening, he also provides an important linkage into the Third. It was in the decades after the Civil War that the social gospel, at the heart of the religious contribution to the Third Awakening and seen by Hopkins as 'America's most unique contribution to the great ongoing stream of Christianity' (1940, 3), began to emerge in the USA. Learning from the practical and theological struggles to overthrow the system of black slavery, Protestants began to turn their attention to similarly overcoming the new emerging evils of industrialization, of wage slavery. It was Beecher who captured this progressive transition by declaring 'Now that God has smitten slavery unto death, he has opened the way for the redemption and sanctification of our whole social system' (quoted by Hopkins 1940, 22). It was that great extension of the social, economic and political agenda of reform that best characterizes the emerging contribution of this Third Awakening to a more comprehensive pursuit of greater human wellbeing.

The challenges facing churches and society in the rapidly evolving later nineteenth century were immense. Almost overnight, 'the Industrial Revolution converted a peaceful and agricultural country into an urban nation of bustling factories' (Hopkins 1940, 22). The dramatic effects of the combination of industrialization and urbanization were all-embracing in their magnitude, intensity and speed. Between 1860 and 1890, national wealth increased from $16 billion to $78 billion, accompanied by the paradox of development as vast inequalities in income and wealth. Between 1880 and 1890, Chicago's population grew by an astounding 100 per cent, soon reaching a million from almost nothing a century earlier, and with all the accompanying problems of poverty,

THE AMERICAN CASE STUDY

Picture 2. 'The Atlantic Cable Projectors' by Daniel Huntington, depicting members of the New York Chamber of Commerce and the first transatlantic telegraph in 1893 (New York State Museum).

unemployment, industrial conflicts, poor housing, vice and political corruption. These forces combine to present the starkest of challenges to the prevailing social and religious belief that all life was integrally part of a 'divinely-regulated and unchangeable social order' (Hopkins 1940, 23).

The growth of large industries, monopolistically dominating their sectors, presented the most powerful challenges to an existing 'unchangeable social order' but equally thereby to its supposed embodiment of that American dream of equal opportunity and robust social mobility. The great wealth and conspicuous consumption of these new industrial and financial elites stood in increasingly stark contrast to the harsh lives of the labouring classes in their appalling urban context. Their great riches and power, not surprisingly, generated the powerfully evocative descriptive concepts of 'the gilded age', the 'great barbecue' and the 'robber barons'. In my study I have a brochure standing on my window ledge with a picture of a group of men responsible for the first transatlantic telegraph in 1893 (see Picture 2). They were members of the New York Chamber of Commerce, and exude power, influence and wealth. The portrait was part of a remarkable collection at Princeton's University Art Museum in 2013 called 'Picturing Power: Capitalism, Democracy and American Portraiture' – and there the robber barons all were – Vanderbilt, Chase, Mellon, J. P. Morgan, Carnegie – the captains representing the elites' capturing of strategic industries from finance, rail and steel, to petroleum (Kusserow 2013). Confronted with such extreme concentrations of power, Lincoln's promise, that *'all should have an equal chance'* (Fogel 2000, 5) was increasingly experienced as unachievable by most. A land of small farmers and businessmen – yes, such a dream was possible. A land of Carnegies and Vanderbilts – no. As McLoughlin judged, by 1890, 'the world seemed to be closing in on many groups in America; freedom and equal opportunity seemed to be dying out'. Instead, 'A stratified social system with restricted mobility seemed about to replace the classless open society upon which the American dream rested' (1978, 150–1).

It was against this increasingly apparent series of disjunctions rapidly reaching new degrees of intensity and extent that the Third Great Awakening began to emerge. It was again initially focused on the reactive and energizing strategies of conversions and emotions but now centred on the urban masses. Moody's great revivalist meetings, often funded by evangelical businessmen who supposed the divinely informed market would correct itself, were intended to reach the new labouring urban classes (McLoughlin 1978, 142–5). Facing growing unemployment and industrial conflict, it was assumed conversions would exercise a calming influence. Yet these new tensions inevitably continued to grow despite the renewed efforts of the greatest national prophet in the 1890s, Billy Sunday, and an increasingly professional revivalism, which was continued in the 1950s by Billy Graham. Again, it amounted to facing crises by resorting to old time religion, the old great evangelical beliefs and values, the old light religions and theologies. Powerful in its inherited core beliefs and practices, it was equally strident in what it therefore opposed, whether Darwinism or immigrants (especially from Catholic Europe); but increasingly the new light religion of liberal Protestantism or modernism began to take over the religious landscape. Yet it was still involved in reform movements inherited from the Second Awakening, including prohibition campaigns. But it rejected the great extension of the reformism of the social gospel, now seeking to address the new problems of industrialization and urbanization, focused, for example in the ecumenical Federal Council of Churches Social Creed of 1912. Protestant support for such social action was anathema to them: 'We've had enough of this godless social service nonsense' (McLoughlin 1978, 148–9). The rise of fundamentalism and Pentecostalism in the early twentieth century continued much of this tradition, initially driven out of public notice but then reappearing into growing prominence after the Second World War.

It became increasingly clear that the problems generating the Third Great Awakening were beyond the reach of the old time, old light revived and revivalist religion. The challenges presented by the new collective corporate realities generated a loss of confidence in these old beliefs, values and order. From the 1870s there therefore emerged what became the core of the Third Awakening, the social gospel. This attempted to redefine and relocate God, to constructively 'sacralize a new world view' (McLoughlin 1978, 152), engaging with Darwin, the natural sciences, technology and the new biblical studies. The result was to reformulate Christian tradition as a progressive orthodoxy in ways resonating with the liberal Catholicism of Christian socialism in Britain again in the late nineteenth century. It is important to note that despite this reformulating of tradition, the social gospel continued to focus on individual conversion but extended that process to engaging the social structurings of the emerging new social order. So it maintained a strong purchase on the great central beliefs of Christianity but sought to reformulate them in order to engage more effectively the great features of the new world of daily life. That was the task of working for the coming of the kingdom of God, a task embodied best in the work of the greatest leader and exemplar of the social gospel, Walter Rauschenbusch. Along with other proponents, including urban reformers such as Washington Gladden and Josiah Strong, for Richard Niebuhr, they kept 'relatively close to evangelical notions of the sovereignty of God, of the reign of Christ and of the coming kingdom. In Rauschenbusch especially the revolutionary element remained pronounced; the reign of Christ required conversion and the coming kingdom was crisis, judgement as well as promise' (Niebuhr 1988, 194). Yet the old light, more conservative tradition always continued to influence society. For example, William Jennings Bryan, the Democratic candidate for the presidency in 1896, 1900 and 1908, represented their more progressive side (Fogel 2000, 23). But it was the social gospel side of the Third Awakening that more directly linked religious beliefs to the great social reform platforms. These were both far more extensive and innovatory than in the first two awakenings not least because the accelerating impacts of industrialization and urbanization in the later nineteenth century generated a whole series of reforms. These involved national and local governments and business – for example, the Sherman Antitrust Act of 1890 – and profoundly affected and improved the material wellbeing of the world of daily life. The significant contribution of Christianity to these developments needs to be located in these processes, and like them, also represented a major growth in their nature and extent.

The social gospel's influence on such reform was best illustrated and symbolized by the Federal Council of Churches Social Creed of 1912 (itself adapted from the Methodist 1908 Social Creed). Its importance as a process was that it exemplified the growing emphasis in the twentieth century on intrafaith collaboration between Christian denominations (in the Federal Council of Churches' case, 33 different churches). This was especially evident in their convergences over social witness matters. The Social Creed embodies these in some detail, again resonating remarkably with William Temple's six objectives in his 'Suggested

Programme' in his *Christianity and Social Order* (1942, 99–100), published in 1942, some 30 years after the Social Creed. Both, too, were deeply informed by the motivating implications of what, in Temple's case, was a strongly incarnational theology, and for the social gospel, by a similar transfer of emphasis from God as transcendent to God as immanent, as among the world of daily life. In both British and American traditions this linking of divine immanence and consequential and progressive social involvement, this process, which was essentially one of transmission, was encapsulated in the slogan the Fatherhood of God requires the brotherhood of man.

The Social Creed summarized both American Christianity's contribution to the pursuit of greater wellbeing in an urban–industrial age and important elements of the reform programmes themselves. It included: equal rights and complete justice for people in all stations of life; the protection of the family through marriage and proper housing; the fullest development of every child including through education and recreation; the regulation of women's work to safeguard the community's physical and moral health; the abatement and prevention of poverty; the conservation of health; the protection of the workers' health and safety; the rights of all for the opportunity for self-maintenance, safeguarding against encroachments from outside bodies, and as protection from the hardships of enforced unemployment; suitable provision for old age and injury at work; the right to organize in labour unions, and for conciliation and arbitration processes; at least one day a week's holiday; the gradual reduction of working hours to the lowest practical point and therefore for adequate leisure time, all being conditions for the effective pursuit of a flourishing human life; a living wage and for the highest wages affordable by industry; and Christian principles for the acquisition and use of property and the most equitable distribution of the products of industry. It's a remarkable creed for a variety of reasons central to this book. Its objectives are closely related to the pursuit of greater wellbeing in a post eighteenth-century world, reflected, for example, in the three perspectives of income, health and subjective wellbeing, and all the other related domains or realms of wellbeing, say education, family life and participation in government, and in the engagement with inequalities (Hopkins 1940, 290–1). They are in addition so wellbeing – encompassing as to constitute a continuing agenda still central to today's pursuit of greater human flourishing. They reflect, too, a pragmatic willingness to enter into negotiations to achieve progressive ends. This was illustrated by coalition building and its associated compromises, which were evident in the religious involvement in the political realignments required by the anti-slavery movements of the Second Awakening. And, of course, they also thereby address a Christianity, too, now located in a religious studies which must therefore negotiate reformulated traditions through interacting with changing contexts. It's a reminder that doctrinal creeds must be complemented by social creeds if religious traditions are to embrace the pursuit of greater human wellbeing, of that godly abundance of John's Gospel, of Irenaeus's focus on 'the glory of God is the person fully alive' (Cairns 1973, 82). Flourishing and God are the two inseparable sides of the same coin.

What followed in American history demonstrated the accuracy and feasibility of that Social Creed's interaction with an evolving programme of social reform, not least through the influence of the social gospel and the Social Creed on the younger Roosevelt. The New Deal of the 1930s – forged out of the need to address the great depression and representing that political realignment stage of an awakening, with the Democrats capturing the federal government through to the 1960s – inaugurated a series of legislative reforms from the Social Security Act (1935) and Full Employment Act (1946) to Johnson's War on Poverty through Medicare and Medicaid, from opening access to higher education through the GI Bill of Rights after the Second World War to continuing the processes left unfinished by the Civil War through the Civil Rights Act (1964), the Voting Rights Act of 1965, the Twenty-Fourth Amendment (ratified in 1964) eliminating important barriers to black equality in political life and the Civil Rights Act of 1966 (Fogel 2000, 133). The campaigns for women and gay equal rights extended this long commitment to the continued evolution of the historic American focus on equal rights and opportunities.

As Wayland illustrated the close relationship between Christianity and economics in the Second Awakening, so Ely, perhaps even more strongly, performs the same role in the Third Awakening (Frey 2009, 105–09). He certainly embodies the interactions between the progressive orthodoxy of the social gospel and the development of professional economics. For example, he was a leading founder of the American Economic Association in 1885 (Angus Deaton, author of the *Great Escape,* important source for my book, is a past president of the Association). Of the 30 who gathered for that occasion, Ely was one of the 20 who were either clergy or from clerical families. They also represented a strong commitment to social reform not least, in terms of Ely particularly, because of their critique of classical economic theories and their associated underwriting of laissez-faire economics. The social changes Ely and many of the other economists sought were strongly opposed by the tradition that viewed economics and economic affairs as governed by unchangeable economic laws with no reason to incorporate any ethical perspectives. Against this understanding, as espoused earlier by Wayland, Ely argued for the reform or development of economics because it was fundamentally a human construct and therefore, among other things, open to ethical influence (Bateman and Banzhaf 2008, 293). Much of this new economic methodology was derived from American involvement in the German historical school of economics. Economic life was therefore contingent in human history and therefore not the manifestation of fixed laws with their focus on deductive method. This approach to and understanding of economics was incorporated in the American Economic Association's statement of principles – that 'we look, not so much to speculation as to the historical and statistical study of actual conditions of economic life', to the economic world of daily life (Bateman and Banzhaf 2008, 309). But where Ely and the others got this perspective from is of particular interest. For Ely's visits to Germany suggest that the roots of his economic methodology were also informed by developments in German liberal religion, particularly in biblical studies and historical theologies. Both German economics and German liberal theology used analytical methods, tracing historical developments in terms of preceding cultural patterns. In economics, this approach replaced universal economic laws with the analysis of economic practices and institutions, including their historical development, as contingent as the culture in which they emerged. Similarly, in German liberal theology, theology begins as subjective religious experience, an empirically verifiable fact, say for Schleiermacher. The empirical study of religion was therefore entirely appropriate, regarding religion, among other things, and therefore like economics, as a human construct. Both, therefore, could and did change. From this German historical school of economics' extrapolation of significant trends in liberal Protestantism into economic understandings, Ely then extrapolated from both into the development of American economics. And his interaction as an economist with his social gospel involvements confirmed these economic developments through immersion in the equivalent developments of progressive orthodoxy. It was therefore in Ely, particularly, that the economic and religious imperatives converged in the promotion of social and economic reform, say as convergence of social creed and New Deal and their deployment of the emerging state for the promotion of greater wellbeing. So, for Ely, 'Government should interfere in all instances where its interference will tell for better health, better education, better morals [including Prohibition], greater comfort of the community' (McLoughlin 1978, 171). But then, as Fogel observes, confirming Keynes's similar judgement on the British experience in the 1860s, economics grew 'far beyond the religious issues that marked their emergence as professions' (Fogel 2000, 134). And that's where we are now, in the last and Fourth Awakening. Yet this brief reflection on Ely's connecting of economic and religious sources of social reforms has wider implications for the wider arguments of this book. For both economic and religious involvements strongly promoted the significance of supportive institutional arrangements for developing greater human wellbeing in the centuries following 1800. They are essential for economic growth, for reducing inequalities, for health policies and for greater subjective wellbeing. In terms of Ely's and American economics, their development through involvement with German historical economics, and therefore with German liberal Protestantism, certainly illustrates the significance and feasibility of my transmission theories. Maybe more importantly, this little case study within a case study also illustrates the viability of developing a reformulating religious studies alongside a reformulating economic tradition, the one powerfully able to learn from the other. There is therefore clearly room for a religious studies sharing and deploying empirical, verifiable and historical methods, for example, in developing its contribution to the pursuit of greater wellbeing.

The Fourth Great Awakening: 1960–? Unfinished business

In view of the recurring main features of the first Three Great Awakenings, there are significant indicators that a Fourth Awakening may well be beginning to emerge, not least because the end of each cycle has consistently overlapped with the early emergence of a new cycle. Many of the distinctive markers of say McLoughlin's trilogy of revivals, awakenings and reform and of Fogel's interacting of technophysio evolution, religious revivals and political realignments can also be discerned in the period running from the 1960s–1970s to the present.

After the stabilities of post Second World War reconstruction, reinforced, as in Britain, by a more traditional, ordered society and religion, a generation emerged which began to face major changes and disruptions. Economically, the rapid increase in economic growth and material standards of living generated increasing freedoms to be and to do, freedoms reinforced by the now very evident impacts of the historic improvements in life expectancy and health, all the positive developments related in Chapter 2. Yet the paradox of development meant that these changes also helped to create new anxieties, for example symbolized, for the positive psychologists, as an emerging age of melancholy, of rapidly increasing incidences of mental illness, especially depression, despite or because of astonishing improvements in material wellbeing. Or maybe these disturbing trends in mental disorders have been accentuated by the slowing down of economic growth from the mid 1970s and the accompanying increasing inequalities. A generation of people beginning to struggle to maintain, never mind increase, their living standards, not surprisingly has not resulted in improving happiness levels. Other features of the crisis were more clearly political in origin and character, including domestic conflicts over the Vietnam War and nuclear weapons, the increasing intrusions of an ever-enlarging state, welfarism and bureaucracy, and profound differences over the shape and quality of family life and associated issues of sexuality (McLoughlin 1978, 179–80; Fogel 2000, 25–7). Again, the old inherited consensus of the 1950s was unable to cope with such serial and deep-seated change, an inability represented also by the recurring gap between ever-accelerating technological change and the ability to develop norms and values to engage it effectively.

As in previous awakenings, the initial response to such disruptive change manifested itself in profoundly religious responses spearheaded, again, by the growth of an enthusiastic religion characterized by spiritual intensity linked to conversion. And, again, it initially took the form of a return to old time religion and old light theology, expounded by the increasingly professional mass urban campaigns of Billy Graham, but also reflected in other denominations, for example in the writings and broadcasts of the Roman Catholic Bishop Sheen (McLoughlin 1978, 186–9). This religious resurgence, particularly of a multi-streamed evangelicalism, was reinforced, for the first time, by the major decline of the historic mainstream churches. Again, initially, the transmission of resurgent religious values into wider society and social reform focused on traditional family values, relationships and sexualities, and again centred on mechanisms to achieve its objectives principally in the form of the usual single issue movements like the Moral Majority (1979). But then, given their inadequacies, and again treading in historically familiar paths, these energies moved into broader coalitions, which attracted the support of more mainstream denominations, including the Roman Catholic (Fogel 2000, 31). Linked to these reform movements there also occurred, as in previous awakenings, major political realignments in terms of the movement of evangelicals, particularly in Southern states, from the Democratic to the Republican Party.

What is not yet clearly and decisively apparent is the existence of strong new light radical progressive social reform. Putnam notes that the growing strength of African Americans and Latinos is 'highly religious and very supportive of antipoverty policy'. Yet the more religious commitment to government policies to reduce inequality fades to below that of the most secular Americans. The deeply religious volunteer and give more to help the poor, preferring 'private provision to public action'. They are 'somewhat less supportive than the general population of public policies to address poverty and inequality' (Putnam and Campbell 2010, 255, 257). And that constitutes a major change for the worse, compared to the performance of the religious in previous awakenings, most particularly in the Third. It was then that a Salvation Army leader, facing a rapidly growing class inequality, as we do now, as illustrated so starkly in Chapter 2, recognized the inadequacies of volunteering and giving for addressing such poverty and inequality: 'To right the social wrong by charity is like bailing the oceans with a thimble' (Putnam and Campbell 2010, 258). Putnam's judgement on the performance of Christianity in this Fourth Awakening is therefore stark: 'The failure of American religion (and especially evangelicals) today to mount a more vigorous campaign against class disparities could thus be seen as a sin of omission, *especially compared to the struggles for social justice that people of faith mounted in comparable periods of American history*' (2010, 258; my emphasis). The fact that George W. Bush mused publicly about whether we were in another Awakening, 'this time with conservative political consequences', is no answer (Putnam and Campbell 2010, 232). That conservative reform strand has always been present in the Awakenings. As Putnam observes 'God in American history has not been a consistent partisan of left or right'. Yet without the other and more dominant radical reform strand, always so present in the Awakenings, it is very difficult to judge that we are as yet in a full-blown Awakening. As yet! For 'Not all religious based movements are progressive, but most American progressive movements have had powerful religious roots' (Putnam and Campbell 2010, 252). We still await that progressive alliance.

I say 'as yet', because the shortage of decisive evidence covering all the main features of awakenings suggests that the case for and elaboration of a Fourth Great Awakening is clearly unfinished business. But that's not at all surprising. McLoughlin published his contribution in 1978 and Fogel in 2000, both too early in the cycles of this Awakening. The major social reforms of the Third Awakening only occurred half a century into the process. Only from the perspective of succeeding generations will we be able to judge whether there has been a Fourth Awakening according to the criteria embedded in the previous three. McLoughlin's and Fogel's development of the awakening thesis as part of 'only a suggestive model of social change' (McLoughlin 1978, xiv) is precisely that, a tool for interpreting US history from the early eighteenth century, but a model, then robustly tested, particularly by Fogel. He therefore rightly regards it as 'a descriptive model of what happened rather than as a forecasting model'. Again, he then rightly qualifies this by recognizing that 'when used cautiously, this model, as with other empirical models, may provide a rough guide to some aspects of future developments' (Fogel 2000, 29). That 'rough guide' is now being tested in current US history, but it will need at least another generation of testing to illustrate its adequacy in and as this fourth generation of awakenings.

5

An Ecclesiastical History of the English Peoples' Journey to Greater Wellbeing
The British Case Study

St Paul's Jarrow is a beautiful modest church, Saxon in origin, and monastic home to the Venerable Bede and his monumental study *The Ecclesiastical History of the English People*, completed in 731 CE. It's a profound and detailed critical survey of Christianity in an 'England' located in a much wider, what we would now call, British and then European context. This astonishing account was also located in political, economic and cultural contexts, all interwoven into one great narrative. The world of daily life and the world of religious life were then strongly and very consciously interconnected in ways since lost in much of the modern world.

This chapter takes that complex story ten centuries forward into a journey from the early eighteenth century to today, a journey through the emergence and growth of those Industrial and Mortality Revolutions so central to the arguments of this book. It is a journey which, in turn, illustrates in some detail the profound interactions of Christian and secular perspectives in the development of greater human wellbeing, including in and through the continuing and always disturbing paradoxes of development. It therefore performs a twofold task. First, by testing the wider historical contexts and frameworks described in the introduction to Part 2, by analytically elaborating that thesis in the narrative details of the last two and a half centuries and the historic breakthrough in social development. And second, by also thereby illustrating the contributions of Christianity to constructive social change. Like Moore, in his fine study of Methodism's activities in the Durham coalfield from 1870 to 1926, but addressing a much wider field of study, religion has 'made some kind of *positive* contribution to the development of modern society' (Moore 1974, 1; my emphasis). Using Ellen Charry's contemporary work on systematic theology and psychology, it is that combination of her 'positive theology' and Moore's 'positive contribution' which summarizes this account of putting Christianity to work in and through the details of over two centuries of British history. And, of course, that is never to make any special pleading for the Christian case, but rather to acknowledge its proper and fitting place, with many other disciplines, practices, ethics and beliefs, in the promotion of greater wellbeing, in this case, through an exploration of the histories of Britain in this seminal last 250 years.

Is there any connection between this contemporary account and Bede's? Both address 'a total web of interconnected political, economic, social and religious factors' even though in fundamentally different historical contexts (Hylson-Smith 1997, 271). In this sense, they have certain common agendas, but it's more than that. For the ancient Saxon church of St Paul's Jarrow now lies in the midst of densely industrial, commercial and urban developments reflecting the turbulent changes this historic area has undergone in the last 150 years. To look down on this site is to look down on that continuing industrial and economic history. It reminds me of another view, which confronted Engels when he stood on top of the Pennine Hills separating Yorkshire from Lancashire and looked down on one of the great origins of the industrial and urban revolutions: 'If we cross Blackstone Edge ... we enter upon that classic soil on which English manufacture has achieved its masterwork and from which all labour movements emanate, namely, South Lancashire with its central city, Manchester' (Engels 1969, 75). In that city, in its ancient cathedral, I served as canon theologian for 20 years, next to the Chethams Library, where Marx and Engels conducted some of their early research into English political economy. From Bede to Engels is not an impossible journey, after all!

THE BRITISH CASE STUDY

In terms of how to address such an agenda, growing familiarity over many years with modern and economic history in particular, and with the traditions and their histories which generated the contemporary discipline of Christian social ethics, revealed that their separate vertical accounts of this period of British history from the eighteenth century indicated substantial horizontal resonances between them, across historical periods and changes in social development. For example, the age of evangelical Nonconformity in ecclesiastical history linked to economic history's early industrial period, the emergence of classical economics and the age of voluntary activity in a free market, and all powerfully resonated, indeed clearly interacted with, the Age of Atonement in Christian social thought. These will form our first 'Age of Voluntarism and Atonement'. By the late nineteenth, and through most of the twentieth century, the problems generated by the processes of industrialization and urbanization increasingly required the attentions of what became, over a century, a strong interventionist local and national state. This second age, of the state, was closely paralleled, and indeed clearly interacted with, a Christian Age of Incarnation. The series of changes that appear to herald the passing of that age, occurring in this generation from the late twentieth and into the present century, could be leading to a growing demand for partnerships and its resonances with an emerging, third, Age of Reconciliation.

Constructing such a typology or classification of social phenomena is of intrinsic value, but it also allows a constructive comparative engagement with the models of Great Awakenings used in the American case study. Both are essentially tools for interpreting complex historical change within which, with other forces and disciplines, religion clearly plays an important role. But there are also, and inevitably, considerable differences between them. There are no equivalent awakenings clearly linked to religious revivals, economic change, political realignments and social reform. The British model can only trace serious connections between dominant cultural–religious 'moods' and social, economic and political change and developments. Both models often lack precision, yet both are open to the development of the tools of scientific as well as traditional history, although the American model and case study has made more progress in this field, particularly through Fogel's contribution. Despite these differences, the British model is therefore also able to play an important part in the reformulation of a contemporary religious studies.

In constructing this British model, representing as already noted a typology or classification of social phenomena, various issues must be addressed. For example, the scale and complexity of the material crossing disciplines and periods ensure it will always be, to some extent, arbitrary – or, rather, 'chainsaw art'. There are always alternative plausibility structures. But an important test is whether it works reasonably, as Morris argued with his social development index, whether in the past or present. Such testing against previous and current experience will be the task of this chapter. Yet even if such evidence demonstrates the viability of the model, it can still only provide a provisional, yet purposeful working framework. Clearly, too, such a typological model is never tidy. There are, as with the awakening model in America, always overlaps between different 'ages', and the regulatory principles of previous 'ages' always continue to exercise influence.

Why link theological and secular typologies? As an exponent of Christian social thought and practice, my starting point is a theologically based typology interacting with secular history movements. The starting point is always the intimate relationship between Christian developments and their changing contexts. Like a study of recent socialist political movements in Europe, religious history is 'inseparable from the history of the economic and social structures which shape it and against which it strives' (Sassoon 1997, 22, xxv). That is why I have taken two of the major concepts, the ages of atonement and incarnation, from a secular historian, Boyd Hilton. I therefore begin with a secular view of Christian contributions in precisely the same way and for precisely the same reasons that I began the exploration of what was it about Christianity that provides greater wellbeing by similarly drawing first from secular sources. In this way, this model of putting Christianity to work in and through the British history of contemporary wellbeing complements the modelling of the

Christian contribution to subjective wellbeing. Their combination can therefore also be seen to be a form of public theology deploying contemporary Christian resources to be 'critically related to the contemporary debate among social philosophers, political scientists', economists, psychologist and sociologists. They will, in the words of Duncan Forrester, formative Scottish theologian to whom many of us owe so much, emerge out of 'the particularities of Christian faith while addressing issues of public significance' (Forrester 1997, 56, 33). You can't get an issue of greater public significance than the wealth, wellbeing and inequalities of nations, and how and why religious studies has contributed, and can now do so even more effectively according to this study, to such greater wellbeing.

The model for this case study is essentially a multilayered construct. It was first elaborated in my *Public Theology for Changing Times* in 2000. By sheer coincidence, Fogel published his model, *The Fourth Great Awakening and the Future of Egalitarianism* in the same year. My model was then developed further in an article in the *International Journal of Public Theology* in 2011, particularly using Methodist sources. The original model had been especially dependent on the rich tradition of Anglican social Christianity. This chapter, while drawing from these earlier versions, also makes use of a variety of additional sources from secular and religious studies disciplines. It is also reinforced with references, where appropriate, illustrating the evolving relationship between Christianity and economics, making use of relevant material from economic history, economics, the histories of economic ideas and the traditions of Christian social ethics.

The First Age of Voluntarism and Atonement (1750–1860)

Knowledge as science and technology was the primary driver of the Industrial and Mortality Revolutions. Living in Engels's South Lancashire as child and then clergyman, I was surrounded by the stories and effects of such inventions, particularly those that drove the foundationally important textile industry revolution in the eighteenth century. The flying shuttle for weaving was invented by John Kay from Bury (1733), where I was a curate. Samuel Crompton's spinning mule of 1779 was invented in Bolton, where I was brought up. I used to walk past the little house where Crompton was born and the merchant's house he moved to, and the grave he ended up in, just outside Bolton Parish Church's front door. He combined features of James Hargreaves's spinning Jenny (c.1764) (from Blackburn, the diocese in which I now reside; with Hargreaves being one of my family names) with Richard Arkwright's water frame (1769), and he originated from Preston, now my county town. The Industrial Revolution is in my bloodstream. Yet behind these faces are the facts, so cleverly collected and analysed by Allen in his chapter 'Inventors, Enlightenment and human capital' (Allen 2009, 238–9). He identifies these major inventors from the major technological breakthrough industries of steam, cotton, iron, porcelain and engineering, analysing their social networks, their application of scientific method to the study of technology through experimentation and their class (interestingly often from literate artisan and shopkeeping backgrounds). I now visit the same familiar places but see them through the quite different eyes of the longer term statistical analysis as well. It's monovision in action in South Lancashire. That's what this brief survey seeks to achieve in terms of looking at the multilayered relationship between secular and religious fields and their contribution to progressive change.

The Lancashire inventions of the mid eighteenth century gradually became focused in the great mills, symbols of new industrial organizations, the concentrating of people and resources in bigger and bigger units, controlled by the timing of machines and the new inanimate energy power of steam. This represented the great breakthrough in productivity, main driver of economic growth, and with the most profound repercussions across the whole of society, human living and religion, particularly with the latter's historic focus on persons and their relationships and traditions formulated in a past now rapidly left behind forever. Allen, summarizing his analysis of inventors behind the Industrial Revolution, including my 'Manchester' men, noted that '[t]he transition from a world in which people prayed to improve their lot to one in which they calculated may have made it easier for intellectuals to imagine the world as governed by mathematical laws rather than by a personal god' (2009, 267). We will see that the world of daily life is never quite so isolated at all, but, in this first stage, regularly and frequently interacts with the world of religion.

These transformations in economic life were accompanied by equally dramatic increases in population. The nineteenth century therefore witnessed a fourfold population growth but this was resourced by a fourteenfold increase in GNP. There were similar supportive changes in the field of political economy beginning with Smith's foundational text, *An Inquiry into the Nature and Causes of the Wealth of Nations* in 1776, and its emphasis on encouraging the role of markets, supported by the division of labour, as effective and efficient ways to produce and distribute wealth. These views and economics developed into the Manchester School's full-blown laissez-faire understanding of the free market and its wealth-creating capacities free from the overbearing state interventions of mercantilism. One of its leading exponents, Cobden, argued that such free trade should also be a major force for peace, the 'doux commerce' argument (Pinker 2011, 77), a clear-cut and intentional combining of economics, ethics and religion – as Boyd Hilton acknowledges by judging evangelicalism to be 'as much public ethic as personal credo'. So Cobden's stated premise in his economic policy was, for Hilton, that 'providence had designed commerce to unify and "moralize" mankind, and that Free Trade was the international law of God "to spread *Christianity through commerce*, over the world"' (Hilton 1988, 203, 246).

In the political context, the growth of nation states was not accompanied by the growth of large government at this stage. The state was a dyke against sin, no active intervener as yet in the promotion of a good society. And the churches underwrote this order, with their 'perceived allegiances' lying with the 'Interested' rather than the 'Oppressed' (Lee 2007, 89). In 1810–20, the Durham Church owned ten seaside pits and nine out of seventeen landside pits. Even in 1873 it owned 11 per cent of the land in County Durham. That reactionary alliance was notoriously confirmed in the development of a social policy to complement a laissez-faire economic policy. The hated Poor Law Amendment Act of 1834 (my father still spoke of its workhouses with great anger even in the 1960s) – powerfully endorsed and indeed initiated by such leading Christian political economists as John Bird Sumner, Thomas Malthus and Thomas Chalmers – illustrated the movement from traditional societies, from status to contract relationships, from estates to classes. Through its carrot and stick approach, determined to pay benefits less than the lowest wage and concentrating the destitute in punitive workhouses (separating men from their wives and children!), the task of the Poor Law was to encourage individual self-help in a free competitive market as the way to improve life. The benefits of such policies were dramatic in terms of the creation of wealth. The costs were also enormous in terms of the destruction of familiar lifestyles and their replacement by initially appalling conditions in the new industrial cities and urban communities. In the early stages of the Industrial Revolution, most people still experienced chronic malnutrition. As we know from Fogel's research used in Chapter 2, in 1800 20 per cent of the population were unable to work because they lacked the necessary dietary (calorific) energy. This, in turn, was linked to low body mass index, early onset of chronic diseases and very low life expectancy. The latter was only 32 years in 1725, rising to 36 years in 1800 and 48 in 1900 (Fogel 2004, 39–42). Wearmouth notes that for labourers life expectancy was 17 years in Manchester and 18 in my home town of Bolton, in an 1845 report (1937, 248). Any gains in real income were offset by poor diets and miserable conditions in the new urban industrial centres: 15 people lived in one room in Radcliffe, my local town when I first moved to Manchester cathedral (Wearmouth 1959, 19). Not surprisingly, it was a period of deep inequalities. The economists' Gini coefficient, which measures income inequality with total inequality as 1 and total equality as 0, was as high as 0.65 in 1700 (Fogel 2004, 39). De Tocqueville, master observer and commentator on American life in this same period, summarized this profound paradox of development at the heart of the Industrial Revolution when he commented so memorably on Manchester that 'from this filthy sewer pure gold flows' (Hobsbawm 1962, 42). But it's the economic historian Landes whose judgement is most accurate, that on balance the benefits for wellbeing significantly outweighed the losses, confirming the conclusion of Chapter 2, that 'no superior authority could have effected an industrial revolution so rapidly and efficiently as the impersonal market' (Landes 1969, 549).

The spiritual certainty of the early exponents of self-help in commerce and industry was provided particularly by evangelical Nonconformity but increasingly also by evangelical Anglicanism. Indeed, free market and Christian beliefs were readily combined by people and culture. So laissez-faire was underwritten by Christian convictions like Burke's that the laws of commerce are the laws of nature and therefore the laws of God (Winch 1996, 213), and by theological comment, like the *Congregational Journal* in 1846, affirming the view that '[e]conomical truth is no less divine than astronomical truth. The laws which govern the phenomena of production and exchange are as truly laws of God as those which govern day and night' (Cocks 1943, 35). It is important to note that this popularizing of earlier Christian engagements with economics profoundly distorts much of the work of early Christian economists. Their skill was to explore the connections between Christianity, the new economics and the dichotomy between wealth and poverty, roughly in the same period as the Reverend John McVicar was asserting something similar in 1825 in the USA. For him, it was about recognizing that 'science and religion eventually teach the same lesson, is a necessary consequence of the meeting of truth, but it is seldom that this union is so satisfactorily displayed as in the researches of Political Economy' (May 1943, 14). The history of these early Christian political economists in Britain in the first generation of the nineteenth century is of importance for both the contemporary Christian engagement with economics and the history of economic ideas itself. For example, Malthus is arguably the founder of this Christian tradition in terms of modern economics, and was a major contributor to population studies (a key source of life expectancy trends) but also to developing the basic economic assumption of scarcity. He was a close friend and colleague of the economist Ricardo. John Bird Sumner was another contributor to early Christian political economy and, like Adam Smith, compared 'the poverty of many in more prosperous societies with the poverty of the majority in others' (Atherton 1992, 104), observing that the former operated on free-market principles, but, as importantly for this book, arguing for the significant positive contribution of inequalities to human wellbeing. Yet despite the problems of such poor societies, he also sought to demonstrate that 'political economy also reveals that the genuine evil associated with the inevitable outcome is remediable' (Waterman 1991, 170). Copleston and then Whately (who once occupied the Drummond Chair in Political Economy at Oxford and was a close friend of the economist Nassau Senior) also saw the significance of economics for Christianity. They both acknowledged its central role in modern life and the need 'to clarify the relationship between economics and Christianity' (Atherton 1992, 104–05). Whately did the latter by understanding the difference between economics as the study of means, and the study of ends as informed by moral and theological principles. This also provides an important point of connection with Sen's contemporary work on the two traditions of engineering and ethical economics. Sadly, these Christian political economists were often promoted to become bishops and stopped contributing to economics (the moral is, as I told my students, that if you want to carry on thinking about the world of daily life, don't become a bishop!). Their contribution to the economics–Christianity dialogue was an equivalent, in terms of serious value, of Ely's in the USA in the later nineteenth century of the Third Great Awakening.

Yet the age of voluntarism did not refer to the emergence of modern free market economies alone but also to the reinvigoration of civil society and religion, including their contribution to the pursuit of more progressive societies. The two, economic and civil society, were closely linked since the freedom that spawned entrepreneurs also promoted a vast array of organizations and societies, of what we would now call voluntary bodies constituting civil society. It was as though '[o]nly liberty and competition in both the political and economic realms – could accommodate the needs and nature of the self-willed individuals who formed civil society' (Appleby, Hunt and Jacob 1994, 122). As in America, these societies and organizations covered a vast range of interests and concerns, from the Church Missionary Society (1799) and the British and Foreign Bible Society (1804) to the Manchester Statistical Society (1833). The latter is still in existence, and in its earlier days generated the research to influence for the good the adoption of evidence-based public policies in fields like public health and education. The new Bishop of Manchester, David Walker, mathematician and contributor to ordinary and empirical theology, is a member today. These interests soon tapped into the aspirations and skills of the working classes, with their concern for improvement through self-help and thrift and their necessary inclinations to mutuality, eventually feeding into the cooperative movement and then the trade unions. These, in turn, were reinforced by religious movements, particularly Christian socialism and Methodism. They nurtured mutual support in times of frequent and dire need, and generated that self-confidence vital for survival, revival and growth in the deeply disruptive emerging urban societies. As schools of democracy for acquiring participative and governance skills (remember the seven features of the Christian model in Chapter 3), they also influenced the development of modern democracies in mass societies: 'In a market economy, dependent upon voluntary efforts, the cultural element is critical, because it is through explicit social values that people are given the personal ambition and essential knowledge to keep the system going', and, indeed, to transform it for the better (Appleby, Hunt and Jacob 1994, 120). By 1821, Lancashire had the highest proportion of friendly society members to total population, an astonishing 17 per cent. The Royton Temperance Society splendidly exemplifies them all. Founded in 1843, near Manchester, its membership was mostly restricted to young male cotton operatives 'who had taken the pledge of abstinence, refused to gamble and were of good character'. After only 20 years, they had produced 'five master cotton spinners, one clergyman, two managers of cotton mills in Russia ... [and] many others had attained respectable positions as managers, overlookers, head mechanics, certified school masters, or had become respectable shop keepers' (Hobsbawm 1962, 247).

It is through the strategic importance of such social values and practices stretching across these economic and voluntary activities that the continuing interaction between the secular age of voluntarism and the theological age of atonement occurs. This latter concept was particularly developed by the secular historian Boyd Hilton in his *The Age of Atonement* (1988). It was deeply informed by the rapid growth of evangelicalism through Methodism from the eighteenth century, and then in the Church of England, as in America it centred on the sin and conversion of the individual, regarding life on earth as a journey through a veil of tears to an eternal destiny, a testing place therefore for faith and conduct, and thereby producing characters imbued with what has become known as the Protestant work ethic. It was a clear, decisive, conviction faith with immense social as well as personal consequences. As in America, it was profoundly a 'religion of the heart', 'written in the feelings' (Hilton 1988, 8), through conversion and grace, believing in both the potential of the human as well as its depravity.

Again, as in America, the evangelical revival spread quickly, as did its influence on society, through transmission processes which Hilton refers to as 'permeation by filtration' (1988, 27). By 1850 it influenced a whole range of theological positions (for example, Prime Minister William Gladstone, who till his death kept a daily detailed diary 'accounting' for his time) certainly including a third of Church of England clergy, and 2 to 3 million out of an 8 million population. Wesleyan Methodists' membership in England particularly grew from 22,410 in 1767 to 77,402 in 1796 and 285,000 in 1851 (Gilbert 1976, 31).

This evangelical atonement-based gospel profoundly affected individuals but also society, even if sometimes unintentionally. It was a conversionist Christianity in theology and purposes, summarized as what God does *for us* through Christ's atoning death (Rom. 1.16–17), and then what God does *in us* as the fruits of the Spirit (Gal. 5.22–6). Its beliefs therefore centred on a strong conviction of the importance of the individual in its relationships with God, and therefore on responsibility for its life to God. So it began by recognizing that all are born and live in sin. William Wilberforce declared: 'We should not go too far if we were to assert that [the corruption of human nature] lies at the very root of all true Religion, and still more, that it is eminently the basis and ground-work of Christianity' (Vidler 1948, 39). It is from this that we are forgiven, but only through God's gracious gift of Christ's atoning death on the cross. From our acceptance of that flows those gifts of the Spirit, transforming our lives.

With such beliefs, evangelical Nonconformity engaged urban society with a vigour and effectiveness rarely since experienced other than in the growing churches of developing economies today. Using an itinerant non-professional ministry, often lay, preaching that simple gospel unencumbered by ancient buildings and separated from the established orderings of society, they generated a strong sense of religious community with a clear, distinct identity. Through leaders like Wilberforce, Venn and Simeon, and then John Bird Sumner – Bishop of Chester in 1828 (he consecrated St George's Church, Hulme, Manchester, where I became rector and was the last bishop to wear a wig!), and then Archbishop of Canterbury in 1848 (Scotland 1995) – it soon also made deep inroads into the established Church of England. In the latter, through the Clapham Sect, Christianity promoted often progressive policies but through a restrained and more measured evangelicalism, much like Jonathan Edwards in America, but more suited to constructive political engagement with the governing classes in England (Tomkins 2010). Wilberforce epitomized this through the campaign against the slave trade initially (leading to the 1807 Act), and then slavery itself (leading to the 1833 Act), again, strongly resonant with equivalent campaigns in America's Second Awakening. The anti-slavery movement, although it attracted a wide variety of supporters, represented the 'supreme example of the politics of atonement' providing public evangelicalism with its 'most potent raison d'etre' (Hilton 1988, 208). Yet it is important to note that even official Methodist, as well as the to be expected Church of England position, also underwrote government policies, including the repressive Poor Law, with mainstream Methodism adopting an 'apolitical and anti-radical approach' (Moore 1974, 12).

The personal experience of change as salvation intentionally and unintentionally promoted social change and reform across a wide spectrum of society. As Moore's study of Methodism and the Durham miners suggests, Weber's work ethic still encapsulates much of this complex interaction between evangelicalism and social change. On the one hand, religion's worldly asceticism reinforced connections between beliefs and economic and political activities. The development of a reformed spirituality influenced the whole of life (as we have seen in Chapter 3 from Roman Catholic, Evangelical, Muslim and Buddhist sources). This included, for converted Durham miners, leading a 'disciplined and planned life' of hard work, thrift, committed family life and abstinence from alcohol, gambling and violence (Moore 1974, 26, 118). Such lives clearly set the converted working class apart from the nasty, brutish and short way of living provoked and reinforced by awful industrial and urban conditions. On the other hand, Weber also points to the elective affinity between religion and other trends, for example, the deeply influential (for social, economic and political reform in the later nineteenth century implemented through legislation, and the growth of local government) relationship between Methodism and Liberalism in the later nineteenth century, but also between progressive forms of organization. So the power of the small Methodist classes informed the character of leaders and members within the churches, but also their transposable leadership skills which influenced the emerging trade union movement. As a disturbed Methodist preacher in the North-East, near to Jarrow and Bede's church, observed: 'if men are to be drilled at missionary and Bible meetings to face a multitude with recollection, and acquired facility of address, and begin to employ the mighty moral weapon thus gained to the endangering of the very existence of the Government of the country, we may certainly begin to tremble for the consequences' (Wearmouth 1937, 103)! Indeed, so successful was this Methodist organizational form that it was also adopted by major secular reform movements. So the Rochdale Chartist Conference of 1839 decided 'that the country should be formed into districts, and that the system of classes pursued by the Methodists should be adopted by the Chartists in every district' (Wearmouth 1937, 217). It's yet another example of the transmission processes, but in this case, of practices and not just values or beliefs.

To illustrate further these deep connections between atonement and voluntarism, a parable does this best, as it did in the nineteenth century. John Bird Sumner's biblical commentaries were written when he was Bishop of Chester (a diocese then including Liverpool and Manchester), as resources for clergy and lay visitors in their mission to promote a Bible-based family life. His reflection on the parable of the talents therefore illustrates well this deep interaction of atonement and voluntarism in its economic and civil society forms: 'And it is the nature of that state of moral trial in which we are placed on earth, that every man, in every rank, shall have the power to improve or abuse his talents of fortune, his talents of authority, his talents of grace, his talents of education' (Sumner 1838, 345). That is the age of atonement and voluntarism. Yet here's a story to show it's never so simple. I purchased for Manchester Cathedral an original copy of Sumner's *Practical Exposition of the Gospel of St Matthew and St Mark* from a bookshop in Ilkley in Yorkshire. Inside was written a dedication from a caring mother to her wealthy landowning son, exhorting him to read, mark and inwardly digest its contents. I found pages still stuck together, never slit open! He'd never read it!

The Second Age of the State and Incarnation (1850–1990)

A century of continuing, ever accelerating, extending and disturbing change from the later nineteenth to the later twentieth century inevitably transformed people's lives, communities and nation. Two stories, from events running through this chapter, illustrate such paradoxes of development in a most graphic way. At the beginning of this stage, two great drivers of the Industrial Revolution, dominant in two great regions of Britain, Bede's Durham and my Lancashire, coal and textiles respectively, were unchallenged kings. By the end of the stage, both industries had disappeared completely leaving behind them disturbing heritages, particularly in the North-East. And Christianity, in different forms and in different ways, made important contributions to affecting change for the better in both regions and nation.

Towards the end of the nineteenth century, the age of voluntarism in a dominant laissez-faire era began to wither away. The concentration of resources in bigger and bigger units was increasingly inimical to philosophies and policies of non-intervention in the free market. It was a period witnessing the arrival of great corporations and mass media, of explosive population increases concentrated in ever-expanding urban areas, all accompanied by struggles for democracy and labour movements. It witnessed the rise of collectivism and the consequent waning of individualism. There would be no going back to that earlier age of voluntarism, despite recent romantic protestations in Church and society. The age of the state, symbol of the new collectivism, made sure of that.

The maturing Industrial Revolution in Britain related to new capital intensive developments, which in turn, as in America, were expressed in the concentration of resources in ever larger production centres. This size issue was accompanied by Malthus's continuing geometrical increase in population, concentrated in great industrial cities and towns, often dominated by these large companies and industries, whether textiles in Dundee or chemicals in Widnes. There was a profound interaction between these expanding industries and urban populations, through the provision of mass markets and large scale consumerism. Department stores emerged in the later nineteenth century. Integrally part of these progressions was the arrival of mass cultures aided and abetted by technological innovations, like the mass press, radio and then television. An age of mass production, markets and populations was in turn linked to political trends, to universal suffrage, education and mass working class organizations. All combined to push governments into deeper social reforms and the management of economic affairs. Life from now on was about an increasingly wide electorate dominated by the common people. And it needed to be, because even in 1900, the year my uncle was born and died, as children did then, a large proportion of volunteers for the Boer War were rejected as unfit, 'a concern heightened by data that seemed to show that men who reached maturity about 1900 were shorter than those who had reached maturity at the time of the Crimean War in the mid 1850s'. Rowntree's great survey also revealed 27 per cent still living in deep poverty at that time (because they consumed insufficient calories to support physical efficiency) (Fogel 2000, 140). All these trends towards mass economies and societies reflected, for Dicey, the decisive if disturbing trend (and particularly for historically individual and small community focused Christianity) from individualism to an age of collectivism, a trend most strongly centred on the emergence of the modern state (Hobsbawm 1994, 54). Initially emerging as strong local government in the later nineteenth century, it developed increasingly also as central government in the twentieth, particularly driven by the two World Wars which 'multiplied the occasions when it became essential for governments to govern' (Hobsbawm 1994, 140). Growing proportions of the population became involved in such economic activity, covering more and more parts of life in dense complex urban societies. It was embodied initially in the town halls, municipal parks, libraries, housing and schools of the later nineteenth century. (When the great leader of the American social gospel, Walter Rauschenbusch, visited England he landed in Liverpool and found it awful, but went on to Birmingham and found it a municipal paradise in comparison, not least due to the great Liberal efforts of Chamberlain!). It was this local state's growing domination of more and more areas of life in advanced economies which epitomized best this transition from the age of voluntarism and free market. And the great town halls so splendidly epitomized this – in my home town of Bolton, but also in Rochdale and Manchester, all 'gigantic and monumental buildings whose purpose was to testify to the wealth and splendour of the age in general and the city in particular'. In 1858, the great Leeds Town Hall was built at the gigantic cost of £122,000, 1 per cent of the total British income tax yield (Hobsbawm 1975, 329). Less obvious, but more important, was the proportion of the work force employed through national and local government, rising threefold in Britain between 1891 and 1911.

These developments of a municipal-inspired and informed greater wellbeing were complemented, reinforced and greatly expanded by the growing importance of collective state provision for education, health and social security, embodied in Britain in the construction of a welfare, a faring well, a wellbeing state. They marked the clear transition from voluntarism, with the state taking over functions performed significantly but increasingly inadequately by churches and voluntary bodies in increasingly strategic fields for wellbeing in mass societies like education, welfare and health. The difference was that the state extended these supportive and interventionist measures to a degree undreamt of by voluntary philanthropy, providing cradle to grave support for citizens. And economies were also part of this transition from voluntarism and free market to more state activity. For the great economist, Keynes, faced by the Great Depression in the 1930s and its ruthless spotlighting of the inadequacies of much neoclassical economics, to find 'a way of saving capitalism from itself' meant essentially 'an economy managed and controlled by the state', which turned economics into 'mixed public/private economies' (Hobsbawm 1994, 333–4). Interestingly, another great economist, Sen, writing two generations later, and after another great economic crisis in 2008, questioned whether a 'genuine capitalism' actually exists, if by that is meant an economic system relying on 'markets for economic transactions' and depending on 'the profit motive and individual rewards based on private ownership'. On the contrary, he argues, most economies now depend partly on transactions and other payments that occur 'largely outside the markets'. These include state-provided welfare payments, education and health care, essentially 'economic entitlements' that are not based on private ownership and property rights, but rather on citizenship (Sen 2009). It's not as much from voluntarism, or free market, to state, but a transition which now centrally involves both. Yet to achieve that, this transition had to occur from voluntarism to state. So, for Landes, the new assumption is that 'the hand of the state is indispensable in good times as well as bad; that, indeed, only the state can assure continued economic growth in an atmosphere of social harmony; further that the economy, like any other aspect of national life, should serve the state rather than the reverse' (1969, 399).

Alongside and interacting with these developments as cause and effect, new developments emerged in Christian social practice and thought. This age of incarnation embodies the transition from the age of atonement, which regarded life on earth as a testing journey through a vale of tears to an eternal home, to now regarding life on earth as a calling to help transform God's good world for the better. In that process of change, the incarnate Christ was both model and means. In that process, Christian social reformers increasingly embraced the state as a principal means for achieving greater wellbeing thereby linking the age of state and incarnation.

In other words, by the 1850s, the more evangelical retributive version of society, linked to a more static Malthusian understanding of agriculture and trade, was visibly and tangibly losing ground to a more optimistic achieved and achievable economic growth. This was accompanied by growing concern for social reforms resourced by improvements in state machinery, revisions in law and progress in housing, industrial relations, work conditions, psychiatry and penology. It represented, and was also informed by, a change of mood including in 'religious sensibility' reflecting the transition to 'evolutionary gradualness and the rejection of apocalyptic change' (Hilton 1988, 263, 267, 274). It was a move from holding to Christ as saviour to Christ as enabling exemplar.

The process of such incarnational faith being embodied in society inevitably placed increasing emphasis on interpreting and engaging the signs of the times in and through contemporary contexts. Since they were increasingly recognized as essentially and profoundly changing contexts, faith itself was also transformed in and through promoting society's transformation for the better. These interactions between such faith and contexts, embedded in the acts of incarnation, were initially and most clearly expressed by F. D. Maurice, Anglican social thinker and reformer, in his recognition that such commitments involved a dual interacting process of Christianizing society and socializing Christianity (Norman 1987, 18, 31).

In terms of informing the reformulation of faith in the light of (and as a contribution to) that interaction, the work of Gore, strongly influenced by Maurice, in the collection of essays in *Lux Mundi: A Series of Studies in the Religion of the Incarnation* (1889) interpreted incarnational theology as liberal Catholicism using current developments in Darwinian evolutionary thinking, biblical and historical criticism, and T. H. Green's English philosophical idealism and his positive views of citizenship and state. It represented developments similar to the progressive orthodoxy of Gladden and Rauschenbusch in America's Third Great Awakening, though the latter made greater use of sociology and economics. Both movements focused on the reformulation of faith for and through more effective and progressive social change, and certainly not its erosion through an accommodation to this context.

The other side of the coin of this interactive incarnationism was the strategic intent of changing society for the better in order to realize further God's purposes in and for the world. Maurice, Kingsley and Ludlow's attempts from the mid nineteenth century to Christianize socialism through cooperatives (initially producer and then consumer), trade unions and pamphleteering, undoubtedly contributed, with movements like Primitive Methodism, to eroding the chasm between Christianity and socialism so destructively evident on the European Continent. That linking of Christianity and social reform continued throughout the nineteenth and into the early twentieth century, for example through the Christian Social Union (CSU), founded in 1889 by the promoters of the theology of *Lux Mundi*. The CSU was particularly involved in the campaign for a living wage and its promotion in legislation, including through the Trade Boards Act of 1909. Westcott, the great reforming biblical scholar, and subsequently Bishop of Durham, embodied this theological and reformist strand through his early leadership of the Christian Social Union and his mediation in the great miners' strike of 1892. For him,

Christ came 'to effect the perfection no less than the redemption of finite beings ... to bring a perfect unity of humanity without destroying the personality of any one man' (Hilton 1988, 335). It was a faith in the cooperation of men replacing the competition between them. Like the historian Seeley's emphasis in his influential *Ecce Homo* (1865) on Christ's humanity, it represented the transition from an apology for humankind to an 'enthusiasm for humanity', from evangelical atonement's morality as restraint to being an 'inspiring passion' (Hilton 1988, 334).

The socializing Church was also to play a central role in the age of incarnation, becoming a vehicle for God's transforming of the world. It therefore moved from being predominantly support for reaction to more agent of social change and betterment. It was a move from the 'squarson', the alliance of parson and squire, including parsons as repressive justices of the peace, to great campaigning socialist parsons like F. Donaldson, leading the great unemployed march to London in 1905 and arguing that 'Christianity is the religion of which socialism is the practice' (Bryant 1996, 115). In particular, it developed into a variety of Christian social reform and socialist groups (the former arguably the more effective), and came to dominate, as in America, the official Church's thinking and practising on and in social affairs, including after the Second World War through bodies like the Anglican Board for Social Responsibility (of which I was a member in the 1970 and 1980s) and the Roman Catholic Justice and Peace Commission, and through the great church reports like *Faith in the City* (1985; I was an advisor), *The Common Good* (1996) and *Unemployment and the Future of Work* (1998) in England, paralleling in the USA, for example, *Economic Justice for All* (1986), and all very influential for the better on public life. Thus had Maurice's strategy of socializing Christianity and the Church, as agents of social change, come to fruition. And this ecclesiological emphasis on sacramental living and social reform can also be linked to the growing embodiment of the churches, in England up to the 1950s, in local living in mass societies, as cradle to grave service, providing educational, leisure and social welfare facilities. In stable, dense urban communities surrounding mills, factories and mines, working class life was profoundly influenced by the Church's calendar, moving from Christmas through Lent to Easter, to Whit walks, Sunday school sermons, summer treats and camps, to harvest festivals; it was a rich social life, exemplifying the strong tangible intermingling of sacred and secular, of the world of daily life and religion.

In terms of Christian practices, ethics and beliefs, the Christian tradition's incarnational theology continued to have formative social consequences. At the heart of the tradition was belief in God's intervention in the world through the life, death and resurrection of Jesus Christ. Powerfully dependent on the Johannine tradition, it emphasized the incarnation as God reclaiming his own, as fundamental affirmation of the world, now embodied in the Trinity through the humanity of Christ. For example, when I was a young curate in Aberdeen in the early 1960s, the Mass always ended with the great incarnational Gospel reading from John 1.1–14, ending with: 'And the Word became flesh, and dwelt among us'. And then you went out and embodied that faith in rebuilding a centre for inner city youth, in Labour Party ward meetings and in CND demonstrations. But it was William Temple who produced the classic expression of this interpretation in his *Readings in St John's Gospel* (1961). Interestingly, these were formulated partly on a really densely crowded Blackpool beach, in the Manchester diocesan missions to working class folk who descended from places like my own town of Bolton on that great leisure facility every summer for the cotton town's 'Wakes Week holiday'. This Christ coming into his own, in and through the great working masses; the rise of the social welfare state as the means for transforming their lot for the better; and the age of incarnation and state – it's all there. And that latter obvious and tangible connecting of state and incarnation was again best represented by William Temple, fine exponent of incarnational theology, yet also the person who named the welfare state, epitome of the age of the state. His great little masterpiece *Christianity and Social Order* was published as a Penguin classic in 1942 (I have a first edition, published on cheap war economy paper costing sixpence – two and a half pence today – and advertising cigarettes!)

THE BRITISH CASE STUDY

and was often read alongside his good friend Beveridge's great report on the welfare state, the one underwriting the other, the ethics, religion and practice of greater wellbeing, the one therefore influencing the other in formation and practical implementation in society; two sides of the same coin. And there you have it; the age of incarnation and state.

The constructive interaction between Christianity and society was especially strong in extent and intensity from the late nineteenth to the early twentieth centuries, and the North-East of England, Bede's country, provides a particularly creative location in which to explore this interaction a little further. The Durham coalfield (the diocese of Durham then included the diocese of Newcastle, so covering the whole North-East of England), like Lancashire, also saw its population dramatically increase from 165,293 in 1811 to 1,479,033 by 1913, and its coal output from 2 million tons in 1810 to 41.5 million by 1913 (Lee 2007, 5). Christianity's engagement with such change was represented particularly by the Church of England and the Methodists, with the latter having by far the more significant and progressive impact. Yet despite all their efforts, the historic 1851 Religious Census indicated that 75 per cent of the population in their area attended neither Anglican or Methodist churches, nor indeed any other church (Lee 2007, 45–6). The efforts of the Church of England had at best a modest impact, thereby highlighting the much greater achievements of the Methodists. For most of the century, Anglicans struggled to shake off their early nineteenth-century involvement with, indeed complicity in, the land and mine-owning interests. By the 1840s, the Reverend John Allen recognized in a great understatement that 'the presence of a pitman or his family in the parish church is, in most colliery neighbourhoods, a somewhat unusual occurrence' (Lee 2007, 9). Indeed, the very mission of this church was often dependent on the money of the coal interests. Not surprisingly, therefore, 84 per cent of the Anglican clergy voted for Conservative Party candidates in the Parliamentary elections between 1832 and 1865 (Lee 2007, 123). Towards the end of the century, the leadership of Bishop Westcott and others began to change this Anglican contribution by recruiting candidates for the ordained ministry from the middle and working classes in the hope that they would establish a more positive relationship between churches and pit families, to offer 'the hope of a new era of connection and engagement' (Lee 2007, 80). Westcott embodied this concern to engage the world of daily life of the Durham coalfield (as his late twentieth successor, the fine Bishop David Jenkins, who recruited me into the William Temple Foundation, also did). His regular meetings with representatives of his area always included miners. Their leader John Wilson greatly welcomed the fact that Westcott 'sought on all occasions to make himself acquainted with our conditions', not least in mediating in the 1892 miners' strike (Lee 2007, 172). Yet, despite such efforts, the Church of England failed to attract miners to church; the parish of Usworth reported that even by 1912, it 'regularly saw just sixteen miners, out of a parish population of 8,000' in church (Lee 2007, 225). The Anglican Church simply 'did not have sufficient answers to the problems of everyday life' (Lee 2007, 286).

Why were the Primitive Methodists far more effective in engaging with and changing the Durham coalfield for the better? Because, unlike the Anglicans, they were 'involved in every aspect of working life and associational culture' (Lee 2007, 285). Building on its organizational strengths, its practices, ethics and beliefs, it generated remarkable contributions to trade unionism and politics. In terms of trade unions, the very secular Sidney Webb, founder of the Fabian Society and the London School of Economics (where I conducted my doctoral research on Webb's friend, R. H. Tawney), observed: 'it is the men who are Methodist and in Durham County especially, local preachers of the Primitive Methodists, whom we find taking the lead and filling the posts of influence. From their ranks have come an astonishingly large proportion of Trade Union leaders, from checkweighers and lodge chairmen up to County officials and committee men' (Wearmouth 1937, 227). The great contemporary historian Hobsbawm confirms this earlier judgement: 'among the northern miners ... Primitive Methodism was so closely identified with the trade unions as to become practically a labour religion' (quoted by Lee 2007, 136). If ever there was the most clear, robust, evidence-based illustration of the transmission of my Christianity's concern for wellbeing in and through the world of daily life, it was here in this region. For the Primitive Methodists' 'self-help communal structures ran against the grain of the ideology of paternalism, for it was a "true church *of* the people, not simply a middle class church *for* the people", more interested in actively campaigning for social legislation than in setting up charities or missions' (Lee 2007, 136). As one of its miners' leaders, Jack Lawson, described it: 'Among the Methodists, my growing tendencies were encouraged, stimulated, and given opportunity for development ... Every house was an "open house" ... We talked pit-work, ideas, the Bible, literature, or union business' (Lee 2007, 136).

Webb also rightly notes the political as well as the industrial influence of the Methodists. Moore's detailed study of Methodism in the Deerness pit valley near Durham reaches the conclusion, confirmed by historians Pelling and Martin, that Methodist involvement in progressive politics ensured that 'the cultural influence and the leadership of the Labour Movement have been more Liberal than Socialist due to their Methodist origin'. By 1875, the North-East miners were represented by two MPs; by 1894, Durham miners began to take control of local parish councils, then district councils; and, in 1919, chiefly as the Labour Party, they took control of the County Council (Moore 1974, 190, 146).

Wearmouth charts this Methodist contribution through 80 full-time trade union leaders, operating from the late nineteenth to the early twentieth century, in the North-East. They all owed their positions to their religious experiences, particularly as Primitive Methodists (whose origins in camp meetings in the early 1800s linked closely to such similar manifestations of resurgent religion in the First and Second Great Awakenings in America). Of the 80 leaders under consideration, 70 were Methodist (of which 46 were Primitive Methodists and 55 were local preachers). Twenty-nine of them began work at less than 12 years of age, representing a local Methodism which 'fashioned and moulded their character and conduct' (Wearmouth 1959, 38).

Peter Lee (1864–1935) particularly embodies this interaction between religion and progressive change, even a new town is named after him. Lee rose to be general secretary of the Durham Miners Association, with 100,000 miners as members, and then county councillor, after beginning work at ten years old. His Primitive Methodism gave him 'a passion for learning, for service, and for religion. They taught him to speak, to pray, and to preach, eventually entrusting him with the office of a local preacher' (Wearmouth 1959, 44). And I know the truth of these accounts of such processes of transmitting Christianity because my father was brought up in a Primitive Methodist family, was an active trade union official all his life, was a strong Labour Party supporter and passed on these concerns to me, centred on a deep religious enthusiasm for a progressive humanity. He passed the test for grammar school, was too poor to go and handed on successfully his determination to be educated to me, his only child.

Theology's involvement with economics was not as eventful! By 1900, in fitting with the interactions between incarnation and state, there had been a movement from regarding people as victims of economic conditions, from Burke's aphorism that 'the laws of commerce are the laws of nature and the laws of God', through F. D. Maurice's conviction that 'competition is put forth as a law of the universe. That is a lie ... I see no way but association for work' (Maurice 1884, 32), to commitments to conquer and regulate such economic conditions (1884, 32), including through government actions. In the later nineteenth century, out of the *Lux Mundi* and Christian Social Union tradition, Wilfrid Richmond combined Maurice's and Westcott's commitment to cooperation, but like Marshall, founder of modern neoclassical economics, his economics celebrated 'the marvellous growth in recent times of honesty and uprightness in commercial matters'. Of greater interest to this book's thesis, particularly with regard to the importance of income for material wellbeing, he argued in his *Christian Economics* (1888) that 'The enjoyment of wealth means ... the freedom of energy, a system of life in which all objects of desire fulfil their function in evoking energy, and in giving the pleasure which attends its exercise, in which the energies of all are called to their fullest extent' (Hilton 1988, 332). By the early 1900s, the original energies of Christian political economics had been transferred into the contribution of ethical economics through Marshall and then Keynes (both, but certainly the first, were examples of Gill's transposing of Christian values into the secular). Tawney's attempts to develop a community-oriented alternative to neoclassical welfare economics met with little success (Bateman and Banzhaf 2008, 212–13). Indeed, as the twentieth century unravelled, positive economics dominated the discipline, leading to the growing marginalization of ethical economics as well as religion.

Not surprisingly, the story from the Christian gospels most used by incarnationalists was the parable of the Good Samaritan (Luke 10.29–37), the great narrative of love in practice, of what it means to embody it in society. My father, as good trade unionist out of the Primitive Methodist tradition, interpreted and developed that parable true to this age of incarnation and state. From that story, he argued for state intervention in society, making the road from Jerusalem to Jericho safe for travellers, having a health service to bind up the wounds of those who fell by the wayside, being tough on crime but equally on the causes of crime through better and fairer management of the economy, full employment and the tackling of poverty, marginalization and inequality. It all fits, doesn't it?

A Third Age of Partnership and Reconciliation? 1980s–

As a generation of changes affecting all areas of life and on an increasingly global stage, the 1980s onwards was an era of turbulence and upheaval, like the 1780s and 1880s before it, and affecting both America and Britain. In the latter, these dates signalled a transition to the age of voluntarism and atonement, and then to state and incarnation. It is not therefore surprising that our generation's greatly changing context should communicate a similar strong sense of the ending of an age and the need to begin to discern any signs of its replacement in what is always a confusing overlapping period. Then the new age can be named and its implications for the changing context acknowledged. For the

American case study, the work done by McLoughlin and Fogel in terms of identifying recurring stages in each awakening cycle made the attempts to begin to discern and then analyse what they describe as a Fourth Great Awakening more feasible. Yet both scholars undertook such a task with some hesitancy, not least, indeed particularly, because they were clearly still in the early stages of what might become more obviously a Fourth Awakening, a transition judged more effectively from the perspective of a succeeding generation. The task of tracing the emergence of a possible third age in the British example is far more difficult and for a variety of reasons distinctive to the British study. For example, the lack, as yet, of recurring stages in an age removes the value of being able to locate an age in such a feasible identifiable process. The transition from age to age, for example from the first to the second in the mid to late nineteenth century, was perceptively described as formative change of *mood*, suggested and substantiated as it was from a wide variety of political, economic, social and religious sources. That 'slippery' concept may be matched by contemporary Christian missiological understandings of 'liquid' and 'messy' church (groups often meeting in secular spaces using mixtures of more informal play, food and drink, and incorporating such features of my seven features of Christianity as singing, readings and networking) (Ward 2002). It is present too in the contemporary philosophy of religion, pastoral theology and public theology, and their deployment of 'blurred encounters' as the focus of fuzzy understandings which cross boundaries or spectrums (Reader 2005). These indicate, somewhat hesitantly, possible mood changes but also confusions, lacking as yet, a generally recognized strong and identifiable embodiment in recurring practices across a variety of groups and engagements.

My earlier work on this case study, in 2000 and 2011, came to a very provisional conclusion, describing a possible Third Age as maybe one of Partnership and Reconciliation. I am now even more cautious, questioning whether the very limited and very early evidence was sufficiently robust to allow such a description to be used with any serious confidence. By working from that material, and using further more recent evidence, possible hints of the likely contours of such a new age may be emerging which warrant further exploration – particularly in this and the next generation. These possible changes include changes in context and religious life, evolving (reformulated) models of Christian and other faiths' involvements in such change in partnerships with government and other sectors, the fruitfulness of the relationship between religion and capital, the growth of religious involvement in interdisciplinary studies of wellbeing, and finally openings in relationships between Christianity and economics.

The context continues to evolve and change with often predictable accompanying turbulences from the painful re-emergence of a more market-oriented economy and society in the 1980s and 1990s to the 2007–08 financial crisis and following deep recession in the West. The latter reinforced the renewed importance both of state oversight of, and involvement in, economic activities, and of the continuing search for and necessity of an associated viable ethical economics. It also further exacerbated the existing trend of the slowdown in economic growth from the 1970s and the consequent squeeze on incomes and standards of living for most people, and particularly for the poorest in society, all in ever stark contrast to the greatly increasing wealth of a small elite. This growth of grave inequalities returned Britain to the earlier part of the twentieth century in terms of such unequal distributions of income, wealth and opportunities. The young unemployed have paid a particularly heavy price in the recent damaging changes, creating the possibility of a lost generation if not addressed quickly. The signs of a return to modest growth in 2014 in the West may begin to alleviate some of these negative wellbeing conditions. All these changes are occurring in an increasingly plural society, including in religious life (Hunter 2010, 200–10).

Interacting with this turbulent generation of changes is the re-emergence and reformulating of religious contributions to such change. These include, as in the American awakenings, resurgent religion, now increasingly also on a global scale. Although this has certainly impacted on Britain, with the growing importance, in size and impact, of evangelical, Pentecostal and Black-led churches, it has also been accompanied by declining mainstream and more liberal churches. And by decline I mean decline! Attendances in the Church of England fell by 50 per cent between 1960 and 1985 (Hastings 1986, 603). In my own diocese of Manchester, at the heart of historic industrialization and urbanization processes, church attendances dropped by two-thirds in 30 years. Between 1960 and 1994, baptisms fell from 19,423 to 6,000, Easter Day communicants fell from 92,450 to 36,600 and confirmations from 10,571 to 1,836 (Atherton 1997, 58). Yet, as Davie observes, changes in religious landscapes are also more complex, subtle and more potentially significant, if linked, as in previous ages and awakenings, to contextual changes (Davie 1994). The picture painted from research material generated by the AHRC/ESRC Religion and Society programme, overseen by the splendid Linda Woodhead, indicates a 'broad and changing British religious landscape of the postwar decades, from new Christian forms and the settling of Islam, Hinduism and other religions in British society to new public ritualizations and the spiritualities in youth culture and popular music' (Woodhead and Catto 2012). Yet, although it can be argued that American religion is more successful because it operates competitively in a free market without an established church (Davie 2002), the British model suggests that churches and religion have and do inform the public realm in equally powerful, if different, ways.

A brief review of religion's current involvement in aspects of progressive social change suggests a growing recognition by government both of their value for greater social wellbeing, and of collaborative partnership ways of working. For example, the then Prime Minister Blair observed in 2001 that faith groups play 'a fundamental role in supporting and propagating values which bind us together as a nation ... [including developing] some of the most effective voluntary and community organizations in the country' (Baker 2007, 63). Research by the North West Regional Development Agency reinforced that judgement by costing the actual contributions of faith groups to its region. It concluded that they contributed between £90.7 million and £94.9 million worth of voluntary action each year, not including their major contributions to the education of children, students and adults.

Importantly, much of this work was self-funded: 73 per cent of respondents said they received no government funding (NWRDA 2005, 3).

These faith contributions to society, including in partnerships with others, also reflect a growing recognition of the importance of civil society for human wellbeing. For the Italian economist Zamagni, an advisor to the papacy on economic affairs, a long-term rebalancing may be occurring, from the dominance of market as exchange of equivalents and the state as commitments to equity, to also include civil society as promoter of reciprocity (Bruni and Zamagni 2007, 19). Fogel similarly recognizes the growing importance of both resources and time for leisure, strongly including what he calls 'volwork', lying at the heart of civil society organization and endeavours, and important source of wellbeing through giving and volunteering (Fogel 2004, 38). It is here that there's a growing convergence between resurgent and mainstream Christianity, whether evangelical and Pentecostal or Roman Catholic and Protestant denominations. These findings, more carefully and rigorously researched, offer a different perspective on what the present British coalition government initially (now essentially dropped off the main agenda) referred to as the 'Big Society', with its strong theological support from Radical Orthodoxy's Phillip Blond and John Milbank (the former wrote *Red Tory: How Left and Right Have Broken Britain and How We Can Fix It* (2010) and is also leader of the think-tank Respublica). The convergences between what they and others promote as Blue Labour and Red Tory led them to argue for an 'Anglican polity and the politics of the common good', and for 'rebuilding Britain's institutional fabric: the transformative role of the Church of England' (two recent interesting articles in the journal *Crucible: Jan–March 2014*, a national journal of Christian social ethics, which I edit). This, they could argue, is a Third Age equivalent of the social engagements in social reform and wellbeing of the Anglican and Primitive Methodists of the previous two ages. Beginning with traditional church volunteering and giving, they then widen its brief greatly, to include, for example, engaging personal and household debt, and unjust wages and unfair prices. Their recognition of traditional church involvement in volunteering and giving is already well researched, as we have already noted. The related claim of the new Archbishop of Canterbury, Justin Welby, that he and the churches would drive the payday loan company Wonga out of business by using the 16,000 local churches to 'build an alternative banking network by supporting the growth of credit unions' (*Crucible* 2014, 12) is both admirable in its prophetic hyperbole, and probably hare-brained in its understanding of the capacity of churches for such sophisticated economic activity. I did a survey in the first years of this twenty-first century, in Manchester. Defining churches facing acute difficulties as those with a Sunday attendance of fewer than 25 persons, and those with an electoral (membership) roll of less than 51, 42 churches met one or both criteria (Atherton 2003, 100–1). Their capacity is restricted to doing nothing much more than surviving, with sometimes occasional contributions made to local life. That urban picture is confirmed by a colleague, parish priest of eight pre-seventeenth-century churches in wealthy rural Oxfordshire, stuffed with skilled influential people. He struggles to get churchwardens, secretaries and treasurers for the churches, never mind providing complex contemporary financial and social services.

Another, and I think more fruitful, avenue to pursue is to trace, reinforce and enlarge the connections between religious and human capital. There is growing research-based recognition of human capital's increasing importance, in quality and extent, in economic and technological activities. This begins to interact powerfully with current British research, as I have already noted, on religious and spiritual capital's significance for human well-being. These represent both the distinctive added value of religious contributions to society and their robust transmission processes.

In terms of Christian involvements in and contributions to multidisciplinary and interdisciplinary work, both increasingly essential for analysing and engaging practically the increasingly complex worlds of the Industrial and Mortality Revolutions, there is important evidence of such partnership working in both practice and theories. The theologian Luke Bretherton, now in the USA, talks out of experience with church involvement in local coalitions of political and community action in the East End of London and its interaction with the financial hub of Canary Wharf, including successful campaigns for a living wage for local service workers in these economic hubs. He notes a shift from a service 'to' and 'for' model of social action, to a model of service 'with' a range of partners – and the 'with' models 'involve all parties with an interest in the common life of the community or institution' (Noyes and Julian 2014, 23). On the theory aspect of partnership working, so strongly evident in secular interdisciplinary working in economics' engagement with psychology and other related disciplines in both health and subjective wellbeing studies, there are important even if only early signs of religious involvement in such studies, particularly in wellbeing, in both the USA and Britain, as I have illustrated. The holding together of such a variety of disciplines, experiences and interests for the promotion of greater human wellbeing is often both messy and creative. Try getting different disciplines to work together, as Easterlin, the economist, recognized: 'We are left, then, with this basic dilemma. When one looks at the world's problems, the trend in needs is toward multidisciplinary scholars. But the trend in supply is toward disciplinary specialists. Whether this worrisome gap can be bridged remains an open question' (Easterlin 2004, 249). Yet that gap has to be bridged, in theory and in practice, for the sake of human wellbeing. Trying to hold together such often profound differences is the subject matter of what Christians describe as reconciliation, its necessity, its costs and its prize. I know that because as I write the first draft of this book, I'm nearing Holy Week in 2014, moving from cross to resurrection experiences, of those greater Christian beliefs and narratives which clarify and lend depth 'to the moral insights which are based upon common human experiences' (Grenholm 1993, 313).

These collaborations lead naturally into a brief reflection on the relationship between Christianity and economics in an Age of Partnerships and Reconciliations. The growing body of interdisciplinary research into wellbeing has provided much of the basis for my Christian model for engaging the three perspectives of income, health but particularly subjective wellbeing, on the wealth, wellbeing and inequalities of nations. It is both dependent on such research but then feeds back into it. And it is but a modest representative of the work of other Christian theologians in this same wellbeing field. Most importantly, they may also be a sign of major ongoing change in economics, paralleling and enabling those in religious studies. The economist Beccatini observes: 'I could be making a mistake, naturally, but if I don't go wrong, a paradigmatic revolution is being prepared at the present time quietly, marginally, almost clandestinely, in economic studies' (Bruni and Zamagni 2007, 233). I have traced and deployed some of these changes in economics and related disciplines, particularly in wellbeing research. I have also observed the recent reaffirmation of Sen's ethical economics in economic theory and practice, which, as Bateman and Banzhaf note in their report of a research project on the historical relationships between Christianity and economics from the eighteenth century to the present, 'may actually make this an unusual moment for the history of economic thought' (Bateman and Banzhaf 2008, 339). For my model deploying Christianity as practices, ethics and beliefs or theories, these provide an obvious and tested field for future cooperation between the two disciplines and practices. It may mean, for this Third Age, a movement beyond the great gulf between Christianity and economics to one of an alliance between them for the promotion of greater human wellbeing. This reflects what Waterman's work on British political economy in the First Age suggested with reference to the relationship between natural theology and science in the eighteenth century as allowing 'the natural sciences to be recruited as allies, not subjects of theology' (Waterman 2004, 108). Alliances for progressive change in the twenty-first century are surely representative of partnerships and reconciliations.

Afterword

On Living in More Than One Place at Once

Journeying through the continuing story of the Industrial and Mortality Revolutions generates two contrasting emotions, two sides of the one coin. Their achievements are extraordinary mostly in themselves but also when contrasted with life before 1800. To increase the average income eightfold for the world's inhabitants in only 172 years (1820–1992) gave people the resources to be and to do, freed from the ever present threats of absolute poverty. For that is also what happened when we take into account that even in only 27 years (1981–2008) 700 million people were released from poverty. The results of the Mortality Revolution were maybe of even greater historic significance for human wellbeing. In America, life expectancy increased from a meagre 47 in 1900, with 20 per cent dying before the age of one, to 77 in 2008. My little uncle, John Robert Atherton, was one of those who died before his first birthday in 1900. I am now 75. Wellbeing cannot but profit from the near doubling of life year chances to be and to do, to pursue one's own self-chosen purposes. I am left with a great sense of eucharistic awe when faced by such achievements.

But then there always comes the deep awareness of the paradox of such development, always also present throughout long history, say from the end of the last Ice Age around 14,000 years ago, but starkly evident in the post-1800 changes, and summarized in the massive inequalities between and within nations. It really is astonishing to see that the world's wealthiest nation is now 256 times richer than the poorest, that in terms of people's height (such a key indicator of nourishment and health adequacies), the impressive growth in Europeans' height from 166 cm to 178 cm in only 130 years (1850–1980) contrasts so starkly with the 151 cm in height of Indians, and that it could take an astounding 200 years for Indian men to catch up with where we Englishmen are now. That fills me with great sadness and sense of shame.

That response to the paradox of development is only compounded by possibly the greatest threat of all resulting from such economic and population growth, one of my five great horsemen of the apocalypse, climate change, so deeply associated with the other horsemen of famine, disease, migration and state failure. In the last 650,000 years, carbon dioxide never reached 300 parts per million (ppm) molecules of air until 1958. By 2010 it was 393 ppm, and, if left unchecked, it will reach 550 ppm by 2050, higher than for 24 million years (Morris 2011, 599). The effects could be irreversible and catastrophic.

Describing, measuring and analysing such changes in human wellbeing is now a profoundly interdisciplinary exercise. For the economist Easterlin, the world's greatest problems are not the problems of any one discipline alone, with their often very protective walls, whether say economics or psychology. Rather, the solutions to today's problems 'recognize multidisciplinary training and research' (Easterlin 2004, 249) using a variety of relevant and related disciplines. Given the impressive performance of religion in promoting greater subjective wellbeing, religion too becomes a partner in such cross-disciplinary studies. But such a religious studies must increasingly move beyond any thought of living 'entirely within a religious grammar'. For the tasks of theology and sociology, psychology and economics 'are united in at least as much as they address the human condition in exploratory and interpretative terms'. All these disciplines, and certainly including religious studies, must therefore 'be concerned in their distinctive ways with life and with how things are, with the world of daily life' (Gill 2012a, 49, 219) and that's about them all 'living in more than one place at once' (Clements 2013), about being able to see things from another perspective as well as from one's own. Interestingly, that profoundly accurate understanding of the human and its better workings comes from a well-researched

AFTERWORD

study of the ecumenical movement, of the historic struggle to bring together very different and frequently warring (literally say through the devastating seventeenth-century Wars of Religion) Christian denominations into the shared space of the World Council of Churches. That journey was the recognition that it was no longer sufficient to be and to have through pursuing one's own self-chosen purposes (Marcel 1949). The task was now also to be profoundly relational, to also 'belong to another outside of ourselves' (Clements 2013, 201). It's what Adam Smith regarded as central to any adequate *Theory of Moral Sentiments*, to put one's self into the other's shoes, to see any problem also from the other's perspective as well as from one's own, to always include in one's judgements, whether personal or corporate, the views of the impartial spectator. And putting the different perspectives together was about 'higgling', Smith's glorious concept (a bit like 'happifying' in the American case study) to describe the actual messiness involved in negotiating prices, in trying to hold together the very different interests involved, in contrast to the efforts of aloof, tidy economic theory (Phillipson 2011, 219).

'Living in more than one place at once' must therefore inform agendas for an emerging religious studies for the twenty-first century, including with relevance for other disciplines. Necessary developments in religious studies illustrate this shared agenda in a number of ways. For example, it involves understanding and appreciating the contributions of different religions in their own terms. It requires accepting the reality and value of a religious pluralism. Interestingly, the Christian laity, with their ordinary theology and church are often much better at this than their clerical leaders. Putnam's survey of contemporary religiosity in America revealed 88 per cent of Christian laity saying heaven was not reserved for their particular faith alone, therefore accepting the legitimate claims of other beliefs and even of the non-religious. In contrast, 60 per cent of Protestant clergy were very clear that heaven was attainable through faith in Jesus Christ alone, and therefore through no other way (Putnam and Campbell 2010, 538).

'Living in more than one place at once' is about living in one religious tradition or discipline and being prepared also to live in another religious tradition or discipline. Yet it is not about being lost or absorbed by the other. For Fingarette, we should be a 'sensitive and seasoned traveller, at ease in many places, but one must have a home' (Bellah 2011, 605). Religious studies is about exploring religion from a variety of perspectives and disciplines, secular as well as religious. Yet it necessarily and indeed essentially also involves the irreplaceable perspectives drawn from living within a particular religious or secular tradition. William James, so foundational for any adequate evidence-based religious studies, knew this and felt it. He realized the importance of the profound religious experiences seen from the inside and so strongly evidenced in the conversion accounts from the American great awakenings, even though he had not himself, as he sorrowfully admitted, experienced one. For him, '[m]y personal position is simple. I have no living sense of communion with God. I envy those who have, for I know that the addition of such a sense would help me greatly' (James 1985, xxiv).

That way of working and seeing things from different vantage points, for Clements, drawing from his reflections on the ecumenical movement, expresses this as a kind of 'double vision', as 'seeing the social world from *there* as well as *here*' (Clements 2013, 195). It's about inhabiting and then bringing together the differences of scientific and traditional history, of a monovision with the brain combining the close detailed work of the reading eye with the longer view of the distance eye. It's about examining aggregates and long-term trends, and yet seeing these essential facts on the particular faces of people at particular times and places.

Of course, 'living in more than one place at once' deeply informs much of religious studies' historic and contemporary engagement with economics. Many theologians today have never seriously entered into the other world of economics, preferring the pontifical statements issued from the safety of their own restricted view of Christianity. Yet it can be done. It must be done, because it has been done. Over 100 years ago, Ely illustrated how the development of a more historically and empirically sensitive economics could be achieved, including through learning from developments

AFTERWORD

in historical and evidence-based religious history, practices, ethics and beliefs. In today's world, the engagement of economics in wellbeing studies illustrates the potential for the reformulating of economic traditions. There are early signs of similar developments in a religious studies also engaged in wellbeing studies. That shared interest in and commitment to understanding better and then promoting greater human wellbeing therefore provides a real opportunity for constructive engagements between these two traditions of Christianity and economics for their mutual benefit. The work on a Christian model for doing this as described in this book illustrates the feasibility of that task. And why? Because it's about being in more than one place at once.

Such living in more than one place at once particularly informs the foundations of Christian beliefs, those energizing forces of spiritual capital behind so much of the effectiveness of its transmission processes, seen, for example, in the British case study's successfully interacting an age of incarnation with an age of the state. In the great prologue to John's Gospel, at the heart of the incarnation story, is the proclamation that 'the Word became flesh ... and lived among us' (John 1.15). For this *living* among us, this living in more than one place at once, literally means 'pitched his tent' among us in the way God dwelt among the Israelites 'in the tent of the tabernacle in the wilderness', as sharing in or living in 'the conditions of skin-thin tented life and human vulnerability' (Exod. 25.30) (Clements 2013, 212). And such Christ-like godly living in more than one place at once therefore means, for Christians, that they too, through faith, share in that energizing double residency. This is described most beautifully in the Collect for the First Sunday of Christmas where we pray 'grant that, as he came to share in our humanity, so we may share the life of his divinity'. It is about Christian beliefs and stories giving greater depth and meaning to the ordinary, necessary and hopefully increasing collaboration between disciplines, traditions and practical partners for the pursuit of greater human wellbeing.

Bibliography

Allen, R., 2009, *The British Industrial Revolution in Global Perspective*, Cambridge: Cambridge University Press.
Alkire, S., 2005, *Valuing Freedoms: Sen's Capability Approach and Poverty Reduction*, Oxford: Oxford University Press.
Appleby, J., Hunt, L. and Jacob, M., 1994, *Telling the Truth about History*, New York: W. W. Norton.
Arrighi, G., 1994, *The Long Twentieth Century: Money, Power and the Origins of our Times*, London: Verso.
Arrow, K., 1963, 'Uncertainty and the Welfare Economics of Medical Care', *The American Economic Review* 53, no. 5 (December), pp. 941–73.
Astley, J. and Francis, L., 2013, *Exploring Ordinary Theology: Everyday Christian Believing and the Church*, Farnham: Ashgate.
Atherton, J., 1979, 'R. H. Tawney as a Christian Social Moralist', Manchester, PhD thesis (unpublished).
Atherton, J., 1983, *The Scandal of Poverty: Priorities for the Emerging Church*, London: Mowbray.
Atherton, J., 1988, *Faith in the Nation: A Christian Vision for Britain*, London: SPCK.
Atherton, J., 1992, *Christianity and the Market: Christian Social Thought for our Times*, London: SPCK.
Atherton, J., 1997, 'Church and Society in the North West 1760–1997', in C. Ford, M. Powell and T. Wyke (eds), *The Church in Cottonopolis: Essays to Mark the 150th Anniversary of the Diocese of Manchester*, Manchester: Lancashire & Cheshire Antiquarian Society, pp. 32–71.
Atherton, J., 2000, *Public Theology for Changing Times*, London: SPCK.
Atherton, J., 2003, *Marginalization*, London: SCM Press.
Atherton, J., 2010, 'Developing the Tradition of Ethical Economics and the Contribution of Christian Social Ethics', in E. Namli, P. Sundman and S. Yngvesson, *Etiska Undersokningar: Om samhallsmoral, etisk teori och teologi*, Uppsala: Uppsala University Press, pp. 153–68.
Atherton, J., 2011, 'Public Mission for Changing Times: Models for Progressive Change from American and British Experience', *International Journal of Public Theology* 5, pp. 410–34.

BIBLIOGRAPHY

Atherton, J., Baker, C. and Reader, J., 2011, *Christianity and the New Social Order: A Manifesto for a Fairer Future*, London: SPCK.

Atherton, J., Graham, E. and Steedman, I. (eds), 2011, *The Practices of Happiness: Political Economy, Religion and Wellbeing*, Abingdon: Routledge.

Baker, C., 2007, *The Hybrid Church in the City: Third Space Thinking*, Aldershot: Ashgate.

Baker, C., 2013, 'Moral Freighting and Civic Engagement: A UK Perspective on Putnam and Campbell's Theory of Religious-Based Social Action', *Sociology of Religion: A Quarterly Review* 74, no. 3, pp. 343–69.

Baker, C. and Skinner, H., 2006, *Faith in Action: The Dynamic Connection between Religious and Spiritual Capital*, Manchester: William Temple Foundation.

Bateman, B. and Banzhaf, S. (eds), 2008, *Keeping Faith, Losing Faith: Religious Belief and Political Economy*, Durham, NC: Duke University Press.

Bede, 1994, *The Ecclesiastical History of the English People*, Oxford: Oxford University Press.

Bellah, R., 2011, *Religion in Human Evolution from the Paleolithic to the Axial Age*, Cambridge, MA: Harvard University Press.

Blond, P., 2010, *Red Tory: How Left and Right Have Broken Britain and How We Can Fix It*, London: Faber and Faber.

Bonhoeffer, D., 1995, *Ethics*, trans. and ed. N. Smith, London: SCM Press.

Brown, M., 2004, *After the Market: Economics, Moral Agreement and the Churches' Mission*, Bern: Peter Lang.

Browning, D., 'Human Dignity, Human Complexity and Human Goods', in R. Soulen and L. Woodhead (eds), 2006, *God and Human Dignity*, Grand Rapids, MI: Eerdmans, pp. 299–316.

Bruni, L. and Zamagni, S., 2007, *Civil Economy: Efficiency, Equity, Public Happiness*, Bern: Peter Lang.

Bryant, C., 1996, *Possible Dreams: A Personal History of the British Christian Socialists*, London: Hodder and Stoughton.

Cairns, D., 1973, *The Image of God in Man*, London: Collins.

Charry, E., 2010, *God and the Art of Happiness*, Grand Rapids, MI: Wm. B. Eerdmans.

Charry, E., 2012a, 'The Necessity of Divine Happiness. A Response from Systematic Theology', in B. Strawn (ed.), *The Bible and the Pursuit of Happiness*, Oxford: Oxford University Press, pp. 229–48.

Charry, E., 2012b, 'Loving Near – Loving Far: Augustine's Psychology of Monovision', *Augustinian Studies 43:1–2*, pp. 89–107.

Charry, E., 2013a, 'Positive Theology: Doctrine as a Guide for the Emotions', Paper 1.

Charry, E., 2013b, 'Positive theology: Virtues, Emotions and a Flourishing Life'. Concordia College USA, Paper 2.

Clark, G., 2007, *A Farewell to Alms: A Brief Economic History of the World*, Princeton: Princeton University Press.

Clements, K., 2013, *Ecumenical Dynamic: Living in More Than One Place at Once*, Geneva: WCC Publications.

Cocks, H., 1943, *The Nonconformist Conscience*, London: Independent Press.

Cooper, N., 2014, 'Restoring Welfare: Renewing the Safety Net in an Age of Food Poverty and Hunger', *Crucible* July–September 2014, pp. 8–16.

Crucible, 2014, 'Deep Purple? Post-Liberalism and the Churches', *Crucible*, January–March 2014.

Dalai Lama and Cutler, H., 1999, *The Art of Happiness: A Handbook for Living*, London: Hodder and Stoughton.

Daly, H. and Cobb, J., 1990, *For the Common Good: Redirecting the Economy towards Community, the Environment and a Sustainable Future*, London: Merlin Press.

Dasgupta, P., 2007, *Economics: A Very Short Introduction*, Oxford: Oxford University Press.

Davie, G., 1994, *Religion in Britain since 1945*, Oxford: Blackwell.

Davie, G., 2002, *Europe: The Exceptional Case: Parameters of Faith in the Modern World*, London: Darton, Longman and Todd.

Davie, G., 2007, *The Sociology of Religion*, London: Sage.

Deaton, A., 2013, *The Great Escape: Health, Wealth and the Origins of Inequality*, Princeton: Princeton University Press.

Diamond, J., 1997, *Guns, Germs, and Steel: A Short History of Everybody for the Last 13,000 Years*, London: Vintage.

Diener, E. and Biswas-Diener, R., 2008, *Happiness: Unlocking the Mysteries of Psychological Wealth*, Oxford: Blackwell.

Easterlin, R., 1974, 'Does Economic Growth Improve the Human Lot?', in P. David and M. Reder (eds), *Nations and Households in Economic Growth: Essays in Honor of Moses Abramovitz*, New York: Academic Press Inc.

Easterlin, R., 2004, *The Reluctant Economist: Perspectives on Economics, Economic History and Demography*, Cambridge: Cambridge University Press.

Easterlin, R., 2010, *Happiness, Growth, and the Life Cycle*, edited by H. Hinte and K. F. Zimmermann, Oxford: Oxford University Press.

Engels, F., 1969 edition, *The Condition of the Working Class in England*, London: Panther.

Faith in the City. A Call for Action by Church and Nation. The Report of the Archbishop of Canterbury's Commission on Urban Priority Areas, 1985, London: Church House Publishing.

Ferguson, N., 2011, *Civilization: The West and the Rest*, London: Allen Lane.

Fogel, R., 1997, 'Economic and Social Structure for an Aging Population', *Philosophical Transactions of the Royal Society of London* 352, pp. 1905–17.

BIBLIOGRAPHY

Fogel, R., 2000, *The Fourth Great Awakening and the Future of Egalitarianism*, Chicago: University of Chicago Press.

Fogel, R., 2004, *The Escape From Hunger and Premature Death, 1700–2100: Europe, America, and the Third World*, Cambridge: Cambridge University Press.

Fogel, R. and Elton, G., 1983, *Which Road to the Past? Two Views of History*, New Haven, CT: Yale University Press.

Fogel, R. and Engerman, S., 1974, *Time on the Cross*, 2 volumes, Boston: Little, Brown.

Forrester, D., 1997, *Christian Justice and Public Policy*, Cambridge: Cambridge University Press.

Francis, L., 2011, 'Religion and Happiness: Perspectives from the Psychology of Religion, Positive Psychology and Empirical Theology', in J. Atherton, E. Graham and I. Steedman (eds), 2011, *The Practices of Happiness: Political Economy, Religion and Wellbeing*, Abingdon: Routledge, pp. 113–24.

Frey, D., 2009, *America's Economic Moralists: A History of Rival Ethics and Economics*, Albany, NY: State University of New York Press.

Friedman, M., 1953, *Essays in Positive Economics*, Chicago: University of Chicago Press.

Gilbert, A., 1976, *Religion and Society in Industrial England*, London: Longman.

Gill, R., 2012a, *Theology in a Social Context, Sociological Theology Volume 1*, Farnham: Ashgate.

Gill, R., 2012b, *Theology Shaped by Society, Sociological Theology Volume 2*, Farnham: Ashgate.

Gill, R., 2013, *Society Shaped by Theology, Sociological Theology Volume 3*, Farnham: Ashgate.

Gore, C. (ed.), 1889, *Lux Mundi: A Series of Studies in the Religion of the Incarnation*, London: Murray.

Graham, C., 2009, *Happiness around the World: The Paradox of Happy Peasants and Miserable Millionaires*, Oxford: Oxford University Press.

Graham, C., 2011, *The Pursuit of Happiness: An Economy of Well-Being*, Washington, DC: Brookings Institution.

Graham, E., 2013, *Between a Rock and a Hard Place: Public Theology in a Post-Secular Age*, London: SCM Press.

Grenholm, Carl-Henric, 1993, *Protestant Work Ethics: A Study of Work Ethical Theories in Contemporary Protestant Theology*, Uppsala: Uppsala University Press.

Goudzwaard, B., 1997, *Capitalism and Progress: A Diagnosis of Western Society*, Carlisle: Paternoster Press.

Habermas, J., 2010, 'An Awareness of What is Missing', in J. Habermas et al., *An Awareness of What is Missing: Faith and Reason in a Post-Secular Age*, Cambridge: Polity, pp. 15–23.

Haidt, J., 2001, 'The Emotional Dog and Its Rational Tail: A Social Intuitionist Approach to Moral Judgement', *Psychological Review* 108, pp. 814–34.
Haidt, J., 2006, *The Happiness Hypothesis: Putting Ancient Wisdom and Philosophy to the Test of Modern Science*, London: William Heinemann.
Hastings, Adrian, 1986, *A History of English Christianity: 1920–1985*, London: Collins.
Hicks, D., 2000, *Inequality and Christian Ethics*, Cambridge: Cambridge University Press.
Hilton, B., 1988, *The Age of Atonement: The Influence of Evangelicalism on Social and Economic Thought, 1785–1865*, Oxford: Clarendon.
Hitchens, C., 2007, *God Is Not Great: How Religion Poisons Everything*, New York: Twelve Hatchette Book Group.
Hobsbawm, E., 1962, *The Age of Revolution: Europe 1789–1848*, London: Weidenfeld and Nicolson.
Hobsbawm, E., 1975, *The Age of Capital: 1848–1875*, London: Weidenfeld and Nicolson.
Hobsbawm, E., 1994, *The Age of Empire, 1875–1914*, London: Abacus.
Hoogen, J. van den, and Lear, E. van de (eds), 2001, *Rationality in Ethics and Economics: A Sceptical Approach*, Maastricht: Shaker Publishing.
Hopkins, C., 1940, *The Rise of the Social Gospel in American Protestantism, 1865–1915*, New Haven, CT: Yale University Press.
Hunter, J., 2010, *To Change the World: The Irony, Tragedy and Possibility of Christianity in the Late Modern World*, Oxford: Oxford University Press.
Hussain, M., 2011, 'Spirituality: A Muslim Perspective', paper given at a Chester University conference 'Spiritual Progression in an Age of Recession', 17 March.
Hylson-Smith, K., 1997, *The Churches in England from Elizabeth I to Elizabeth II, vol II, 1689–1833*, London: SCM Press.
Inglehart, R., 1988, 'The Renaissance of Political Culture', *American Political Science Review* 82, no. 4, pp. 1203–30.
Iremonger, F., 1948, *William Temple Archbishop of Canterbury: His Life and his Letters*, London: Oxford University Press.
Jackelén, A., 2005, *Time and Eternity: The Question of Time in Church, Science, and Theology*, trans. by Barbara Harshaw, Conshohocken, PA: Templeton.
Jackelén, A., 2013, 'How Should a post-Einsteinian Notion of Time Change Our Understanding of Atonement, Reconciliation, and Forgiveness?', paper delivered at the conference 'Remembering the Past – Living the Future. Lutheran Traditions in Transition', Uppsala University, 2013.
James, W., 1985 edition, *The Varieties of Religious Experience: A Study in Human Nature*, introduction by M. Marty, London: Penguin Books.
Jamison, C., 2008, *Finding Happiness: Monastic Steps for a Fulfilling Life*, London: Weidenfeld & Nicolson.

BIBLIOGRAPHY

Jantzen, G., 2011, *Julian of Norwich*, London: SPCK.
Kahneman, D. and Deaton, A., 2010, 'High Income Improves Evaluation of Life but not Emotional Wellbeing', *Proceedings of the National Academy of Sciences* 107, no. 38, pp. 16489–93.
Kahneman, D., 2011, *Thinking, Fast and Slow*, London: Allen Lane.
Kennedy, G., 1964, *The Unutterable Beauty*, London: Hodder and Stoughton.
Keynes, J., 1932, *Essays in Persuasion*, New York: Harcourt-Brace.
Küng, H., 2010, 'The Age of Globalization Requires a Global Ethic', *Theology* 108, no. 875, pp. 323–38.
Kusserow, K., 2013, *Picturing Power: Portraiture and its Uses in the New York Chamber of Commerce*, New York: Columbia University Press.
Landes, D., 1969, *The Unbound Prometheus: Technological Change and Industrial Development in Western Europe from 1750 to the Present*, Cambridge: Cambridge University Press.
Landes, D., 1998, *The Wealth and Poverty of Nations*, London: Little, Brown and Company.
Layard, R., 2005, *Happiness: Lessons from a New Science*, London: Allen Lane.
Lee, R., 2007, *The Church of England and the Durham Coalfield, 1810–1926: Clergymen, Capitalists and Colliers*, Woodbridge: The Boydell Press.
Long, D., 2000, *Divine Economy*, London: Routledge.
MacCulloch, D., 2009, *A History of Christianity: The First Three Thousand Years*, London: Penguin Books.
McLoughlin, W., 1978, *Revivals, Awakenings, and Reform: An Essay on Religion and Social Change in America, 1607–1977*, Chicago: University of Chicago Press.
Malthus, T., 1798, *An Essay on the Principle of Population*, ed. Anthony Flew, Aylesbury: Penguin Books.
Marcel, G., 1949, *Being and Having*, Glasgow: Glasgow University Press.
Maslow, A., 1964, *Religions, Values, and Peak-experiences*, Columbus, OH: Ohio State University Press.
May, H., 1949, *Protestant Churches and Industrial America*, New York: Harper and Bros.
Maurice, F. (ed.), 1884, *The Life of Frederick Denison Maurice. Chiefly Told In His Own Letters vol. 2*, London, Macmillan.
Meeks, D., 1989, *God the Economist: The Doctrine of God and Political Economy*, Minneapolis: Fortress Press.
Micklethwait, J., and Wooldridge, A., 2010, *God is Back: How the Global Rise of Faith is Changing the World*, London: Penguin Books.
Moore, R., 1974, *Pit-Men, Preachers and Politics: The Effects of Methodism in a Durham Mining Community*, Cambridge: Cambridge University Press.

Morris, I., 2011, *Why the West Rules – For Now: The Patterns of History, and What They Reveal About the Future*, London: Profile Books.
Morris, I., 2013, *The Measure of Civilization: How Social Development Decides the Fate of Nations*, Princeton: Princeton University Press.
Munby, D., 1956, *Christianity and Economic Problems*, London: Macmillan.
Myers, D., 2008, 'Religion and Human Flourishing', in M. Eid and R. Larsen (eds), *The Science of Subjective Well-Being*, New York: The Guildford Press, pp. 323–43.
New Economics Foundation, 2009, *National Accounts of Well Being: Bringing Real Wealth onto the Balance Sheet*, London: New Economics Foundation.
Niebuhr, H., 1951, *Christ and Culture*, New York: Harper & Row.
Niebuhr, H., 1988, *The Kingdom of God in America*, Middletown, CT: Wesleyan University Press.
Niebuhr, R., 1963 edition (originally 1932), *Moral Man and Immoral Society*, London: SCM Press.
Niebuhr, R., 1980 edition (originally 1929), *Leaves from the Notebook of a Tamed Cynic*, Louisville, KY: Westminster/John Knox Press.
Norman, E., 1987, *The Victorian Christian Socialists*, Cambridge: Cambridge University Press.
Noyes, J. and Julian, C., 2014, 'Rebuilding Britain's Institutional Fabric: The Transformative Role of the Church of England', *Crucible* January–March 2014, pp. 17–23.
NWRDA, 2005, *Faith in England's Northwest: Economic Impact Assessment*, Warrington: Northwest Regional Development Agency.
Olson, M., 1982, *The Rise and Decline of Nations: Economic Growth, Stagflation, and Social Rigidities*, New Haven, CT: Yale University Press.
Päivänsalo, V., 2013, 'Lutheran Perspectives on the Right to Health in a Global World', paper given at the Uppsala University Conference, 'Remembering the Past – Living the Future. Lutheran Traditions in Transition'.
Pannenberg, W., 1991, *An Introduction to Systematic Theology*, Grand Rapids, MI: Wm. B. Eerdmans.
Pascal, B., 2003, *Pensées*, trans. W. Trotter, Mineola, NY: Dover.
Phillipson, N., 2011, *Adam Smith: An Enlightened Life*, London: Penguin Books.
Piketty, T., 2014, *Capital in the Twenty-First Century*, Cambridge, MA: Harvard University Press.
Pinker, S., 2011, *The Better Angels of our Nature: The Decline of Violence in History and Its Causes*, London: Allen Lane.
Pomeranz, K., 2000, *The Great Divergence: China, Europe, and the Making of the Modern World Economy*, Princeton: Princeton University Press.

BIBLIOGRAPHY

Poole, E., 2010, *The Church on Capitalism: Theology and the Market*, Basingstoke: Palgrave Macmillan.

Preston, R., 1983, *Church and Society in the Late Twentieth Century: The Economic and Political Task*, London: SCM Press.

Putnam, R. and Campbell, D., 2010, *American Grace: How Religion Divides and Unites Us*, New York: Simon & Schuster.

Reader, J., 2005, *Blurred Encounters: A Reasoned Practice of Faith*, Glamorgan: Aureus Publishing.

Roberts, R., 2007, *Spiritual Emotions: A Psychology of Christian Virtues*, Grand Rapids, MI: William B. Eerdmans.

Sachs, J., 2005, *The End of Poverty: How Can We Make It Happen In Our Lifetime?*, London: Penguin Books.

Sachs, J, 2008, *Common Wealth: Economics for a Crowded Planet*, London: Allen Lane.

Sacks, D., Stevenson, B. and Wolfers, J., 2012, 'Subjective Wellbeing, Income, Economic Development and Growth', in P. Booth (ed.), *... and the Pursuit of Happiness: Wellbeing and the Role of Government*, London: The Institute of Economic Affairs, pp. 59–97.

Sassoon, D., 1997, *One Hundred Years of Socialism: The West European Left in the Twentieth Century*, London: Fontana.

Scotland, N., 1995, *John Bird Sumner: Evangelical Archbishop*, Leominster: Gracewing.

Sedgwick, P., 1999, *The Market Economy and Christian Ethics*, Cambridge: Cambridge University Press.

Seligman, M., 2002, *Authentic Happiness: Using the New Positive Psychology to Realize Your Potential for Deep Fulfilment*, London: Nicholas Brealey Publishing.

Seligman, M., 2006 edition (originally 1991), *Learned Optimism: How To Change Your Mind and Your Life*, New York: Vintage Books.

Seligman, M., 2011, *Flourish: A New Understanding of Happiness and Well-being and How to Achieve Them*, London: Nicholas Brealey Publishing.

Sen, A., 1988, *On Ethics and Economics*, Oxford: Blackwell.

Sen, A., 2009, 'Capitalism beyond the Crisis', *The Guardian*, 14 March.

Smith, A., 1759, *The Theory of Moral Sentiments*, London: Penguin Books, 2009 edition, introduction by Amartya Sen.

Smith, A., 1776, *An Inquiry into the Nature and Causes of the Wealth of Nations*, Oxford: Oxford University Press (Liberty Fund edition of 1981).

Stackhouse, M., 2007, *Globalization and Grace*, London: Continuum.

Stiglitz, J., 2005, 'The Ethical Economist', *Foreign Affairs*, November–December.

Stiglitz, J., Sen, A. and Fitoussi, J.-P. (eds), 2010, *Mis-Measuring our Lives: Why GDP Doesn't Add Up*, London: New Press.

Stiglitz, J., 2012, *The Price of Inequality*, London: Penguin Books.

Strawn, B. (ed.), 2012, *The Bible and the Pursuit of Happiness: What the Old and New Testaments Teach Us about the Good Life*, Oxford: Oxford University Press.
Sumner, J., 1838, *A Practical Exposition of the Gospels of St. Matthew and St. Mark*, London: Hatchard.
Tanner, K., 2005, *Economy of Grace*, Minneapolis: Fortress Press.
Tawney, R., 1914, *The Establishment of Minimum Rates in the Chain-Making Industry under the Trade Boards Act of 1909*, London: G. Bell & Sons, Ltd.
Temple, W., 1942, *Christianity and Social Order*, London: Penguin Books.
Temple, W, 1961 edition (originally 1939–40), *Readings in St. John's Gospel*, London: Macmillan.
Tomkins, S., 2010, *The Clapham Sect: How Wilberforce's Circle Transformed Britain*, Oxford: Lion Hudson.
Tracy, D., 1981, *The Analogical Imagination: Christian Theology and the Culture of Pluralism*, London: SCM Press.
Vasquez, M., 2011, *A Materialist Theory of Religion*, Oxford: Oxford University Press.
Vidler, A., 1948, *The Theology of F. D. Maurice*, London: SCM Press.
Ward, P., 2002, *Liquid Church*, Carlisle: Paternoster Press.
Warren, R., 2002, *The Purpose Driven Life: What on Earth Am I Here For?*, Grand Rapids, MI: Zondervan.
Waterman, A., 1991, *Revolution, Economics and Religion: Christian Political Economy, 1798–1833*, Cambridge: Cambridge University Press.
Waterman, A., 2004, *Political Economy and Christian Theology since the Enlightenment: Essays in Intellectual History*, Basingstoke: Palgrave Macmillan.
Wayland, F., 1837, *The Elements of Political Economy*, New York: Leavitt, Lord and Co.
Wearmouth, R., 1937, *Methodism and the Working-Class Movements of England 1800–1950*, London: Epworth Press.
Wearmouth, R., 1959, *Methodism and the Trade Unions*, London: Epworth Press.
Wikell, A. (ed.), 2009, *Evangelium Idag: tolv artiklar skrivna for prast-och diakonmotet*, Strängnäs stift.
Winch, D., 1996, *Riches and Poverty: An Intellectual History of Political Economy in Britain, 1750–1834*, Cambridge: Cambridge University Press.
Wogaman, P., 1986, *Economics and Ethics: A Christian Inquiry*, Philadelphia: Fortress Press.
Woodhead, L. and Catto, R. (eds), 2012, *Religion and Change in Modern Britain*, London: Routledge.
Zhibin, Xie, 2013, 'Sino-Christian Scholarship in Contemporary China: A Public Interpretation', paper presented to the Kuyper Conference on 'Church and Academy', Princeton Theological Seminary.

Acknowledgements of Sources

Page 66, Table 1 is from J. Atherton, E. Graham and I. Steadman (eds), 2011, *The Practices of Happiness: Political Economy, Religion and Wellbeing*, London: Routledge, p. 12.

Page 114, Figure 1 is from I. Morris, 2011, *Why the West Rules-For Now: The Patterns of History, and What They Reveal About the Future*, London: Profile Books, p. 166, Fig. 3.7.

Page 115, Figure 2 is from I. Morris, 2011, *Why the West Rules-For Now: The Patterns of History, and What They Reveal About the Future*, London: Profile Books, p. 156, Fig. 3.1.

Page 116, Figure 3 is from R. Fogel, 2000, *The Fourth Great Awakening and the Future of Egalitarianism*, London and Chicago: University of Chicago Press, p. 75, Fig. 2.4.

Page 117, Figure 4 is taken from J. Sachs, 2005, *The End of Poverty. How We Can Make It Happen in Our Lifetime*, London: Penguin Books, p. 28, Fig. 2. The figure was originally sourced from A. Maddison, 2001, *The World Economy: A Millennial Perspective*, Paris: OECD.

Page 117, Figure 5 is taken from J. Sachs, 2008, *Common Wealth: Economics for a Crowded Planet*, London: Allen Lane, p. 51, Fig. 2.5. The figure was originally sourced from F. Bourguinon and C. Morrisson, 2002, *Inequality Among World Citizens: 1820–1992*, Paris: Ecole Normale Superieure.

Page 118, Figure 6 is taken from J. Sachs, 2005, *The End of Poverty. How We Can Make It Happen in Our Lifetime*, London: Penguin Books, p. 29, Fig. 3. The figure was originally sourced from A. Maddison, 2001, *The World Economy: A Millennial Perspective*, Paris: OECD.

Page 119, Figure 7 is from N. Ferguson, 2011, *Civilization: The West and the Rest*, London: Allen Lane, p. 147.

Page 120, Figure 8 is from S. Pinker, 2011, *The Better Angels of Our Nature: The Decline of Violence in History and its Causes*, London: Allen Lane, p. 49, Fig. 2-2.

Page 147, Picture 2 is from the front cover of an exhibition guide at the Princeton University Art Museum in April 2013. The painting is titled The Atlantic Cable Projectors, 1895, by Daniel Huntington, and is in the New York State Museum.

Index

Aberdeen 8, 13, 20, 27, 94, 180
academy 15
accomplishment 56, 66, 69, 107, *see also* PERMA
Africa 36, 119
agriculture 34, 113, 114, 146, 177
Age of
  Voluntarism and Atonement 129, 146, 161, 163–73, 185
  State and Incarnation 161, 173–85, 197
  Partnership and Reconciliation 129, 161, 185–92
Alkire, S. 102
Allen, J. 181
Allen, R. 164
American Economic Association 136, 153
Anglican x, 20, 68, 70, 71, 131, 143, 163, 167, 177, 179, 181, 182, 189
apocalypse, horsemen of 3, 16, 104, 109, 194
Appleby, J., Hunt, L., and Jacob, M. 169
archaeology 104, 114, 119
Aristotle 58
  eudaimonia 55
Arkwright, R. 164
Arrighi, G. 127, 134
Arrow, K. 45
Asia 37

Astley, J. and Francis, L. 48, 70, 75, 78, 79, 80, 81, 85
Atherton, J. 8, 10, 13, 41, 87, 97, 168, 188, 190
Awakenings, Great 130–1, 134, 135, 136, 157, 161, 187, 196
  six stages of 133
  First 129, 130, 136–40, 183, 186
  Second 129, 130, 140–6, 152, 153, 171, 183, 186
  Third 130, 143, 144, 145, 146–55, 157, 168, 178
  Fourth 129, 130, 145, 154, 155–8, 186
axial age 103, 106, 110–12

Backus, I. 138–9
Baker, C. x, 20, 82, 83, 84, 85, 88, 139
Bangladesh 44
banks, food 18
Baptists 139
  Southern 145
Bateman, B. and Banzhaf, S. 126, 153, 185, 192
Beccatini, G. 192
Beecher, H. 144, 146
Beecher, L. 142
Begg, Rev. 4
Bellah R. 1, 3, 14, 19, 70, 80, 97, 104, 105, 106, 108, 110, 111, 196
Benedictine 71

Beveridge, W. 8, 180
Bible 16, 72, 78, 88, 96, 144, 172, 173, 183
  societies 143, 169
biblical studies x, 54, 90, 91, 92, 94, 105, 149, 153, 178
biodemography 3, 10, 15
Birmingham 175
bishops 9, 168
  women 4
Blackburn 164
Blackpool 180
Black Death 16
Black-led church 187
Blair, T. 188
Blond, P. 189
Blue Labour 189
blurred encounters 186
Board for Social Responsibility 179
Boer War 175
Bolton 164, 166, 175, 180
Bonhoeffer, D. 25, 26, 80
Bretherton, L. 190
Britain 4, 8, 27, 34, 36, 41, 43, 98, 105, 109, 126, 174, 176, 185, 187, 191
Brown, M. 15
Bryan, W. 150
Bryant, C. 179
Buddhism 20, 73–4, 84, 106, 110, 111, 112, 172
Bury 164
Bush, G. 157

Caird, E. 8
Calvinism 137, 139, 141
Cambridge University Well-Being Institute survey 68–9
camp meetings 142, 183
cancer 42, 59, 97
capital 38, 187
  human 61, 101, 164
  religious and spiritual 84–5, 139, 190, 197
    symbolic, cultural, social and economic 136
cardiovascular disease 42, 59
cartels 37
Catholic, Roman 71, 156, 172, 179, 189
Center of Theological Inquiry ix, 7, 10
chainsaw art 71, 107, 161
Chalmers, T. 166
charitable giving 66, 188
character and virtues 55, 57–8
Charry, E. ix, 10, 19, 54, 73, 75, 77, 92, 93, 94, 99, 160
Chetham's Library 160
Chester
  Bishop of 171, 173
  University x, 72, 101
Chicago 13, 146
child mortality 28, 40
children 2, 31, 33, 40, 41, 42, 44, 51, 67, 68, 80, 81, 94, 98, 143, 166, 175, 188
  nurturing of 80–2
China 9, 14, 16, 20, 35, 36, 41, 85, 106, 107, 108, 111, 112, 113, 118–19
Chopwell parish 41
Chorley 131
Christendom 16
Christian political economy 12, 101, 166, 167, 168, 184
Christian social ethics 18, 71, 90, 91, 134, 161, 163, 189
Christian socialism 149, 169, 179
Christian Social Union 178, 184
Christianity
  and wellbeing 62–102, 135
  causal relationship with wellbeing 26, 63, 70–1
  correlative relationship with wellbeing 22, 26, 63, 70–1
Church Action on Poverty 8
church decline 78, 157, 187–8

INDEX

church, ordinary 48, 75, 76, 78, 80, 125, 169, 195
church, St Katharine's x, 80
Churches
British Council 20
World Council 20, 195
churchgoing 65, 67, 69, 77, 78, 79–90
and volunteering, civic offices 77, 82, 85, 88, 99, 190
Civil Rights 152
civil society 168, 175, 189
Civil War, American 141, 144, 145, 146
Clapham Sect 143, 171
Clements, K. 80, 194, 195, 196
cliometrics 122–6, 127, 134, *see also* history, scientific
Cobb, J. 87, 102
Cook, E. Fig. 2 113–14, 115, 124
common good, 29, 61, 65, 67, 73, 83, 144, 189
Confucianism 20, 106, 110, 111, 112
Congregationalism 139, 167
Connecticut 138
consumption 33, 113, 174
conversions 138, 139, 142, 148, 149, 156, 170
Cooper, N. 36
Copleston, E. 12, 168
credit unions 196
Crompton, S. 164

Dalai Lama 73, 74
Daly, H. 87, 102
Daoism 110
Darwin, C. 149, 178
Dasgupta, P. 17, 86, 128, 135
Davie, G. 78, 188
Deaton, A. ix, 1, 10, 26, 27, 28, 29, 30, 32, 33, 34, 35, 36, 37, 38, 39, 40, 41, 42, 43, 44, 46, 48, 49, 50, 51, 54, 153
Declaration of Independence 136

Deerness pit valley 183
Deism 140
dementia 42, 97
democracy 38, 52, 60, 61, 131, 140, 144, 145, 148, 169, 174
Democratic Party 132, 145, 150, 152, 157
Denham, J. 84
Depression, Great 2, 152, 176
development, paradox of 2, 3, 4, 5, 6, 16, 28, 36, 108, 110, 112, 118, 131, 146, 155, 159, 166, 173, 193, 194
Diamond, J. 104, 106, 108
Diener, E. 15, 30, 51, 52, 53, 55, 60, 64, 78, 79, 80, 96
distributional coalitions 37
domains of life 47, 49, 50, 51, 58, 96
Donaldson, F. 179
Dundee 174
Durham 174, 181–4
church 165, 181–4
coalfield 4, 160, 181–4
diocese 41, 181–4
miners 172
Bishop of 178, 182

Easterlin, R. 25, 28, 30, 34, 38, 39, 40, 43, 44, 46, 47, 49, 50, 90, 101, 123, 191, 194
economic
affairs 135, 153, 174, 189
agents 10, 47, 90
growth 2, 10, 28, 34, 35, 38, 46, 50, 60, 61, 118, 154, 155, 156, 164, 177, 187
systems 9, 10, 29, 61, 176
economics 3, 6, 9, 11, 12, 16, 17, 25, 29, 40, 44, 46, 51, 60, 63, 64, 86, 90, 91, 95, 122, 123, 126, 134, 154, 160, 163, 176, 178, 191, 192, 194, 196, 197
classical 38, 153, 161
engineering 13, 68

211

ethical 13, 168
macro and micro 9, 10, 18
neoclassical 8, 9, 47, 49, 176, 184, 185
positive 185
welfare 91, 185
economics and
  Christianity 6, 7, 11–16, 21, 22, 25, 29, 54, 55, 100, 126, 135, 153, 163, 167, 168, 172, 177, 191–2, 196–7
  ethics 6, 12–14, 29, 61, 86, 165, 185, 187
economics, behavioural 54
economics of wellbeing 15, 22
ecumenical 20, 80, 195, 196
education 1, 2, 5, 26, 32, 33, 38, 39, 61, 69, 78, 100, 101, 135, 144, 151, 152, 154, 169, 174, 176, 188
Edwards, J. 139, 141, 171
Einstein, A. 107
Ely, R. 136, 153–5, 168, 196
emotions 48, 52, 99, 138, 148, 193
  positive 55, 56, 59, 65, 66, 68, 77–82
  and God 94
  emotion-virtues 77–8
  engagement 56, see also PERMA
Elton, G. 104, 106, 122–6
Engels, F. 160, 163
Enlightenment 137, 140, 141, 164
epidemics 3, 16, 109
Europe 39, 42, 51, 107, 114, 119, 130, 162, 194
evangelical 172, 189
  Nonconformity 167, 170, 171
  Anglicanism 167, 170
evolution 3, 45, 70, 81, 89, 104, 132, 137, 150, 152, 177, 178, see also technophysio evolution
Exchange, Old World 109
  Columbian 109

Exodus, Book of 32

family 2, 19, 41, 51, 60, 68, 69, 84, 98, 133, 139, 151, 152, 156, 164, 172, 173, 181, 184
famines 16, 109, 193
Federal Council of Churches 149, 150
  Social Creed 149, 150, 151, 152
Ferguson, N. 35, 101, 118–19
finance 16, 86, 148
financial crisis 187
Fingarette, H. 196
Finney, C. 142, 143
flying shuttle 164
Fogel, R. 13, 30, 34, 39, 40, 43, 44, 45, 86, 104, Figure 3 113–15, 122–6, 127, 128, 132, 133, 134, 138, 139, 140, 142, 143, 145, 148, 150, 154, 155, 156, 158, 161, 163, 166, 175, 185, 189
Fogel's religious-political cycles 133–4
Forrester, D. 163
Francis, L. (also with Astley) 48, 70, 75, 78, 79, 80, 81, 85, 88
free market 161, 165, 166, 167, 168, 174, 175, 176, 188
Free Trade 165
Frey, D. 145
Friedman, M. 13
friends 8, 42, 52, 60, 67, 69, 84

germ theories 28, 84
Germany, historical school of economics 153–5
  liberal theology 153–5
Gilbert, A. 170
Gilbert, P. 98
Gilded Age 37, 148
Gill, R. 70, 77, 80, 81, 82, 83, 85, 86, 88, 98, 140, 185, 194
Gini coefficient 87, 166
Gladden, W. 150, 178

INDEX

Gladstone, W. 170
Glasgow 8
  University 12
global religious ethic 71, 74
globalization 5, 37
Gore, C. 178
Goudzwaard, B. 15
Graham, C. 46, 47, 50, 51, 53, 62
Graham, E 10, 11, 71, 97
Great
  Divergences 26, 27, 28, 34, 36, 41, 61, 118
  Escapes 26, 27, 29, 30, 34, 35, 61, 103
Greece 109
Greek philosophy 106, 110, 111, 112
Green, T. 178
Grenholm, C-H. x, 15, 71, 191

Habermas, J. 71
Haidt, J. 15, 30, 54, 74–5
Hamiltonians 141
happify 140, 195
happiness 10, 27, 45, 48, 52, 55, 62, 72, 99, 156
  biblical 93, 101
  and Christianity 65
  and God 94
  and income 49
  and religion 88
Hargreaves, J. 164
Hastings, A. 188
health 1, 3, 4, 6, 10, 15, 21, 25, 26, 27, 32, 43, 44, 45, 46, 51, 52, 54, 59, 61, 63, 96, 135, 151, 154, 155, 176, 198, 193
  benefits from religion 73, 95, 97
  care 5, 32, 37, 38, 39, 78, 97, 100, 101, 176
  mental 52, 59, 65, 66, 155
  public 28, 44, 109
  and positive psychology 55, 57, 58, 96
height 30, 42–3, 193

Hicks, D. 87, 102
higgling 195
Hilly Flanks 106, 107, 108
Hilton, B. 162, 168, 170, 171, 177, 179, 184
Hinduism 11, 20, 88, 110, 112, 188
history
  economic 10, 15, 17, 18, 33, 40, 104, 134, 160, 161, 163, 167
  narrative 104, 121–6, 132, 161
  scientific, *see also* cliometrics 105, 121–6, 132, 134, 161, 196
  six characteristics of the two histories 123–6, 196
Hobsbawn, E. 167, 170, 175, 176, 182
Holloway, S. 23
Hoogen, J. 15
hope 38, 39, 59, 65, 66, 70, 78, 99, 130, 139, 181, 182
Hopkins, C. 146, 147, 152
hospices 98
hospitals 98, 99
Hussain, M. 73
Hunter, J. 126, 127, 128, 136, 187
Hylson-Smith, K. 160
hymns 66, 68, 79, 80

Ice Age 21, 103, 104, 105, 106, 193
Incarnation 151, 161, 162, 173, 177, 178, 179, 180, 181, 184, 185, 197
income 3, 5, 6, 10, 15, 21, 25, 26, 27, 29, 32, 33, 34, 35, 37, 38, 39, 43, 45, 46, 47, 51, 60, 95, 102, Figure 4: world per capita income 117, 116–17, 121, 128, 135, 151, 166, 184, 187, 191, 193
  and Christianity model 99–102
  and subjective wellbeing 46–50

213

Index

Alkire-Foster Method 102
Belonging, Becoming and
  Participation 88
Human Development 87
Inequality Adjusted Human
  Development 87, 102
Religiosity 88
Religion and Happiness 88
Sarkozy Commission 87
Social Development 87, 104,
  107, 108, 109, Figure 1 114,
  161
Sustainable Economic
  Welfare 87, 102
India 9, 20, 35, 36, 41, 42, 98,
  113, 118–19, 194
industrialization 12, 28, 57, 131,
  146, 149, 150, 161, 188
inequalities 3, 5, 6, 10, 16, 19, 29,
  32, 34, 38, 40, 42, 61, 77, 101,
  103, 128, 152, 154, 156, 157,
  168, 185, 187
  global, Figure 6 113, 118
  health 26, 28, 40
  increasing 36–40
  nations, between 2, 28, 36, 103,
    108, 193
  nations, within 2, 28, 36, 37–8,
    87, 103, 108, 146, 193
  subjective wellbeing 26
infections 28, 40, 42, 59
Inglehart, R. 39
inflation 37
institutions 86, 88, 95, 122, 123,
  125, 135, 154, 189
  positive 55
  support for income, health and
    subjective wellbeing 60–1
interdisciplinary 7, 8, 16, 19, 20,
  54–5, 77, 91, 128, 187, 190,
  191, 194
interfaith 20, 71
interspirituality 20
intrafaith 20, 71, 150

Iremonger, F. 20
Irenaeus 152
Iran 106
Islam 11, 70, 73, 83, 88, 111, 112,
  188
Israel 106
Italy 107

Jackelén, A. 93
James, W. 196
Jamison, C. 72, 73, 178, 191
Jantzen, G. 16
Japan 107
Jeffersonians 141
Jenkins, D. 182
Johnson, L. 132
  war on poverty 152
Jordan 106
Judaism 20, 83, 88, 106, 110
Julian of Norwich 16
justice 65, 68, 151
  social 61, 86
just wage 100, *see also* living
  wage

Kahneman, D. 15, 30, 50, 54, 91
Kaozheng 15
Kay, J. 164
Kenya 50
Keynes, J. 12, 39, 154, 176, 185
kingdom of God 150
Kingsley, C. 178
knowledge 18, 25, 26, 28, 44, 45,
  57, 60, 88, 90, 92, 93, 101, 169
Küng, H. 71, 74
Kuznet, S. 34

Labour 4, 14, 94, 146, 151, 180,
  182, 183, 184, 189
Labour movements 160, 174, 183
Lancashire 160, 163, 164, 169,
  174, 181
Landes, D. 40, 127, 167, 177
Latin America 51
Lawson, J. 183

INDEX

Layard, R. 30, 46, 48, 49, 50, 51, 55, 61, 64, 65
Big Seven 51-2, 99
Lee, J. 140
Lee, P. 183-4
Lee, R. 4, 41, 165, 181, 182, 183
Leeds 175
liberal Catholicism 149, 178
life after death 78
life expectancy 1, 5, 10, 27, 28, 30, 34, 39, 40-5, 61, 87, 96, 97, 118-19, 121, 128, 155, 166, 193
  global Figure 7 113
life, good 1, 2, 39, 40, 48, 111
Lincoln, A. 132, 145, 148
literacy 87, 101, 143, 144
  and education 101, 143, 144
Liverpool 173, 175
living wage 100, 151, 178, 191
London 8, 179, 191
  School of Economics 122, 182
  University College 122
Long, D. 15
Ludlow, J. 178
Lutheran x, 10, 20, 68, 71

MacCulloch, D. 181
Malthus, T. 12, 33, 145, 166, 167, 174, 177
Malthusian Trap 33, 35, 109, 116-17
Manchester 8, 79, 109, 160, 166, 167, 169, 173, 175
  bishop 169
  cathedral 160, 166, 173
  Diocese 180, 188, 190
  men 164
  School 165
  University 92, 134
manufacturing 34, 141
marginal utility 49
Markham chantry chapel 31, 99
market 44, 165, 167
marriage 47, 51, 86, 151
Massachusetts 139

Marcel, G. 195
Marty, M. 136
Marshall, A. 8, 184, 185
Maslow, A. 75
materialist theory of religion 76, 91
Marx, K. 33, 160
Maurice, F. 177, 178, 179, 184
McVicar, J. 167
McLoughlin, W. 130, 131, 132, 133, 134, 137, 138, 139, 140, 141, 143, 148, 149, 154, 155, 156, 158, 185
  meaning 3, 52, 56, 58, 65, 66, 67, 68, 69, 70, 73, 74, 77, 79, 106, 110, 111, 142, 197, see also PERMA
  measurement 17, 28, 47, 52, 89, 105, 106, 128, 135
  measurement of religion 22, 26, 63, 85-9, see also Index
Medicaid 152
Medicare 152
meditation 65, 66, 72
Meeks, D. 15
messy or liquid church 186
Methodists 138, 143, 160, 163, 169, 171, 172, 173, 181, 183
  Episcopal Church 142
  and Liberalism 172
  Primitive 142, 178, 182, 183, 184, 185, 189
  Social Creed 150
  Wesleyan 170
Micklethwait, J. and Wooldridge, A. 11
Middle Ages 11, 31, 100
Middle East 31
migration 3, 6, 16, 37, 109, 194
Milbank, J. 189
Mill, J. 38
mills 164, 167, 179
models 134, 135, 158, 177, 187, 188
  economic 63, 122, 128

215

for Christianity and economics 10, 17, 21, 22, 26, 64–102, 197
American 128–9, Chapter 4, 161–2
British 128–9, Chapter 5, 161–2, 163
for Christianity and health 63, 64, 90, 95, 96–9
Christianity and income 63, 64, 95, 99–102
and subjective wellbeing 89–90
prioritising models' features 69–70
correlative and causal relationships 70–1
sections of:
1. Mapping and modelling 64–82
2. Transmission processes 82–5
3. Measuring 85–9
money 5, 99, 100, see also income
monovision 19, 23, 105, 121, 196
moods 161, 186
Moody, D. 148
Moore, R. 160, 172, 183
moral growth 61, 86
moral freighting 77, 82, 84, 88, see also transmission processes
Moral Majority 156
Morris, I. 1, 2, 16, 71, 87, 104, 106, 107, 108, 109, 110, 111, 112, Figure 1 113, 114, 124, 161, 194
Munby, D. 15
Muslim 10, 72–3, 74, 84, 172
Myers, D. 62, 64, 80, 97, 98, 99

Nepal 44
New Deal 101, 132, 152, 154
New Economics Foundation's National Accounts of Wellbeing 53, 66–8, 70, 87
New England 139, 142
new light theology 133, 137, 139, 141, 142, 143, 146
new science 55
New York Chamber of Commerce 148
Niebuhr, Reinhold 89, 90
Niebuhr, Richard 128, 150
Norman, E. 178
North West Regional Development Agency 188–9
Nottingham 73
nutrition 30, 42–3, 166

Office of National Statistics 53
old light theology 133, 139, 149, 150, 156
Olson, M. 37
Oxford 8, 168

Päivänsalo, V. 98
Pakistan 50
Palestine 30
Pannenberg, W. 92
Pareto principle 29, 90
Pascal, B. 17
participation in governance 26, 32, 51, 52, 61, 65, 66, 78, 88, 135, 152
partnerships 21, 185–92, 197
Peasants' Revolt 16
penicillin 25
Pentecostalism 149, 154
PERMA 56, 59, 69, 87
Phillipson, N. 6, 7, 195
philosophy of life 65, 67, 69, 74, 99
Piketty, T. 38
Pinker, S. 104, Figure 8 199–20, 165
Plato 58
plutocracy 38
political realignments 132, 134, 145, 152, 155, 156, 161
Pomeranz, K. 26

INDEX

Poole, E. 15
Poor Law Amendment Act 166, 171
Porvoo Agreement 20, 68
postmaterialism 38–9
postmodern 25
poverty 8, 9, 35, 57, 100, 101, 103, 109, 117–18, 144, 146, 151, 157, 167, 168, 185, 193
  global Figure 5 113, 117–18
  reduction 14, 27, 29, 32, 33, 34, 35–6, 88
  relative 2, 36
preferences
  revealed 47, 123
  expressed 47, 123
pre-moral goods 87
Preston 164
Preston, R. 15
Princeton ix, 7, 10, 15, 26, 54, 85, 148
progressive orthodoxy 147, 153, 154, 178
Prohibition 149, 154
prophecy 4, 10, 39, 133
Protestant work ethic 83, 170, 172
psychology 9, 15, 17, 18, 21, 25, 46, 49, 50, 51, 63, 64, 86, 94, 122, 126, 160, 191, 194
  positive 15, 54, 55, 57, 58, 59, 68, 73, 94, 155
  and health, cardiovascular disease, cancer and infectious illness 59–60
  of subjective wellbeing 54–60
Puritan 130, 131, 137, 144
Putnam, R. 62, 64, 70, 79, 80, 82, 83, 88, 134, 144, 157, 158, 195

qualitative surveys 75, 85, 122, 123, 124
quantitative surveys 75, 85, 105, 124

Radcliffe 166

Radical Orthodoxy 189
Rauschenbusch, W. 150, 175, 178
Reader, J. x, 20, 186
Red Tory 189
reform 132, 133, 134, 135, 143, 144, 145, 146, 150, 151, 152, 153, 154, 155, 156, 174, 177, 189
religiometrics 121, 124, *see also* cliometrics
religion, sociology of 18
religion, enthusiastic 132, 133, 156
religious revivals 131, 132, 134, 135, 136, 139, 142, 149, 155, 156, 161
religious studies 7, 10, 16, 17, 18, 20, 21, 22, 48, 49, 57, 63, 76, 89, 90, 91, 105, 121, 122, 124, 125, 126, 152, 155, 163, 194, 195, 196, 197
rent seeking 37
Republican Party 132, 157
research, basic and applied 18, 20, 90, 91
Revelation, Book of 16, 109
Revolution
  Industrial, 2, 16, 18, 25, 26, 27, 30, 32, 33, 34, 40, 43, 44, 46, 60, 90, 92, 100, 101, 104, 112, 117, 146, 159, 163, 164, 166, 167, 173–4, 190, 193
  Mortality 2, 18, 25, 26, 27, 28, 30, 43, 46, 60, 90, 92, 98, 101, 104, 112, 159, 163, 190, 192, 193
  scientific 16, 92, 106
Richmond, W. 184
Roberts, R. 77
Rochdale 175
Rochdale Chartist Conference 173
Rolfe, J. 131
Rome 108
Roosevelt, F. 132
Roosevelt T. 152
Rowntree Foundation 36

Royton Temperance Society 169–70
Russia 51, 169
Ryan, J. 100

Sachs, J. 36, Figures 4, 5 and 6 113–18
Sacks, D., Stevenson, B., Wolfers, J. 49–50
Salford 19
Salvation Army 157
sanitation 35, 44, 109
Sarkozy Commission 53, 87, see also Index
Saxon 159, 160
Science of Man 6, 12
Scotland, N. 171
scriptures 6, 16, 19, 65, 68, 99, 102
secularization 136
Sedgwick, P. 15
Seligman, M. 15, 18, 35, 53, 55, 56, 57, 58, 59, 60, 62, 64, 69, 70, 73, 74, 78, 87, 96
Sen, A. 8, 13, 29, 48, 53, 61, 87, 88, 89, 168, 176, 192
services 34, 35
sexuality, human 4, 156
shamanism 97
Sherman Antitrust Act 150
Sierra Leone 41
slavery 123, 133, 171
  abolition 135, 143, 144, 145, 146, 152, 171
  economics of 124
Smith, A. 6, 8, 12, 139, 145, 165, 168, 195
social development 22, 103, 104, 108, 109, 113, 159, 161, see also Index
  religious contribution to 103
social gospel 101, 146, 149, 150, 151, 153, 154, 175
social sciences 16, 47, 86, 90, 112
social security 5

socialism 179
sociology 10, 15, 63, 64, 80, 86, 178, 194
spinning jenny 164
spirituality 14, 20, 26, 38, 39, 52, 63, 71, 72, 73, 74, 98
secular 74–5, 84, 172
St John's Gospel 1, 2, 152, 180, 197
St Mary Magdalene church 30–1
St Paul's Jarrow 159, 160
Stackhouse, M. 15
Standish, M. 130–1
Stanton, E. 144
state 3, 5, 16, 45, 109, 110, 112, 119, 120, 121, 136, 137, 140, 141, 142, 143, 156, 157, 161, 165, 173, 174, 175, 176, 177, 178, 180, 181, 184, 185, 187, 189, 194, 197
  welfare 176, 180, 181
  failures 3, 16, 109, 194, see also apocalypse, horsemen
statistics 17, 18, 19, 41, 43, 63, 86, 87, 116, 122, 132
steam 164
Steedman, I. 10, 97
Stiglitz, J. 8, 29, 37, 38, 53, 61, 86, 87, 88, 89
Storrar, W. ix
Strängnäs diocese 67, 68, 70
Strawn, B. 77, 93, 95, 101–2
Strong, J. 150
subjective wellbeing 4, 6, 10, 21, 25, 26, 27, 30, 32, 45–60, 75, 78, 87, 121, 124, 151, 154, 191
  as life evaluation/satisfaction 46, 47, 48, 49, 50, 51, 52, 54, 62, 95, 104, 121, 151
  as emotional wellbeing 47, 48, 50, 53, 54
  and Christianity 54, 62–102, 128, 162, 194
Sumner, J. 12, 101, 166, 168, 171, 173

INDEX

Sunday, B. 148
Sunday schools 143, 144
Sweden 10, 41, 67, 68
 archbishop 93
Syria 106

Table: Mapping Christianity's Practices, Ethics and Beliefs 64–7, 76
Tanner, K. 15
Tanzania 98
Tawney, R. 8, 100. 182, 185
technology 44, 45, 60, 90, 92, 98, 105, 107, 109, 113, 114, 132, 149, 156, 163, 164, 174, 190
technophysio evolution 45, 87, 132, 145, 155
textiles 163
theologians 9, 10, 25, 30, 33, 48, 54, 56, 75, 85, 99, 100, 127, 139, 142
theology 89, 92
 empirical 169
 liberation 2, 9, 91
 ordinary 48, 75, 76, 78, 85, 91, 125, 169, 195
 pastoral 18, 91, 186
 positive 54, 93, 160
 practical 18, 90, 91
 public 15, 18. 71, 90, 91, 126, 163, 186
 sociological 91
 systematic x, 18, 19, 22, 54, 90, 91, 92, 93, 105, 160
town halls 175
Tracy, D. 15
Trade Boards Act 178
transmission processes 23, 63, 82–5, 95, 97, 135, 136, 143, 151, 155, 156, 170, 173, 182, 184, 188, 190, 192, 196, 197
 as belonging, becoming, participation 83, 84–5, *see also* Index
 as moral freighting 83–5

 as transposing beliefs, values and practices 82–3, 95, 98, 173, 185
transport 35
Turkey 106
typology 161, 162
 theological and secular 162

UK 2, 19, 21, 22, 29, 35, 36, 37, 86, 101, 103, 119, 124
ummah 73
unemployment 4, 19, 51, 57, 147, 148, 151
unions 146, 151, 178, 182, 183, 185
Uppsala University x, 10
urbanization 12, 57, 131, 146, 149, 150, 161, 188
US 2, 15, 22, 29, 32, 34, 35, 36, 37, 39, 41, 44, 50, 57, 59, 69, 79, 97, 98, 100, 101, 105, 118, 119, 126, 130–58, 167, 168, 179, 190, 191
Usworth Parish 4, 182

Vasquez, M. 76, 91
Venerable Bede 159, 160, 172, 174, 181
Vietnam 44
violence 104
 history of Figure 8 113, 119–21
virtues 60, 65, 73, 83, 98, *see also* character and virtues
 six main 57–8, 74
 24 routes to 58, 74
virtue ethics 57
vocation 51
voluntary 57, 65, 66, 83, 143, 161, 168, 169, 170, 173, 176–89
voluntary bodies 168, 170, 176, 188

Walker, D. 79, 169
Ward, P. 186
Warren, R. 72, 73

Wars of Religion 17, 119, 195
water frame 164
Waterman, A. 12, 168, 192
Watson, N. x
Wayland, F. 145, 153
Wearmouth, R. 166, 172, 173, 182, 183, 184
Webb, S. 182, 183
Weber, M. 83, 172
Welby, J. 190
welfare 32, 38, 61, 101, 135, 156, 176
 state 180, 181
Westcott, B. 178, 181, 182, 184
Whately, R. 12, 168
Whitefield, G. 138
Widnes 174
Wikell, A. 68
Wilberforce, W. 171
Wilkinson, R. 44
William Temple 8, 20, 101, 150, 151, 180
William Temple Foundation x, 8, 9, 68, 82, 182
Winch, D. 167
Wilson, J. 182
Wogaman, P. 15
women's rights 143, 145, 152
Woodbine, Willy 94
work 52, 70
workhouses, 166
World Health Organisation 55, 59
world of daily life 1, 3, 4, 5, 14, 19, 31, 32, 76, 89, 107, 110, 111, 112, 137, 150, 151, 159, 168, 180, 183, 194
worship or ritual 65, 66, 68, 72, 78–9, 84, 94, 99
Wright, T. 78

York 80
Yorkshire 160, 173

Zamagni, S. 189, 192
Zhibin, Xie 85

www.ingramcontent.com/pod-product-compliance
Lightning Source LLC
Chambersburg PA
CBHW051356290426
44108CB00015B/2035